Hitler's Plans for Global Domination

HITLER'S PLANS FOR GLOBAL DOMINATION

Nazi Architecture and Ultimate War Aims

Jochen Thies

Translated by
Ian Cooke and Mary-Beth Friedrich

Berghahn Books
New York • Oxford

Published in 2012 by
Berghahn Books

English language edition
©2012 Berghahn Books

German language edition
@1976 Droste Verlag

Originally published as
Architekt der Weltherrschaft. Die „Endziele" Hitlers
By Jochen Thies

Printed in the United States

ISBN 978-0-85745-462-1
Book Club Edition

In memory of my friends

Jonathan Carr
Christopher Cviic
Harry Weinberger

CONTENTS

PART III. HITLER AND MILITARY ISSUES: FROM WHALE BAY TO LAKE ERIE

PART IV. HITLER IN 1940–1941: WHEN VISIONS BECOME REALITY

ABBREVIATIONS

ADAP	Akten zur Deutschen Auswärtigen Politik
AHR	American Historical Review
BA	Bundesarchiv Koblenz
BA/MA	Bundesarchiv-Militärarchiv Freiburg i.Br.
CEH	Central European History
FS	Festschrift
GWU	Geschichte in Wissenschaft und Unterricht
HZ	Historische Zeitschrift
IfZ	Institut für Zeitgeschichte München
JCH	Journal of Contemporary History
JMH	Journal of Modern History
IMT	Internationaler Militärgerichtshof
KTB	Kriegstagebuch Halder
MBB	Messerschmitt-Bölkow-Blohm
MfT	Mitteilungen für die Truppe
MGM	Militärgeschichtliche Mitteilungen
MR	Marine-Rundschau
NPL	Neue Politische Literatur
Ortenau	Veröffentlichungen des Historischen Vereins für Mittelbaden
PA AA	Politisches Archiv Auswärtiges Amt
PRO	Public Record Office London
PVS	Politische Vierteljahreszeitschrift
RGBl	Reichsgesetzblatt
Slg	Sammlung
Tb	Tagebuch
VfZG	Vierteljahreshefte für Zeitgeschichte
WWR	Wehrwissenschaftliche Rundschau

FOREWORD

The last two decades have seen yet another noticeable upsurge in the academic study of—and public interest in—the Hitler dictatorship and German society under National Socialism. The old question of how the Germans got into the Third Reich has received renewed attention in works on the Weimar Republic, attention that has been further expanded by research on the continuities and discontinuities in modern German history from Bismarck to Hitler.

As far as the Nazi period in the strict sense is concerned, research has focused both on how the country "ticked" in the 1930s at the grass-roots level and, above all, on the sociopolitical history of World War II with its 70 million dead and its mass murder of Europe's Jews and other minorities. To some extent, the topics of military violence and geno-cide received a considerable boost after the 1995 publication of Daniel Goldhagen's *Hitler's Willing Executioners*, which identified the murderous depths of German anti-Semitism as being a root cause of the Holocaust.[1] This bestseller asserted that when the Nazi regime provided the ideologi-cal justifications and administrative structures that permitted genocide, a preexisting "eliminationist" hatred of the Jews in Germany flipped over into an "exterminationist" racism. It was these prewar forces and wartime conditions that, according to Goldhagen, mobilized not only a relatively small number of fanatics through the SS, but also "ordinary" German men through the Wehrmacht and police units sent into the occupied Eastern territories to kill.

Following Christopher Browning and others, Goldhagen rightly drew at-tention once again not just to the cold-blooded industrial mass murder at Auschwitz and other extermination camps, but also to the Holocaust in the villages of the East, where soldiers and policemen, often under the

---

[1] Daniel J. Goldhagen, *Hitler's Willing Executioners. Ordinary Germans and the Holocaust*, New York 1996.

guise of antipartisan warfare, took Jewish women, children, and elderly people into the woods and ravines adjacent to their village, forced them to dig their own mass graves, and shot them under circumstances that defy sober historical description.[2] Apart from some praise, Goldhagen received very vigorous and often well-founded criticism that we can reference only selectively in a footnote here.[3] No less significant than the Goldhagen Debate is the wave of fresh, meticulous research now available on the subject of the murder of Europe's Jews, Sinti and Roma, Slavs, and others.

Much of this work—which, again, can be mentioned only selectively here—is concentrated on retrieving the fate and the responses of the victims from the records.[4] However, historians and sociopsychologists have also turned to the study of the perpetrators. There are now a number of major books on the developments and decision-making processes within Hitler's wartime headquarters and in Berlin's Reich Security Main Office down to the level of the higher SS, police leaders, and administrators who organized the ghettoization, deportation and "resettlement" of millions of victims.[5] Finally, recent work has also been concerned with the grassroots level and the men in the rear areas who not only gave the orders to kill, but who also actively participated in the killing.[6]

This research has in turn revived an interest in the role of the Wehrmacht, although without focusing on the alleged "Lost Victories" or the strategic and tactical blunders that the German generals and fieldmarshals laid at Hitler's door after 1945.[7] This kind of purely military history that began in the early postwar period shifted in the 1970s to an expanded notion of the history of World War II, one that was interested in how actual German warfare was linked to the evolution of the campaign in the rear areas, the badly underestimated logistical problems, and the brutal treatment of the population in the occupied territories. Due to this research, we now have a much more comprehensive and less compartmentalized

---

[2] Christopher R. Browning, *Ordinary Men. Reserve Police Battalion 101 and the Final Solution in Poland*, New York 1992.

[3] See e.g. Robert R. Shandley, *Unwilling Germans? The Goldhagen Debate*, Minneapolis 1998.

[4] See e.g. Saul Friedlaender, *Nazi Germany and the Jews*, Chapel Hill 1995.

[5] Michael Wildt, *Generation des Unbedingten. Das Führungskorps des Reichssicherheitshauptamtes*, Hamburg 2002.

[6] Edward B. Westermann, *Hitler's Police Battalions. Enforcing Racial War in the East*, Lawrence 2005.

[7] Erich von Manstein, *Lost Victories*, London 1958. See also Barry Leach, *German Strategy against Russia, 1939-1941*, Oxford 1973.

picture of the SS and the Wehrmacht's *Weltanschauungskrieg*, which the regime began first in Poland, then later conducted in the Balkans and the Soviet Union, as well as in occupied Western Europe.

However valuable all this work has been for understanding the larger dynamics of the Third Reich and the causes of its ultimate defeat by the Allies—as well as its self-defeat through its inner contradictions and irrationalities, even in the face of impending collapse—one key question is not addressed in much of this recent literature, whether the literature provides sweeping analyses of *Hitler's Empire* or the *Nazi Empire*[8] or whether it is narrowly monographic. This is the question of the ideas and policies the Nazis conceived of for the world after Operation Barbarossa, the invasion of the Soviet Union in June 1941.

Of course, it could be argued that the study of post-Barbarossa planning is counterfactual and hence irrelevant. After all, Hitler never defeated the Soviet Union, and he himself was soon defeated, first in the East by the Red Army and later in Western Europe. But there is something special about this particular counterfactual, in that the Wehrmacht came very close to defeating Stalin in the summer and early autumn of 1941. Indeed, the regime was at that time so confident that the war in the East would be won as quickly as the earlier campaigns in Western and Northern Europe that Hitler's headquarters began preparations to reduce the mass mobilization that it had accomplished in the spring 1941. At the same time, the planning for the world post-Barbarossa that had begun as far back as 1937–38 continued, accompanied by expert discussions about how to establish a New Order in the vast spaces of a defeated Soviet Union and the rest of conquered Europe,[9] as well as by the continuing construction work on the buildings that architect Albert Speer had designed with Hitler's approval. All this was not just a utopian "dream of empire"; the foundations had been laid before Barbarossa, and concrete measures had been taken.[10]

As Jochen Thies mentions in his book, there have been earlier studies of whether Hitler was merely a conqueror of "living space" in the East and of a Continental European empire, or whether he was preparing for a struggle against Britain and the United States for world domination. Hugh Trevor-Roper had been among the first to raise this question in a short article in 1961, where he discussed evidence that Hitler's ambi-

---

[8] Shelley Baranowski, *Nazi Empire*, Cambridge 2011; Mark Mazower, *Hitler's Empire*, New York 2008.

[9] Arno Sölter, *Grossraumkartell*, Dresden 1941.

[10] Albert Speer, *Inside the Third Reich*, London 1970; W.W. Schmokel, *Dream of Empire*, New Haven.

tions were indeed, he believed, global ambitions.[11] Andreas Hillgruber and Klaus Hildebrand subsequently wrote big books in which they put forward the argument, backed up by plenty of empirical evidence, of a Nazi *Stufenplan*, or the notion of a calculated expansion in two stages: first on the European Continent, and then, once this position had been secured, in a war against the two major "sea powers," Britain and the United States.[12] Milan Hauner and Robert Hertzstein also wrote a few much shorter studies of this question.[13] Students of Hillgruber and Hildebrand have also published monographs on the subject, such as Jost Dülffer's study of Hitler's naval rearmament program and the so-called Z Plan, as well as the buildup, well before the invasion of Poland in 1939, of planes—developed by Messerschmitt and others—that were capable of transcontinental warfare.[14]

However, the most comprehensive and compelling treatment of the long-range aims of Nazi imperialism was written by Jochen Thies, another student of Andreas Hillgruber. A long overdue translation of this important book, first published in German, has now finally been undertaken. It is a good example of the fact that even in the age of instant information and sound bites, there are still studies that, although published some time ago, have lost none of their importance over the years.

Against the background of the enormous destructiveness of the Nazi dictatorship—which should never be forgotten or minimized—the fact that a New Order had begun to be built on the ruins of the "Old Europe" has been largely overlooked. But, as Jochen Thies demonstrates, the Nazi ambitions went well beyond the murderous conquest of *Lebensraum* ("living space") in the East. His book shows the concrete preparations the Nazis made for military operations after Barbarossa, preparations that included trans-Atlantic naval and air warfare with ships and planes capable of attacking the United States. Colonial administrators were learning Swahili in preparation for service in African colonies. Ultimately, Thies draws a connection between these ambitions and Hitler's architectural rebuilding plans. In many ways, this is the most fascinating, but also the

---

[11] Hugh Trevor-Roper, "Hitlers Kriegsziele," in: Vierteljahrshefte für Zeitgeschichte, vol. 8 (April 1960), pp. 121–133.

[12] Andreas Hillgruber, *Hitler's Strategie. Politik und Kriegführung, 1940 – 1941*, Frankfurt 1965; Klaus Hildebrand, *The Foreign Policy of the Third Reich*, New York 1973; Gerhard L. Weinberg, *The World at War*, New York 2005..

[13] Milan Hauner, "Did Hitler want a World Dominion?", in *Journal of Contemporary History*, vol. 13 (1978), pp. 15–32; Robert Hertzstein, *When Nazi Dreams Com True*, London 1982.

[14] Jost Dülffer, *Hitler und die Marine*, Düsseldorf 1973.

most terrifying aspect of this book, not least because Speer not only prepared scale models of gigantic buildings and rally grounds for Hitler, but
actual work on constructing such projects continued as late as 1943, one
example being the huge area just outside Nuremberg where the annual
Nazi Party conventions would to take place, with granite constituting
one of the key building materials. The Nazi utopia had begun to turn into
a grim reality not merely in the way the regime destroyed millions of human beings and their homes, but also in the blueprints for the buildings
that would be constructed—or that were already being constructed—upon
those homes, as well as in the post-Barbarossa military plans for world
domination.

This book is the best digest of Hitler's imperial New Order, and it
should be read alongside the many volumes available on the Holocaust
and other racist programs in order to gain a comprehensive impression
of what the world would have been like had Hitler won the war against
Stalin in 1941. Had this happened, the minimum effect would have been
a much longer struggle to defeat not only the brutal imperial conquests of
the Nazis, but also those of Japan in the Far East and Mussolini in Africa.
This is why the year 1941 is a more crucial divide in the history of human
kind in the twentieth century than 1939 or 1945; it was the year when
Hitler expected to defeat Stalin and initiated the Holocaust, as well as
the year when the United States entered the war after the Japanese attack
on Pearl Harbor.

Volker Berghahn

INTRODUCTION

It is the artist, the critic, the quick mind of the so-called "man in the street" or the detached skeptical observer and outsider who, from time to time, can best expose the character of authoritarian leadership, whether through striking commentaries or through other means of irony. Thus Charlie Chaplin in his 1940 film "*The Great Dictator*" played the role of a potentate who closely resembled Hitler, and who juggled with a huge globe until it fell to the ground, smashing into pieces. And thus in Munich and Berlin, crowds reacted with a joke to the frenetic pace of construction of monumental state buildings during the last three years of relative "peace" that preceded the war: saying that it was a four hundred and sixty meter "Reichseinheitsfassade" (a façade of the Unity of the Reich.)[1]

While on a tour of European capitals on the eve of the Second World War, Romanian Foreign Minister, Grigore Gafencu summarized his April 19, 1939, meeting with Hitler with the words that the "Führer" intended—whether Great Britain acted as a friend or a foe—to take control of the entire world.[2] In the first few years after the war, he wrote the following about Hitler:

> He had given himself the role of a reformer. He wanted to create a new world order, in which the old values would be robbed of their meaning, Europe robbed of its historical function, the world robbed of its balance, law robbed of the concept of justice, morality robbed of the sense of mercy, religion robbed of the existence of God. He believed he could bring about such a plan if he modestly proceeded towards this end in stages. The Aryan race would then populate heaven and earth with German people and German Gods.[3]

A study of Hitler's ultimate goals first requires an explanation of terms. The German word for ultimate goals is *"Endziele,"* a heavy pleonasm that stems from the inhuman vocabulary of the Third Reich (*End* meaning final, *Ziele* meaning aims or goals). *Endziele* describes the visions Hitler had about the internal and external state of the empire he was striving to create in the distant future. Yet a study of Hitler's *"Weltanschauung"* (world view) must at the same time include an analysis of the structure and practices of the National Socialist regime, for which the continuity of German foreign policy prior to the regime can provide a framework. A possible conclusion—not an accurate guideline that might pave the way to an investigative study concentrating on Hitler—could be that Hitler intended to conquer the world on a racial basis, as Gafencu once pointed out.[4]

Plans to acquire world power are a general theme within the progress of history. The decisive difference between the more or less "classical" imperialism found from antiquity to the early modern period and the imperialism of National Socialism—in terms of reality and consequences, a revolutionary imperialism, however counter-revolutionary it may have appeared in conceptual terms—is found in the close connection between the politics of internal and external power that takes over, seeking total und ubiquitous control and conformity, when one moves beyond the typically Middle Ages notion of world power as a supranational regime oriented toward universal peace.[5] It cannot be discussed here in detail whether or not this was also the aim of Soviet Communism with its idea of global revolution. Without a doubt, however, from the early 1950s to 1989, the balance of fear tactics practiced by both world powers, the United States of America and the USSR, did express their mutual respect for the opponent's potential to obtain world hegemony.

The Third Reich's foreign policy must be analyzed logically against the backdrop of continuity of hegemonic, geopolitical, and racist goals that had existed since the German Kaiserreich, continuing through World War I until the collapse of Germany's dreams of great power and world rule in 1945.[6] Understanding and accepting this continuity should not diminish the importance of Hitler's singular role, his personal room for maneuvering, his capacity and will to act, and the range of his decisions within National Socialism. Although the German dictator was subject to a set of social conditions, it is critical, in deciding, whether there was a qualitative difference between his concepts and those of a Bismarck, a Tirpitz or a Ludendorff, to describe the extent to which Hitler could act autonomously. Only by identifying and systematically explaining the contribution that his personality and his politics made, can it be understood why National Socialism represented the most radical variant within the spectrum of European Fascisms. Did Hitler want to solidify the status quo, or were there tendencies towards the overthrow of capitalism that he wittingly or unwittingly encouraged in order to make way for a pre-modern utopia?[7] Only an analysis of Hitler's ultimate goals will provide a firmer answer to the question of whether the involvement of the victors of 1945 and an almost global mobilization of forces to crush Hitler's Germany were necessary. The proven extent to which Hitler gave priority to politics and the extensive level of autonomy contained within his "program" culminated in the still unanswered question of whether his program of conquest was continental or global. In examining the development of the National Socialist system, it is therefore necessary to take Hitler's plans and intentions into consideration, although it will always remain controversial whether Hitler, considering the internal political chaos within Germany, could have had any goals at all that he was ever able to act upon in an organized manner. A study of his ultimate goals might therefore bring together the until now immeasurable concepts of the "dynamics" and "program" of the Third Reich.

Finally, it is a matter of great investigative interest to use new questions and methodogical innovations in order to overcome the hurdle of "historical helplessness" (Klaus Hildebrand) with regard to "Hitler" as a phenomenon in an attempt to shed light on a historical figure who "challenged the world and history; which distinguished him from contemporary dictators and puts a question mark behind the terms totalitarianism and fascism."[8]

In his study of Hitler's foreign policy program, Axel Kuhn encountered the difference between Hitler's short-term and long-term goals, and limited himself in his work to the aims of the German dictator, which research on Hitler has unanimously identified. Thus Kuhn also formulated a desideratum of research to offer a monograph about Hitler's long-term and ultimate goals.[9]

Research into Hitler's ultimate goals has been divided and identified as two separate schools of thought since the beginning of the 1960s, schools that may be referred to as either "continental" or "global." One school believes that the ambitions of Hitler's foreign policy encompassed only continental Europe, while the other direction of research understands his goals as reaching far beyond Europe to include complete global conquest. It was Hugh Trevor-Roper who, in a study of Hitler's war aims,[10] opened up the real debate, after the topic had already been investigated by public opinion in countries that were at war with the Third Reich, thanks both to H. Rauschning's controversial books and to other pre-war documents written by German emigrants, as well as to the first pre-war publications.[11]

In his essay, Trevor-Roper took a position that not only opposed the widely accepted opinion which had prevailed, especially since Alan Bullock's biography of Hitler,[12] that showed Hitler as an unscrupulous opportunist both in his domestic and foreign policies, but that also demonstrated through key documents that the German dictator, utilizing a core program he had adhered to in effect for over twenty years, was planning an Eastern empire, meaning the conquest of the western part of the Soviet Union. Shortly after this, Günter Moltmann moved in the opposite direction by focusing on Hitler's *concepts* of world power.[13] Due to the difficulty in securing sources at the time of his writing, Moltmann was cautious about committing to any details. However he suspected that behind the three stages of Hitler's foreign policy, i.e., coming to power, the revision of the Treaty of Versailles, and the imperial expansion to the East), there was a fourth stage which carried global implications. The particulars of the plan had not been conceived, but the guidelines had been set for what was to be the centuries-long, consistent struggle of the "Nazi movement."[14]

The works of Andreas Hillgruber made decisive progress toward clarifying Hitler's ultimate goals. While Trevor-Roper still understood Hitler's "program" to mean a continental European empire, Hillgruber could now expand upon this term in his fundamental study of Hitler's strategy[15] and define it as a continental empire that also included a position of global power beyond Europe. The evidence regarding the role the United States had played in Hitler's thought process since the end of the twenties was decisive. The term "multi-stage plan" that Hillgruber had coined also proved to be a useful instrument of analysis for Hitler's foreign policy. In the first stage, according to Hillgruber's theory, Hitler planned the conquest of an empire stretching across all of Europe right up to the Urals. Then, after the collapse of the existing world powers France and Russia, with the added colonial territories acquired through expansion in Africa, and the development of a fleet that has Atlantic bases, Germany would become a power on a par with Great Britain, the United States and Japan. The consequence of this policy would make it inevitable that at some point in the future the two strongest "world powers," Germany and the United States, would have to engage in an ultimate fight for the domination of the world.

The ever changing meaning of terms such as: "great power," "world power," "world supremacy" and "world rule" should be defined here, albeit using provisional definitions. Within this study, the question of what Hitler understood by these terms will have to be dealt with frequently, as well as how he used these terms and whether or not their definition and use were constant. According to the meaning of these expressions, the struggle to become a great power has to be understood as the aim to reach a status comparable to that of France or Italy. On the other hand, the goal of attaining world power would imply an engagement reaching far beyond the boundaries of Europe. The description of world supremacy or world rule can only be applied when in both cases a dominating position of power is reached on a global scale that would not necessarily exclude other world powers, but that would cause the world leader no longer to face any military challenge from them.

In his already mentioned study of the decisive two years of the war 1940–1941, Hillgruber could define Hitler's intention of obtaining world power, with its obligation to be in constant military conflict, as the only logical consequence of Hitler's biological thinking process which was fuelled by overpopulation and, the resulting need for more living space as well as continued population growth. Hitler's true aims could not be satisfactorily determined from existing sources.[16] Only later, with the help of newly-discovered documents, could Hillgruber defend his theory that Hitler, after having carried out a worldwide Blitzkrieg, then planned to attack the United States in order to gain world supremacy. Measures to be taken in 1941 were to form the foundation for the great, decisive military clash with the Anglo-Saxon powers that was intended to take place in the following steps:

- Bringing the Soviet Union to its knees in three to four months.

- An operation in autumn 1941 with three combat wedges thrust towards Iran, Syria/Iraq and Palestine aimed at shattering Britain's hold on the Middle East. Then the establishment of an operational base in Afghanistan aimed at causing the collapse of British power in India.

- The Japanese advance to Singapore in spring 1941 was to create a pincer effect around India from the East, while avoiding a conflict with America in the Philippines.

- The takeover of Gibraltar in the autumn of 1941, and afterward, the building of a base in Northwest Africa to create a war front position against the United States.[17]

According to Hillgruber's theory, Hitler still had these objectives in mind during the weeks of July 1941 when he met with the Japanese ambassador Oshima, on July 14, 1941, to offer Japan a military pact between the two countries that would create an offensive spearhead meant to destroy their mutual enemies the Soviet Union, the United States, and Great Britain.[18] Had this all come about, then the National Socialist global reach that Moltmann had forecast for the coming centuries would have been moved up to the immediate future.[19] However, in terms of world supremacy, the extremely relevant problem of "Japan" remained unsolved.

Hildebrand verified Hillgruber's starting point in a branch of foreign politics, as represented within colonial politics,[20] and developed them in subsequent works.[21] Like Hillgruber, he also suspected that Hitler planned to attack the United States with Japan's support in the summer of 1941.[22] In an analysis of racist motives and motives born of a quest for political power, he named the following three stages in Hitler's "program": by foregoing the invasion of Great Britain and becoming its ally instead, Hitler could first conquer the Soviet Union. In a second step, going far afield for overseas territories, with the United Kingdom as a partner, "the allies" could tackle together the conflict with the United States in order to resolve the question of world supremacy between North America and Europe. In the last stage, through the takeover of the world by a racist elite, the historical process would be brought to a halt, and the dynamics of world history known up to now would be replaced by the "biologically fixed utopia."[23]

There have been, if not exactly direct disagreements, at least some objections to the theories of Hillgruber and Hildebrand coming from Eberhard Jäckel,[24] Kuhn,[25] and sometimes Hans-Adolf Jacobsen.[26] They do not contest the fact that Hitler had a "program," but they see its scope as being continental rather than global.

A revitalization of the discussion about Hitler's ultimate goals took place thanks to the theories of a group of neo-revisionist historians around Martin Broszat[27] and the Institute for Contemporary History (IfZ), as well as Hans Mommsen.[28] Based on the inner structure of the Third Reich, this branch of research supports the view that Hitler's foreign policy was a "dynamic system without direction."[29] Although it seems that some representatives of this group did not wish to dispute the theoretical idea of world supremacy, their theory seemed to be rather on the same level as that of Rauschning and Bullock, which saw Hitler as an opportunist without scruples. Most importantly, Broszat even rejected the idea of the war against the Soviet Union as being part of a calculated plan. "The goal of gaining new living space in the East had, to a large degree, played the role of an ideological metaphor until 1939–1940, as a symbol for ever increasing activity in the area of foreign policy."[30] This had to be translated into action in 1941 in order to satisfy the internal political dynamics that had been set in motion.

From the vast array of literature on National Socialist foreign policy, Gerhard Weinberg's[31] diplomatically and historically oriented study, a complementary study to Jacobsen, as well as the work on peace initiatives and power politics of WWII by Bernd Martin[32] must be mentioned. While Weinberg simply infers the potentially limitless expansionist character of the Nazi system by observing its programs and dynamics, Martin leaves no doubt that Hitler's aims during the war were for world supremacy. The foundation of these goals, he claims, was similar as a concept to that of the American President Roosevelt, with the fundamental difference that the Americans dreamed of a political and economic system that resembled that of the United States, an open and globally aligned system.

The authors of two Hitler biographies in the 1970s took no position on the issue of world supremacy versus a continental empire, and in fact treated aspects regarding this possibility only marginally. Compared to other parts of his book, Joachim Fest, in his milestone study of Hitler, went into the war years and the accompanying analysis of Hitler's policies much too briefly. However, he did emphasize, as he had in earlier works, the global alignment of the National Socialist system.[33] Unfortunately, David Irving also only glossed over this problem, although one would have expected him to deal with the decisions and reflections of Hitler in more depth, particularly those of July 1941, since the starting point of his study was 1939. His views on Hitler's ultimate goals have remained opaque.[34]

In summary, therefore, as an intermediate stance and temporary result, the conclusion must be drawn that the controversy over "New Lebensraum in the East" versus "Global Supremacy" had not yet been resolved, as works that have not been directly involved in the discussion in recent years have demonstrated, and therefore must be considered as neutral observers.[35]

There has in effect been no change in the position over the past thirty-five years. Those who had spear-headed the debate, above all Hillgruber and Hildebrand, on the one side,[36] and Jäckel, on the other,[37] held on to their views. Having found fresh archival materials, Thies expanded his arguments in a number of further publications.[38] Thus he edited a speech that Hitler had given at Offenburg in November 1930, together with popular reactions to the event.[39] He also published the text of a key speech that Hitler made in Berlin before the commanders of the army on February 10, 1939. The remarks Hitler made on this occasion provide a unique insight into his thought and the global conquests that he was entertaining at this time.[40]

In 1978, Wolfgang Michalka put out an anthology in which he provided a platform to the protagonists and the critics of the hypothesis to advance in compact form their views of whether or not Hitler had aimed at world domination.[41] That same year, Milan Hauner, while favoring

Thies's position on the subject, published an article in which he offered a digest of the debate in English.[42] All the while, the Militärgeschichtliches Forschungsamt (MGFA) in Freiburg moved forward with its large research project of publishing a comprehensive multi-volume history of the Second World War. One of the historians responsible for this project found it difficult to take sides and left the issue unresolved.[43] His colleague at the MGFA, Gerhard Schreiber, took a different line just a few years later. Writing a very important and thoughtful study of how Hitler had been viewed and interpreted over a period of some sixty years, he—having gone through all the arguments that had been advanced up to that point—came down in favor of the world domination hypothesis.[44]

At about the same time, Geoffrey Stoakes examined the concepts that Hitler had developed in the 1920s, carefully weighing the meanings of "world domination" (Weltherrschaft), "world hegemony" (Weltvorherrschaft), and of the world being a "challenge cup" (Wanderpokal) that was passed on from region to region, all of which Hitler had used in his writings.[45] In the end Stoakes opted, surprisingly, for a Eurocentric interpretation of the Nazi's plans of conquest.[46] By contrast, Rainer Zitelmann in his study of Hitler followed Thies's view.[47]

After 1975, due to the growing historical distance from the Nazi dictatorship, the number of books by actual witnesses who had something of value to say about the period declined. Here the memoirs of Nicolaus von Below, Hitler's adjutant representing the air force, should be mentioned. However, his book blended personal recollections with judgments that he had developed after reading the scholarly literature on the subject.[48]

At the beginning of the 1990s, Jäckel continued to adhere to the view that Hitler no longer publicly spoke about his long-term goals after the Nazi Party had expanded its representation in the Reichstag from twelve to 107 seats in 1930.[49] After the early death of Hillgruber in 1989, Hildebrand, on the other hand, sided more firmly with the views that Thies had advanced in favor of the hypothesis concerning world domination.[50] He was supported by Gerhard L. Weinberg in his major study of the Second World War.[51] By contrast, Mark Mazower noted in his study of the Nazis' practices of domination that they ultimately lacked the "transcontinental reach" of the Allies.[52] In the meantime, two books by best-selling authors who had taken up the theme of world domination caused a furor in Britain and Germany. There was Ralph Giordano, who came close to copying the arguments of Hillgruber, Hildebrand, and Thies.[53] In his thriller, Robert Harris, on the other hand, adopted a Eurocentric position and placed the Nazi regime against a backdrop of the huge public buildings that Hitler was planning and that seemed to be emulating those of ancient Assyria and Egypt.[54] Two years later, Harris's book inspired a film, entitled *"Fatherland,"* directed by Christopher Menaul. It was no more than a modest success.

After Joachim C. Fest's biography of Hitler, published in 1973, Ian Kershaw's two volumes made a most important contribution to the field some thirty years later.[55] Since then, the debate has moved increasingly in the direction of the interpretation of Hitler's aims that Hillgruber, whose book was reissued in 1993, had advanced some forty years earlier.[56] Considering that he took up a position against Hillgruber and Hildebrand in the so-called *Historikerstreit* of the 1980s, it may come as a surprise that Hans-Ulrich Wehler sided with the "globalists," as they were now being called. Unlike Jäckel, he attached great value to Hitler's speeches of the fall of 1930, and in particular to the speech he made before a gathering of students at Erlangen University. Without explicitly referring to Hillgruber, he supports the view of the latter by pointing out that, if the war had taken a different course in 1941–42, the final duel for world domination would have taken place between Hitler's Germany and the United States.[57]

Since then, it seems that interest in Hitler's ultimate aims has declined in Germany. It is a different matter in the Anglo-Saxon world. As the American historian Shelley Baranowski, writing of German imperialism from Bismarck to Hitler, put it in her recent book *Nazi Empire*: "The horror of the Third Reich continues to fascinate."[58] She compares the German case with other empires, describing the similarities and differences between Hitler's conquests and other examples that had emerged at various times in the past. And yet, she, too, inclines towards a Eurocentric view. Like many of her American colleagues, the global ambitions of the Nazi dictator are difficult for her to fathom.

The present state of research with regard to specific issues will, as it becomes relevant, be treated at the beginning of the separate chapters.[59]

After taking earlier studies into consideration, the decisive methodological question is: Which questions must be posed in order to ascertain Hitler's ultimate goals with greater accuracy than has been possible up to now? How can we find new sources to investigate his intentions, and what must be pulled into play to judge them? How can the man Hitler be understood, given his statement that he knew of three kinds of confidentiality: "The first being when we talk one on one [as he told admiral Raeder], the second I'll keep to myself, and the third are problems placed far into the future which I don't think through to the end."[60]

The path that Jäckel[61] has chosen to take remains unsatisfactory when speaking of method, because Hitler is only analyzed with respect to his intentions, not in a political and social environment. Kuhn also reduced the problems substantially in the first part of his work, which at the same time makes up the basis of the investigation, when he referred to the foreign policy "program," simply meaning that Hitler's ideas are taken from his written and spoken comments.[62] Hitler's comments with regard to his program must be connected with other material, i.e., written documents, speeches, decisions, to avoid the danger of a Hitler-scholastic that is limited to an exegesis of his own documents.[63]

Going beyond the four source groups listed by Hillgruber to investigate Hitler's foreign policy,[64] a closer look must be turned to Hitler's special areas of interest, people whom he trusted and to whom he was closest, places that were of symbolic significance to him (Munich, Nuremberg, Linz), and people or groups who were of utmost importance with regard to the achievement of his long-term goals (leaders of the SS, architects, generals). Even if the concepts of what is normal (realistic planning and rational designing) break down when studying Hitler, it must still be attempted, within the framework of this methodically difficult tightrope walk, to reach a convincing reconciliation between subjective factors, as far as Hitler's intentions are concerned, and objective factors.

The corrective in the double sense of the meaning is the understanding abroad of Hitler's ultimate goals, especially in the United Kingdom, as well as the survey of his critics and opponents in Germany before 1933, which help to classify Hitler's statements from the distance of the historian's perspective. The "weakness" of the sources at first glance—Hitler's principle of confidentiality, and the turning point of the National Socialist system since the end of 1941—all this requires a new way of thinking by the contemporary historian. Since the quantity of the sources does not offer the hoped-for results, the apparatus must be refined qualitatively and widened at the same time. Propaganda, picture, film, and sound play a role. But it also becomes necessary to use the techniques of medievalists in this case. Also within the field of contemporary history there are sources from the unwritten tradition, which are expressions of their time and their representatives. These need to be analyzed as well.

Hitler's unique position within the National Socialist system permits us to investigate a number of issues that involve foreign policy, but that paradoxically appear to have nothing to do with it. For example, it is well known that Hitler, throughout his lifetime saw himself as an artist and as an architect who could not practice and, who had no certificates. The question therefore becomes whether in the field of architecture there is a correlation between ultimate political goals and the creation of structures in the building sector, or at least a preparation. It is well known that throughout history one can demonstrate that a form of interdependence exists between revolution and architecture. It would be essential in this regard to know exactly when decisions about architecture were made in the Third Reich, or indeed how long prior to political developments or expectations they were made. The research of architecture with a foreign policy premise would be a vitally important instrument to illustrate Hitler's long-term plans. It could possibly even draw the outer limits of a projected plan for the creation of state power in the far distant future. For the interpretation of the symbols of power as they are represented in architecture, its models and parallels, as well as Hitler's understanding of history and art, must all be investigated in order to identify the flow of ideas and the decision-making process. In other words, the entire area of reasoning and conjectural argumentation should be used to comprehend Hitler's ultimate goals.

Another variation of Hitler's passion for architecture was represented by his interest in weapons development. Jost Dülffer[65] was able to show how Hitler, relatively soon after coming to power, became involved in the armaments program of the navy, and in doing so, had probably anticipated his long-term plans in foreign policy. The question that comes to mind is whether or not there were corresponding observations within the armaments program of the Luftwaffe or the army. How openly did Hitler speak to the planners and generals of the Wehrmacht? Were there other social groups, perhaps organizations of the new generation in Germany, elite schools like the "Ordensburgen," with whom he communicated more openly? In the event of further positive findings in such secondary fields of research, proof could be furnished that Hitler actually had a well-defined long-term plan that worked toward a predetermined goal.

The main source of information about Hitler's ultimate goals is characterized first of all by well-known, and to a large degree, published primary material, to which several new editions have been added during the course of the 1960s and 70s. These, however, merely represent secondary resources.[66]

The work began, in the spirit of Waldemar Besson, to find "new meanings rather than new sources"[67] in the research of National Socialism and to take stock of previous discussions about Hitler's ultimate goals. However, it could be expanded in the course of these investigations. Surprising findings, which in one case took the form of a key document on Hitler, have enriched this study with new angles and previously unknown sources.

The attempt to study especially the years 1920–1933, regarding the central aspect of this doctoral dissertation, brought to light a surprising amount of unknown material, showing how desperately necessary a comprehensive Hitler edition has become, and how inadequate even the study of Hitler's own comments has been up to this point. In this light, the 1920–1933 southern German edition of the "Völkischer Beobachter," was used, as well as the files of the NSDAP main archive kept in the Federal State Archives (BA) in Koblenz and the collection of brochures at the Institute for Contemporary History (IfZ) in Munich and in the re-search unit for the History of National Socialism in Hamburg.

With regard to Hitler's architectural policies, the "memoirs" of Albert Speer (which have not yet been analyzed within the framework of a study on foreign policy were of greatest value, as was the extensive official ma-terial from the Third Reich contained in the Institute for Contemporary History and in the Hamburg research unit.[68] With new questions and a different approach, the files of the archives of the Reichskanzlei (the cen-tral governmental office of the Reich), on the field of political history, as well as those of the chief civil architect for Berlin in the Federal State Archives in Koblenz, offered important information about Hitler in the years 1933–1935. Film material from the Institute for Scientific Film in Göttingen broadened the scope in this area, where written memoirs in general were of great value.

With regard to the policies on armaments and the "special relationship" in this field between Hitler and the Wehrmacht, the best sources came, strangely enough, not from the State and Military Archives in Freiburg (BA/MA), but rather the Federal State Archives in Koblenz. The finding here were here the documents of several previously unknown speeches that Hitler gave to officers in 1939–40. Important new discoveries regard-ing the history of the Luftwaffe were provided through documents held at the Public Record Office in London (PRO) and in individual company information from the German aerospace industry as well.

Questioning witnesses was only valuable to a certain extent because the themes discussed understandably forced people, especially former gen-erals and former top civil servants, to be very reticent. In the 1970s, the passing time further reduced the number of sources. Unfortunately, the questioning of witnesses that was done principally by the Munich Insti-tute for Contemporary History hardly dealt with the question of Hitler's ultimate goals at all.

Notes

1. Compare H. Schacht, *Abrechnung mit Hitler* (Hamburg, 1948), 52. *Zum Witz im Drit-ten Reich: Meldungen aus dem Reich. Auswahl aus den geheimen Lageberichten des Sicher-heitsdienstes der SS 1939–1944*, ed. H. Boberach (Munich, 1968); M. Vandrey. *Der politische Witz im Dritten Reich* (Munich, 1967).

2. G. Gafencu, *Europas letzte Tage. Eine politische Reise im Jahre 1939.* (Zürich, 1946), 87f.

3. Ibid., 91. Compare also ibid., 7f (foreword), 27, 56, 64. The French ambassador of many years in Berlin made a similar judgment of Hitler's ultimate goals: A. François-Poncet, *Als Botschafter in Berlin* (Mainz, 1947), 6, 86, 359. Compare M. Braubach, *Hitlers Machtergreifung*. The reports of the French ambassador, François-Poncet, about the occurrences in Germany from July, 1932 until July, 1933. In *Festschrift (FS) für L Brandt*, ed. by J. Meixner and G. Kegel (Cologne-Opladen, 1968), 460.

4. Also: H. A. Winkler, *Gesellschaftsform und Außenpolitik. Eine Theorie von Lorenz von Stein in zeitgeschichtlicher Perspektive*, in *HZ* 214 (1972), 349ff.

5. K.D. Bracher, W. Sauer, & G. Schulz, *Die nationalsozialistische Machtergreifung* (Cologne-Opladen, 1962), 220.

6. Standard, A. Hillgruber, *Kontinuität und Diskontinuität in der deutschen Außenpolitik von Bismarck bis Hitler* (Düsseldorf, 1969). Revised version now in *Großmachtpolitik und Militarismus im 20. Jahrhundert. 3 Beiträge zum Kontinuitätsproblem* (Düsseldorf, 1974). Also compare to that the older work of L. Dehio, *Gleichgewicht oder Hegemonie. Betrachtung über ein Grundproblem der neueren Staatengeschichte* (Krefeld, 1948). Further: K. Hildebrand, „Hitlers Ort in der Geschichte des preußisch-deutschen Nationalstaats," in *HZ* 217 (1973), 584–632; Hildebrand, „Innenpolitische Antriebskräfte der nationalsozialistischen Außenpolitik," in *FS für H. Rosenberg* (Göttingen, 1974), 635–651.

7. In addition: H. A. Turner, Jr., *Faschismus und Anti-Modernismus*. In *Faschismus und Kapitalimus in Deutschland* (Göttingen, 1972), 157–182.

8. K. Hildebrand, *Weltmacht oder Untergang. Hitlers Deutschland 1941–1945.* (MS, Bielefeld, 1974),15.

9. A. Kuhn, *Hitlers außenpolitisches Programm. Entstehung und Entwicklung 1919–1939.* (Stuttgart, 1970), 13.

10. H.R. Trevor-Roper, *Hitlers Kriegsziele*. In *VfZG* 8 (1960), 121–133.

11. The following gives an overview: M. Michaelis, "World Power or World Dominion? A Survey of the Literature on Hitler's Plan of World Dominion. (1937–1970)," *The Historical Journal* 15 (1972), 331–360.

12. A. Bullock, *Hitler. Eine Studie über Tyrannei* (Düsseldorf, 1953). In the completely revised edition of 1964, Bullock takes the position of Trevor-Roper.

13. G. Moltmann, "Weltherrschaftsiden Hitlers," In *Festschrift für Egmont Zechlin* (Hamburg, 1961),197–240.

14. Ibid., 234f,. On this level, there are also the interpretations of foreign policies based on examinations of the structure of National Socialism: F. Neumann, *Behemoth. The Structure and Practice of National Socialism* (New York, 1942), 37; H. Arendt, *Elemente und Ursprünge totaler Herrschaft*, 2nd ed. (Frankfurt am Main, 1962) 209ff, 609ff, and elsewhere; H. Buchheim and E. Eucken-Erdsiek & G. Buchheit & H.G. Adler, *Der Führer ins Nichts. Eine Diagnose Adolf Hitlers* (Rastatt, 1960),41; Bracher, Sauer and Schulz, 220; H. Grebing, *Der Nationalsozialismus. Ursprung und Wesen*, (Munich-Vienna,1965), 66f.

15. A. Hillgruber, *Hitlers Strategie. Politik und Kriegführung 1940–1941* (Frankfurt am Main, 1965).

16. Ibid., 584.

17. Ibid., 317ff; Hillgruber, *Der Faktor Amerika in Hitlers Strategie 1938–1941. Aus Politik und Zeitgeschichte. Beilage zum „Parlament".* B 19/66 (May 11, 1966), 14ff.

18. Hillgruber, *Faktor Amerika*, 17.

19. Hillgruber, *Deutschlands Rolle in der Vorgeschichte der beiden Weltkriege* (Göttingen, 1967), 68, 120.

20. K. Hildebrand, *Vom Reich zum Weltreich. Hitler, NSDAP und koloniale Frage 1919–1945* (Munich, 1969), 88, 694, and elsewhere.

21. Representing further studies: *Deutsche Außenpolitik 1933–1945. Kalkül oder Dogma?* (Stuttgart, 1973).

22. Ibid., 114.

23. Hildebrand, *Außenpolitik*, 27f.

24. E. Jäckel, *Hitlers Weltanschauung. Entwurf einer Herrschaft* (Tübingen, 1969), 29, 52.

25. Kuhn, 13, 135.

26. H. A. Jacobsen and W. Jochmann, eds., *Ausgewählte Dokumente zur Geschichte des Nationalsozialismus 1933–1945*. 3 vols. (Bielefeld, 1960–1966), 118; H.-A. Jacobsen, *Nationalsozialistische Außenpolitik 1933–1938* (Frankfurt am Main-Berlin, 1968), 7, note 23, 446ff.

27. M. Broszat, *Der Staat Hitlers* (Munich, 1969).

28. H. Mommsen, „Nationalsozialismus," in *Sowjetsystem und demokratische Gesellschaft*, 4:703.

29. B. Freudenfeld, ed. *Stationen der deutschen Geschichte 1919–1945* (Stuttgart 1962), 148. A discussion by Brozat about Trevor-Roper's seminar paper can be found in "Hitler's Kriegsziele," ibid., 9–28, compare with note 10 above.

30. M. Broszat, „Soziale Motivation und Führer-Bindung des Nationalsozialismus," in *VfZG* 18 (1970), 408. R. Bollmus takes a mediating position for the group of those representing the continental viewpoint of Hitler's ultimate goals in *Das Amt Rosenberg und seine Gegner* (Stuttgart, 1970), 11, 245, 247. Despite the chaotic structure within the Third Reich, he admits to Hitler having been consistent in seeking new living space in the East and in seeking to exterminate the Jews, without seeing any organized plan in following principles.

31. G.L. Weinberg, *The Foreign Policy of Hitler's Germany. Diplomatic Revolution in Europe 1933–36* (Chicago, 1970), 7, 358. The two-volume work by N. Rich, *Hitler's War Aims* (New York, 1973–1974). Even though Rich considers research results to great extent, he tends more to the idea that Hitler's foreign policies were opportunistic.

32. B. Martin, *Friedensinitiativen und Machtpolitik im Zweiten Weltkrieg 1939–1942.* (Düsseldorf, 1974), 26, 244, 252, 300, 335f, 505f.

33. J.C. Fest, *Hitler. Eine Biographie* (Frankfurt am Main-Berlin-Vienna, 1973), 18, 147, 334, 599, 736, 877, 938ff, 1031; Fest, *Das Gesicht des Dritten Reiches. Profile einer totalitären Herrschaft* (Munich, 1963), 81f, 98; Fest, „Hitler-Skizzen zu einem Porträt," in *Der Monat* 240 (1968), 36.

34. D. Irving, *Hitler und seine Feldherren* (Frankfurt am Main-Berlin-Vienna, 1975), 145, 205, 219, 553.

35. In addition: J. Petersen, *Hitler-Mussolini. Die Entstehung der Achse Berlin-Rom 1933–1936* (Tübingen, 1973), xxi. Petersen shows skepticism toward the theories of Broszat and Hildebrand. Similarly: P. Krüger, *Das Jahr 1941 in der europäischen Politik* (Munich-Vienna, 1972), 14f, 34f.

36. See, inter alia, Andreas Hillgruber, "Hitler und die USA, 1933–1945," in *Europas Mitte*, edited by O. Franz, (Göttingen-Zürich, 1987), 125–44; Klaus Hildebrand, *Das vergangene Reich. Deutsche Außenpolitik von Bismarck bis Hitler* (Stuttgart, 1995), 746ff.

37. Eberhard Jäckel, *Hitlers Herrschaft* (Stuttgart, 1991), 66.

38. See, for example, Jochen Thies, "Hitler's European Building Programme," *Journal of Contemporary History* 13 (1978), 413–31; Thies, "Nazi Architecture - A Blueprint for

World Domination: The Last Aims of Hitler," in *Nazi Propaganda*, ed. David Welch (London, 1983), 45–64; Thies, "Peut-on qualifier Hitler de 'dictateur faible'?," *Revue d'histoire de la deuxieme guerre mondiale* 120 (1980), 33–48; Thies, "Hitler-Architekt der Weltherrschaft,'" in *Faszination und Gewalt. Zur politischen Ästhetik des Nationalsozialismus*, ed. B. Ogan and W.W. Weiss (Nuremberg, 1992), 177–196.

39. Thus Hitler in Offenburg on November 8, 1930. See also the documents relating to Hitler's ultimate aims in *Ortenau* 57 (1977), 296–312.

40. Jost Dülffer et al., eds., *Hitlers Städte. Baupolitik im Dritten Reich. Eine Dokumentation* (Cologne-Vienna, 1978), 289–315.

41. Jochen Thies, "Hitlers 'Endziele': Zielloser Aktionismus, Kontinentalimperium oder Weltherrschaft?," in *Nationalsozialistische Außenpolitik*, ed. Wolfgang Michalka (Darmstadt, 1978), 70–91. See also the counter-position taken up by Dietrich Aigner, "Hitler und die Weltherrschaft," ibid., 49–69.

42. Milan Hauner, "Did Hitler Want World Dominion?," *Journal of Contemporary History*, 13 (1978), 15–32.

43. Manfred Messerschmidt, "Außenpolitik und Kriegsvorbereitung," in *Das Deutsche Reich und der Zweite Weltkrieg*, vol 1, ed. Militärgeschichtliches Forschungsamt (Stuttgart, 1979), 542f.

44. Gerhard Schreiber, *Hitler. Interpretationen, 1923–1983* (Darmstadt, 1988), 365.

45. Geoffrey Stoakes, *Hitler and the Quest for World Dominion* (Leamington Spa, 1986), 161ff, 166, 222.

46. Ibid., 236.

47. Rainer Zitelmann, *Hitler. Selbstverständnis eines Revolutionärs* (Darmstadt, 1989), 81, 103.

48. Nicolaus von Below, *Als Hitlers Adjutant, 1937–1945* (Mainz, 1980), 296.

49. Jäckel, *Hitlers Herrschaft*, 67.

50. Klaus Hildebrand, *Das Dritte Reich* (Munich, 1995),193ff.

51. Gerhard L. Weinberg, *A World at Arms. A Global History of WW II* (Cambridge, 2005), 178.

52. Mark Mazower, *Hitlers Empire. How the Nazis Ruled Europe* (New York, 2008), 579.

53. Ralph Giordano, *Wenn Hitler den Krieg gewonnen hätte. Die Pläne der Nazis nach dem Endsieg* (Hamburg, 1989).

54. Robert Harris, *Fatherland* (London, 1992).

55. Ian Kershaw, *Hitler, 1889–1945*, 2 vols. (London 1998–2000).

56. Kershaw, *Fateful Choices. Ten Decisions That Changed the World, 1940–1941* (New York, 2007).

57. Hans-Ulrich Wehler, *Deutsche Gesellschaftsgeschichte*, vol. 4 (Munich, 2003), 848.

58. Shelley Baranowski, *Nazi Empire. German Colonialism and Imperialism from Bismarck to Hitler* (Cambridge, 2010), 233ff.

59. With regard to the research in the former GDR, it can be said that because of the official Komintern definition of fascism, Hitler was not seen as having had an independent role. With regard to literature about German imperialism striving for world domination, compare: "Historische Forschungen in der DDR 1960–1970. Analysis and reports on the Thirteenth international Historian Congress in Moscow in 1970," special edition of *ZfG* (1970), 581 note 139, 585 note 158.

60. H. Picker, *Hitlers Tischgespräche im Führungshauptquartier 1941–1942*, published by P. E. Schramm in cooperation with A. Hillgruber and M. Vogt (Stuttgart, 1963), 117. This statement was given by Raeder's chief of staff, Admiral Schulte-Mönting. *Der Prozess gegen die Hauptkriegsverbrecher vor dem Internationalen Militärgerichtshof* (IMT), 42 vols (Nuremberg, 1947–1949), 14:341.

61. Cf. note 24.
62. Kuhn, 11f.
63. Petersen is of this opinion, xxf, cf. note 35.
64. A. Hillgruber, „Quellen und Quellenkritik zur Vorgeschichte des Zweiten Weltkrieges," *WWR* 14 (1964), 116 ff.
65. J. Dülffer, *Weimar, Hitler und die Marine. Reichspolitik und Flottenbau 1920–1939* (Düsseldorf, 1973).
66. H. von Kotze, ed., *Heeresadjutant bei Hitler 1938–1943. Aufzeichnungen des Majors Engel* (Stuttgart, 1974); Heinrich Himmler, *Geheimreden 1933 bis 1945 und andere Ansprachen*, ed. B. F. Smith and A.F. Peterson (Frankfurt am Main-Berlin-Vienna, 1974); M. Salewski, ed., *Die deutsche Seekriegsleitung. Denkschriften und Lagebetrachtungen 1938–1944* (Frankfurt am Main, 1973); *Lagevorträge des Oberbefehlshabers der Kriegsmarine vor Hitler 1939–1945*, ed. G. Wagner, (Munich, 1972); *Die Weizsäcker-Papiere 1933–1950*, ed. L.E. Hill (Frankfurt am Main-Berlin-Vienna,1974). With reservations, the writings of E.L. Bird can also be included: *Hess. Der "Stellvertreter des Führers"* (Munich-Vienna-Basel, 1974), as well as the thoroughly quoted, newly reconstructed material brought to light by Irving in the 1970s in the framework of his Hitler biography. Finally: Albert Speer, *Spandauer Tagebücher* (Frankfurt am Main-Berlin-Vienna, 1975).
67. W. Besson in *Die Zeit*, July 8, 1966.
68. A. Speer, *Erinnerungen* (Frankfurt am Main-Berlin, 1969).

Part I

HITLER'S ULTIMATE GOALS
1920–1933
"Lebensraum" Only in the East?

Chapter 1

HITLER AND HIS CRITICS

Two months after the sensational outcome for the NSDAP in the national elections of September 14, 1930, which increased the party's seats in parliament from twelve to 107, Hitler gave a speech in Erlangen.[1] The central theme of his lecture delivered November 13, 1930, in front of the professors and students of the university of that city in Franconia was Germany's role in world domination. According to Hitler, Germany, more than any other nation in the world, was predestined for global supremacy. These comments did not go unchallenged. Bernhard Schmeidler, a professor of medieval and modern history, criticized Hitler's comments on world supremacy very sharply and referred to them as "unbridled demagogy" and "factual nonsense."[2] Three days after Hitler's speech, the National Socialist student organization at the University of Erlangen (NSDStB) demanded a discussion with Schmeidler on the subject of German global supremacy. It was interrupted by riots and failed to offer any solution.

Current research has verified the events of November 1930 in Erlangen.[3] Before Hitler's seizure of power, there existed no organized social or political group in Germany who understood his ultimate goals, and therefore there was no one to provide a warning prior to his rise to power. As long as there is a lack of study in this area, the only references that can be made are to individuals who had more or less clearly predicted Hitler's "program" since 1930.[4] By September 14, 1930, Hitler was a significant political factor and had managed to find a large following among the German public. How, for example, did people react to the foreign policy parts of *Mein Kampf*? Up until 1933, some 287,000 copies had been purchased fairly voluntarily, long before the work became an obligatory addition to every German bookcase.[5]

From among the various books and brochures about Hitler that were in circulation before his "*Machtergreifung*" (seizure of power), three should be taken as an example of how Hitler's ultimate goals were received by his contemporaries during the closing years of the Weimar Republic.[6] The publishers of anti-Hitler literature were certainly not representative of the general public of their time. They were mostly intellectuals, staunch democrats, and defenders of the parliamentary system created during the first German republic. The author of a flyer from January 1931, viewed the "Hitler problem" with scientific distance and great knowledge. "If the 'Third Reich' is not satisfied with the land we have," his analysis of Hitler's foreign policy vision said, "then this part of the Earth should be set on fire. Because in the whole world lives according to Hitler eternally the idea of survival of the fittest."[7] It is interesting in this context that the author refused to see a common identity between Italian Fascism and National Socialism. "For Hitler the state is only an instrument to establish a utopian, racially superior leadership and for his plans of a social revolution."[8]

More encompassing and detailed was the analysis of the Nazi foreign policy in a flyer dated September 1931. In this brochure, meant for distribution in Germany and abroad, the author based his views on an analysis of *Mein Kampf,* the daily "Völkischer Beobachter" (The People's Observer), "Angriff" (Attack), and other National Socialist newspapers, as well as the comments of Nazi Party leaders. He concluded that National Socialism was an issue that was not just limited to Germany.[9] Rather, there existed a much greater danger in Germany failing as a nation and consequently causing a catastrophe in Europe and the largerworld,[10] because Hitler would seek nothing less than world supremacy.[11]

In his book "*Hitler's Weg*" (Hitler's Way), published at the end of 1931, Theodor Heuss, who would later become the first president of the Federal Republic of Germany in 1949, and who at the time was a reader of political science at a special institute in Berlin (comparable to the London School of Economics), didn't go quite as far in his evaluation of *Mein Kampf.* According to Heuss, the core of Hitler's foreign policy was to acquire new territory in Eastern Europe. Heuss felt that this was his "maximum aim."[12]

Notes

1. With regard to details of the speech, cf. 51ff, this volume.

2. The dissertation by M. Franze, *Die Erlanger Studentenschaft 1918–1945* (Würzburg, 1972), 128ff, gives a vivid picture of the attendant circumstances of Hitler's speech.

3. Standard: K. Lange, *Hitlers unbeachtete Maximen. „Mein Kampf" und die Öffentlichkeit* (Stuttgart, 1968); not satisfactory: P.W. Fabry, *Mutmaßungen über Hitler. Urteile von Zeitgenossen* (Düsseldorf, 1969); further: A. Grosser, *Hitler, la presse et la naissance d'une dictature* (Paris, 1959).

4. Such studies should differentiate at least on two levels: they should incorporate the reactions on the NSDAP elections results inside Germany (working class, middle class, young academics, high civil servants, generals etc.) between 1930–1933 and make a difference between the late Weimar Republic and the first years of the dictatorship, when more and more Germans left the country. It is especially difficult to judge the literature of emigrants. What was propaganda and what was serious analysis? The comment of the émigré chancellor H. Brüning at the end of 1941 refers to other problems: "The worst thing is that most emigrants do not know what happened in Germany between the last war and the Nazi's rise to power. You can hardly find three emigrants who can agree. Emigrants often have no possibility to know what people at home really feel. Generally everybody knows something about the city or the province in which he lived. This leads to completely false judgments." –H. Brüning, *Briefe und Gespräche 1934-1945*, ed. C. Nix, (Stuttgart, 1974), 378. Further available literature includes K.R. Grossmann, *Emigration. Geschichte der Hitler-Flüchtlinge 1933–1945* (Frankfurt am Main, 1969); P. Stahlberger, *Der Zürcher Verleger Emil Oprecht und die deutsche politische Emigration 1933–1945* (Zurich, 1970); J. Radkau, *Die deutsche Emigration in den USA. Ihr Einfluß auf die amerikanische Europapolitik 1933–1945* (Düsseldorf, 1971) Generally it should be noted that the study of emigration is still in the phase of collecting material.

For the main questions in this study, the following studies, mostly written in exile, should be mentioned: I. Harand, *„Sein Kampf"*. *Antwort an Hitler* (Vienna, 1935), 6, 332, 337; K. Heiden, *Adolf Hitler. Eine Biographie*, 2 vols. (Zurich, 1936–37), 2: 237ff, 332f; R. Olden, *Hitler* (Amsterdam, 1936), 206; H. Rauschning, *Gespräche mit Hitler* (Zurich, 1940), 42ff, 61ff, 105, 115ff. and elsewhere. Rauschning, *Die Revolution des Nihilismus. Kulisse und Wirklichkeit im Dritten Reich* (Zurich-New York, 1938), 332 (!), 384ff, 477, and elsewhere; A. Stein, *Adolf Hitler, Schüler der "Weisen von Zion"* (Karlsbad, 1936), 31f, 83ff, 108, and elsewhere.

To establish the attitude of the population before and after 1933, W. Kempowski produced a remarkably methodical study worth reading: *Haben Sie Hitler gesehen? Deutsche Antworten*, epilogue by S. Haffner (Munich, 1973).

5. Lange, *Hitlers unbeachtete Maximen*, 31.

6. Further points from Lange, 38ff.

7. G. Schultze-Pfaelzer, *Anti-Hitler. Eine unabhängige Zeitbetrachtung* (Berlin, 1931), 17.

8. Ibid., 28.

9. H. Klotz: *Die Außenpolitik der Nationalsozialisten* (Berlin, 1931), 3.

10. Ibid., 32.

11. Ibid., 19.

12. T. Heuss, *Hitlers Weg. Eine Schrift aus dem Jahre 1932*, ed. E. Jäckel (Tübingen, 1968). Compare also J.C. Hess, *Theodor Heuss vor 1933. Ein Beitrag zur Geschichte des demokratischen Denkens in Deutschland* (Stuttgart, 1974), 99.

Chapter 2

CURRENT RESEARCH

Even after the extensive discussion regarding the emergence and development of Hitler's "program"[1] in the 1970s, there are still important points that controversy.[2] Along with diverging opinions on the content of Hitler's comments[3] and on the extent of his plans for expansion, new studies have shown that there is no clarity about the time frame in which his "program" was to be enacted.

Hillgruber[4] characterized the period from 1919 to 1928 as a time frame in which Hitler's ideas progressed in various "stages," toward a "program" that was solid at its core. Hillgruber believed that Hitler stuck to this plan right up to his suicide on April 30, 1945. Dülffer[5] took a similar line of reasoning. He saw "definite indications" of Hitler's foreign policy views as having existed since around 1920, appearing more in the formation of "solid thought patterns" and less concerned with the political arguments of the day. Dülffer also took the time frame up to 1928, but emphasized that Hitler's "program" was basically finalized with the publication of *Mein Kampf*. Hildebrand[6] attempted to determine the development of Hitler's objectives in a more subtly diverse manner. During the period from 1919 to 1923, a phase he regarded as the time when Hitler's "thought formation" on foreign policy took place, he especially singled out 1922 as the year when certain concepts of Hitler's reached their final form: a synthesis of the issue of race, as well as a form of government and geopolitics.[7] Hildebrand saw 1923 as the year in which Hitler's foreign policy ideas reached their final form,[8] which was newly set down and expanded to include enmity towards the United States in the *Second Book*.[9] Kuhn,[10] who has most thoroughly dealt with the emergence of Hitler's "program," represented the viewpoint that a gradual development between 1920 and 1924[11] led to the completion of Hitlers's foreign policy program.[12] Later, however, Kuhn qualified this assertion and divided Hitler's program into two stages, before and after 1925. Up to 1925, Hitler's "program" is centered on Europe, and after that, it broadens to take in such power factors as America and Japan, without ever changing the priority of the goals regarding continental Europe.[13] Similarly, Jäckel saw 1924 as the decisive date, as that year marked Hitler's change of direction from revisionist politics to imperialistic expansion politics.[14] On the other hand, Jäckel emphasized the importance of the year 1926, the year Hitler's foreign policy views were completed[15], and 1928, the year in which Hitler, in his *Second Book*, brought to an end the foundation upon which his entire historical perception was based.[16] Finally, Fest[17] emphasized the importance of *Mein Kampf*, equating the drafting time of that work to the molding and completion of Hitler's "program." As Fest saw it, the years after the completion of *Mein Kampf* were simply a time of arranging and smoothing off some of the rough edges, but contain no further development.[18]

Regardless of the differences, the common denominator of all the descriptions mentioned above is the decisive importance given to *Mein Kampf*, and to the period in which it was written, 1924–1926, within the framework of Hitler's thinking on foreign policy. Accordingly, *Mein Kampf* should be taken as "last resort" when examining Hitler's goals. But an urgent question to be answered is whether or not *Mein Kampf* also contains any details of long-term objectives along with its programmatic announcement of "short-term goals."[19] In other words, did Hitler differentiate between tactical moves by which Germany might gain a dominant position in Central Europe"a position that could be built up toward the ultimate goal of a continental European empire"and a strategy that went above and beyond his aims in Europe, one oriented toward expansion beyond the borders of the continent? In the latter case, were these plans just part of his goals for achieving" world power" for Germany, or did they represent a decisive step, on the road to world supremacy? In that case, the suspected road map for world supremacy should be examined with the following questions in mind: How concrete are the references to Hitler's goals? What are the geographical regions in question? Which enemies does he mention? What time frame does he foresee? Which instruments of power are to be used, and what conditions are set? Finally, how does the time frame relate to Hitler's lifespan, in other words, what does he think can be achieved within his lifetime? What has to happen after him?

Plans for reaching beyond Europe have been mentioned quite often in connection with *Mein Kampf*. This stems from Hitler's reception of the "Protokolle der Weisen von Zion" (Protocols of the Elders of Zion)[20] which, according to the latest research, came earlier than was previously thought.[21] The appearance of the Protocols not only accelerated the formation of Hitler's thoughts, but also led to the axiom of the racist ideology, formed by socio-Darwinism, that he developed and that climaxed in his utter opposition to Judaism.[22] Bolshevism was the other form taken by his final conception of the enemy, and lesser forms of what he saw as evil could be found in terms such as "democracy" or in the picture he presented of the still undecided fight between "Judaism" and countries with a certain "race content."

Hitler also referred to Judaism with such terms and images as "Internationality" or "international Jewish finance," the socialist "internationals," Pan movements, and every sort of supranational organization. Even Christianity[23] was banished to his "opposing world" from time to time. But for Hitler, the victory of the Bolsheviks had already established "Jewish rule" in Russia, which to him was identical with the absolute rule of "Judaism." According to Hitler, the Western democracies, including the Weimar Republic, were already highly influenced by the Jewish world, although not yet totally lost, since their "ethnic national defenses" were still in working order.

This general situation, which was by no means heading toward a status quo in Europe or in the entire world, made it urgent, in Hitler's view, to set the resistance of the "Aryan race" against the alleged dynamic "Jewish" principle, which would supposedly be the only effective possibility of retaliating. This is a theory often mentioned in the field of Hitler research.[24] Of the European "Aryan core races," which in Hitler's opinion also existed abroad (e.g., in the United States), the German people were the strongest, and they were therefore chosen to take on the fight against Judaism in the name of the entire world. His battle orders could only be suited for "victory or demise," as the world could not be freed of the "Jewish plague" through compromise, according to Hitler. "Victory," for the inmate writing at Landsberg prison, meant the complete annihilation of the opponent, and the establishment of a new status quo the globe would be brought to the level of a "biologically defined statics of an utopia," along the lines of Hitler's racist projections.[25]

The defensive character of Hitler's comments has been pointed out several times in the literature on the subject. It is widely assumed that his plans for world takeover stemmed from his feeling of being threatened.[26] Similarly, only with a positive thrust, considerations of Hitler in the role of a self-proclaimed deliverer and savior of humanity have also been brought forward.[27] Hitler's own vision of a "German history of world power" offers sufficient evidence of this. In Hitler's interpretation of history, which always referred to the present and the future, there was only one empire that had been really a world power, the "Imperium Romanum."[28] According to Hitler, Jews and Christians had undermined that entity, through Paul, who was working as a tool of the Jews, and whose Christianization of Rome had resulted in the destruction of its world power.[29] In this great hour of need, the saviors had been the Teutons, from whom Hitler derived his 2,000 year long "German history of world power," which had come to a decisive interruption three hundred years ago. The Thirty Years War, for which "Christianity" was once again to blame in Hitler's eyes, had robbed Germany of its chance to claim world supremacy during its first run. Based on this view of history, Hitler planned to reach back and further develop humanity to a level dating before the Christian era and before the Jewish religion. He saw no option but to pit his "chosen race" against God's "chosen people." Their extermination would prove the Aryan's elitist supremacy. "The theological fact must be removed in order to make way for the realization of the biological myth."[30]

Notes

1. The term "program," which has been used in the field of research ever since Trevor-Roper's essay on Hitler's war aims, does not mean the National Socialist party program, but rather Hitler's expansionist foreign policy: The formation of a European continental empire, the development of a position of world power. Compare also: Hillgruber, *Strategie*, 21 note 15.
2. In two initial studies that thoroughly deal with Hitler's aims in the foreign policy of his early years, the emphasis was set differently. G. Schubert, *Anfänge nationalsozialistischer Außenpolitik* (Cologne, 1963), 242f. Schubert already saw the basic structure of the National Socialist foreign policy from 1919 to 1923 and referred to this period as the "first stage in the formation of Third Reich foreign policy." F. Dickmann, „Machtwille und Ideologie in Hitlers außenpolitische Zielsetzung vor 1933," in *Spiegel der Geschichte. FS for M. Braubach* (Münster, 1964), 915–941. Dickmann took the position that only source material from *Mein Kampf* onward could securely be accepted, and referred to Hitler's early speeches as unreliable evidence due to the pressures that were in the limelight at the time. –Cf. ibid., 916.
3. Petersen, xxi. He warned of the risks of "Hitler-Scholastics," a danger that exhausts itself in the exegesis of his writings.
4. Hillgruber, *Faktor Amerika*, 3; Hillgruber, *Vorgeschichte*, 67; Hillgruber: „Die ‚Endlösung' und das deutsche Ostimperium als Kernstück des rassenideologischen Programms des Nationalsozialismus," *VfZG* 20 (1972), 134f.
5. Dülffer, 204, 211.
6. Hildebrand, *Weltreich*, 71.
7. Ibid., 75. –Compare Cf. D. Grieswelle, *Propaganda der Friedlosigkeit. Eine Studie zu Hitlers Rhetorik 1920–1933* (Stuttgart, 1972), 178.
8. Hildebrand, *Weltreich*, 87.

9. Ibid., 86. –Also cf. Hildebrand, *Außenpolitik*, 25.

10. Kuhn, 108f.

11. Kuhn justified this division with the closing of the fourth chapter in *Mein Kampf*, as only here are thoughts on foreign policy brought together in the first volume. Cf. ibid., 108.

12. Ibid.

13. Ibid., 138.

14. Jäckel, *Hitlers Weltanschauung*, 157.

15. Ibid., 48.

16. Ibid., 135.

17. Fest, 295.

18. The listed works are simply a selection, an unavoidable measure taken in view of the volume of secondary literature.

19. This differentiation was made by Kuhn, for example, and he also underlined the necessity of answering more extensive questions. Cf. also Hildebrand, *Weltreich*, 77.

20. Schubert, 27; Hillgruber, *Vorgeschichte*, 68; Hillgruber, „‚Endlösung' und Ostimperium," 136; Hildebrand, 7f.

21. W. Horn, *Führerideologie und Parteiorganisation in der NSDAP (1919–1933* (Düsseldorf, 1972). He can prove that the "*Protokolle der Weisen von Zion*" was being passed around in the DAP already in 1920, ibid., 31 note 5.

22. For further comparison: Jäckel, *Hitlers Weltanschauung*, passim; Hillgruber, *Vorgeschichte*, 70; Hillgruber, „‚Endlösung' und Ostimperium," 136; Hillgruber, „England in Hitlers außenpolitischer Konzeption," *HZ* 218 (1974), 71; Dülffer, 206f; Schubert, 30; Hildebrand, *Weltreich*, 73ff, especially 82ff; E. Nolte, *Der Faschismus in seiner Epoche. Die Action française. Der italienische Faschismus. Der Nationalsozialismus*, (Munich, 1963), 405f, 491f, and elsewhere; U. Adam, *Judenpolitik im Dritten Reich* (Düsseldorf, 1972), 22ff.

23. Nolte, *Faschismus*, 406, 491ff.

24. Especially in the previously named studies by Hillgruber, Hildebrand and Dülffer. –Jäckel can only decide to agree with a "theoretical understanding" of Hitler in view of his comments in *Mein Kampf – Hitlers Weltanschauung*, 122.

25. Hildebrand, *Außenpolitik*, 28. –Finally, in addition, „Hitlers Ort," 589, 597; Hillgruber, *England*, 67f.

26. Cf. Hildebrand, "Hitlers Ort," 621 note 178 with further literature references; Nolte, *Faschismus*, 486.

27. Nolte, *Faschismus*, 405.

28. Cf. Hewel's *Diary 1941*. –Entry from June 8, 1941: "In the evening at dinner a wonderful lecture on the Roman Empire and its replacement by Christianity. The Roman Empire was the only real empire that had ever existed. Only with the blood of Roman citizens had it been founded (comparison with England). Where would we be today if Christianity had not been forced upon us. … If we had become Muslim, we would own the world." –Cf. also Picker, *Tischgespräche*.

29. Cf. D. Eckart, *Der Bolschewismus von seinen Anfängen bis Lenin. Zwiegespräch zwischen Adolf Hitler und mir* (Munich, 1924); E. Nolte, „Eine frühe Quelle zu Hitlers Antisemitismus," *HZ* 192 (1961), 584ff; BA NS 6/133, –„A Führer's conversation of November 29, 1944."

30. I. Fetscher, „Faschismus und Nationalsozialismus. Zur Kritik des sowjetmarxistischen Faschismusbegriffs," *PVS* 3 (1962), 61. –About Hitler's role as the "NS high priest," cf. ibid., 90 note 53.

Chapter 3

"MEIN KAMPF"
AS THE CENTRAL SOURCE

Fifty years ago, a milestone essay was published posing the question of Hitler's ultimate goals. The premise was that these goals would possibly go beyond the generally accepted aim of an Eastern European empire. In these "ultimate goals," some milestones were described "that were not to be part of Germany's objectives during WW II but rather much later in the future. They had not yet been systematically organized to form a clear concept, but already existed as ideas that were not to be rearranged."[1] An analysis of *Mein Kampf* within that study concluded that Hitler was seeking a position of world power for Germany that went far beyond the boundaries of Europe. But due to the scarce source material at that point in time, the work lacked a deeper interpretation of *Mein Kampf*.[2] A more recent study of Hitler's book, one that reflects the results of more modern research, opens up the possibility of making far broader comments. It is by no means necessary to delve exclusively into the second volume of *Mein Kampf* for Hitler's scattered thoughts regarding his long-term plans; both volumes are generously peppered with many references.

There are two main groups of ideas or images that must be taken into consideration when examining a compilation of Hitler's comments in *Mein Kampf* regarding his ultimate world view. Although there is a mutual relationship between both groups of images, the following differences must be pointed out:

1. Ultimate goals of his own policies.
2. Negative goals that Hitler assumed were those of the Jewish enemy, and that needed to be addressed.

Hitler used the term "mission," a mission that, according to him, "the creator of the universe had appointed the German people to fulfill."[3] What Hitler meant by this is dealt with at a later point: "Whoever speaks of a mission of the German people on Earth, must know that it can only exist in the constellation of a state who views its highest task as the preservation and promotion of the undamaged remnants of the noblest elements of our race, and even of all humanity."[4] Hitler becomes even more concrete in the discussion of "pacifist ideas" when he writes that he sees the possibilities of eternal peace as becoming possible only "when the highest form of human specimen has conquered and subjugated the world in such a way that he is sole ruler of the Earth."[5] These instances undoubtedly increase and get an even clearer outline in the course of the second volume of Mein Kampf. Hitler determines towards the end of the first chapter "that in the distant future humanity will be faced with problems that only a Herrenvolk, a higher race, will be called upon to solve, with the means and possibilities of the whole world at their disposal."[6] More proof of Hitler's ultimate goals can only be found indirectly. He refers to borders as "coincidences,"[7] and he also refers to letting the powers of the globe run free, which in later years he calls the "challenge cup."[8] The one significant limitation to this is that "the final victory of the healthier and the stronger"[9] is to be permanent, and is the actual goal itself. He states that the path should be opened for the best humans, who, because they have earned ownership of the world, should do what they deem necessary.[10]

While these passages emphasize the principles of world supremacy, one of Hitler's leitmotifs already appears, showing his ideas and thinking as they were well through the start of the war. Hitler felt that Germany had missed out on its chance for world supremacy once before. He blamed German hyperindividualism, a term he placed in contrast to his idea of the "Masse Mensch," which, as "a herd-like unit," would make "the German Reich of today the mistress of the globe."[11] This German populace, which Hitler imagined to be potentially stronger than all other peoples of the world, was to form the "core race" he called for, in order to rise "to a ruling position slowly but surely."[12] At that point, Hitler had consciously chosen a very broad goal because, "as seen in history, the greater the goals in battle are, the more colossal the success will be."[13] A mature race must be created for the moment of great change toward which Hitler felt the world was headed with all its might, for the moment containing "the final and greatest decisions for planet Earth." Hitler felt that whichever "race" took the first step would be the final victor.[14]

From these images it already becomes clear that, even if Hitler's goal of world supremacy was an abstract one, that he considered only the German race capable of attaining world supremacy. His goal would not be to create a place for Germany among other world powers in the style of Kaiser Wilhelm II. Hitler's plan was much more about Germany's "exceptional path" that must lead to world supremacy. Toward the end of *Mein Kampf*, he does revert to using the term "world power,"[15] but at a noteworthy point in the second to last sentence of his epilogue, he strengthens the principal idea he had previously developed: "A state, which in times of contaminated races, commits itself to the care of the noblest elements of its race will become lord over the entire Earth one day."[16]

In examining the second set of images that correspond to Hitler's view of the world, we find his fear that "this impenetrable fate, which for unknown reasons remains hidden from us poor humans, desires the final victory for this small race (the Jews)... Should this race, which has only lived on the Earth, have the Earth promised to them as their reward?"[17]

Hitler wanted to avoid this fate at all costs. The important question of whether this was his subjective conviction or simply an enemy stereotype he employed to conceal his own plans should temporarily be put aside. A point should be made, however. *Mein Kampf* represents a massive expression of fear about Jewish world supremacy,[18] which Hitler viewed as coming closer because of the Bolshevik takeover of Russia, as well as the threat to Germany through the drain on [its] manpower by "Jewish world finance."[19] Hitler felt therefore that, in order to eliminate the danger, Germany had to become the spearhead of an international racist countermovement that represented "the whole world."[20] Further threats came from the western democracies, whom the Jews stood behind, ready for the conquest of the "Jewish world empire they hoped to win."[21]

The most important point for Hitler was that the "Jews," as well as the "English," wanted to achieve their goals for world power, with the least amount of effort. Instead of facing a conflict, they chose indirect methods: sneak in, be subversive, erode the enemy from the inside, fight with "their own weapons:" lies, slander, poisoning, and decline."[22] Hitler tries to counteract this "highly cunning and cold logic used by the Jews in their thoughts and war efforts to gain world control."[23] He is clearly troubled by the fact that the "Jew," according to his own imagination, is of "pure race,"[24] a well-known and decisive prerequisite for success in Hitler's view. Since the "Jews" are better than any other race at preserving these racial characteristics, they will continue on their path until a power of some importance opposes them.[25] In view of Hitler's delusions, one could almost be tempted to speak of a quick change of labels, from "Jewish goals" to "Aryan goals."[26] The similarities are painfully obvious: a pure race, a step by step approach to reaching world supremacy. But one thinks, too, taking into account the "pseudo revisionism" of Hitler's foreign policy from 1933 to 1937–1938, of words such as: "cunning to the utmost degree"and, "ice-cold,"—the latter being a great favorite expression of Hitler.

If one were to summarize Hitler's ultimate goals in view of his expansionist aims as expressed in *Mein Kampf*, there is one crossover that comes from two sources. This crossover is of a vision of expansionist power that, even if it is granted to other races in principle, is the means by which the German people will be led to world supremacy on the basis of race. This vision is the result of Hitler's all too imaginative way of seeing the negative goals of a "Jewish ambition of world supremacy," goals which he ascribes in a bizarre manner to every type of supranational amalgamation, and against which he prescribes a reaction that is not limited either geographically or to a particular time. This reaction will continue until all suspected dangers have been cleared away, and—since it is a germ that is being dealt with—these dangers can never turn up again.

The character of Hitler's ideological campaign of annihilation against Judaism and Bolshevism represents something qualitatively different than the "natural" fighting among the races that will erupt after the elimination of "international Judaism." The removal of a "vermin," the "extermination" of epidemics, should prepare the landscape in a clear and clean way for Germany's entrance into the arena. The struggle against Great Britain therefore takes on, as will be shown later, the character of a sports competition for Hitler. The outlawing of all types of "unnatural" sports, as Hitler regarded the "international machinations" of "Judaism," is therefore simply the forced fulfillment of a duty.[27] Due to a number of factors, Hitler sees the German people as predestined for this task, as well as for achieving his own ultimate goals. One of these factors is the size of the "core race," for which history provides proof; another is the missed chance to rule the world, as well as the consequences that missed chance will have on the future; another is the exceptional value of the German people, a unique constellation in the framework of global history. For Hitler, all these factors mean that the path to world supremacy for the German people is already mapped out.

Notes

1. Moltmann, 197.
2. Ibid., 201ff..
3. The following editions of *Mein Kampf* were used: a) vol. 1, 1933, vol. 2, 1933, b) two volumes in one, 1939 –Ibid., 234.
4. Ibid., 439.
5. Ibid., 315. Cf. the letter from Hess to Hewel from March 30, 1927, 3753 –PS Archives of the Institute for Contemporary History in Munich. Also see Hildebrand, "Hitlers Ort," 621 note 181.
6. *Mein Kampf*, 422.
7. For example ibid., 740.
8. Compare to M. Domarus, *Reden und Proklamationen 1932–1945*, 2 vols., (Würzburg, 1962–63), 1498, 1638f; Picker, 320; Fest, 298.
9. *Mein Kampf*, 577 –this compared to Jäckel, *Hitlers Weltanschaung*, 123.
10. *Mein Kampf*, 422.
11. Ibid., 437f.
12. Ibid., 439.
13. Ibid., 440.
14. Ibid., 475.
15. Ibid., 728f, 742. –The change of use shows that Hitler didn't use these terms precisely. The important thing is that he understood the meaning of "world domination."
16. Ibid., 782. –Cf. also W. Daim, *Der Mann, der Hitler die Ideen gab* (Munich, 1958), 207ff.
17. Mein Kampf, 69.
18. Ibid., 343, 475, 504, and elsewhere.
19. Ibid., 703.
20. Ibid.
21. Ibid., 723.
22. Ibid., 751.
23. Ibid., 761.
24. Ibid., 751.
25. Ibid.
26. Ibid. In addition compare: Jacobsen, *Außenpolitik*, 191f; Heuss, *Hitlers Weg*, 32. Here, Marxism and National Socialism are compared. The key words are not higher quality or class struggle, but blood and race. The psychological scheme of simplicity is exactly the same. "Exploiter" and "exploited" corresponded to the opposites of "superior quality" and "inferior quality" races. As a term of opposition to historical materialism, one could choose the formula of biological naturalism. Cf. also ibid., 114.
27. Jäckel, *Hitlers Weltanschauung*, passim; J. Henke: *England in Hitlers politischem Kalkül 1935–1939* (Boppard, 1973), 20ff.

Chapter 4

HITLER AS BUILDER:
Construction Plans, Armaments, and a Vision of War

There are indeed more possibilities to recognize Hitler's ideas for his global aims. The research for the period 1932–1933 does not solely depend on the exegesis of Hitler's written and verbal comments.[1]

Indications from secondary areas such as architecture, armaments, and war plans that help clarify Hitler's ultimate goals do indeed exist and must be included in the research. When one speaks of the years in which *Mein Kampf* was written and what those years meant for Hitler, one aspect adds an important dimension to our analysis and must not be overlooked. While Hitler was documenting his program in *Mein Kampf*, he formulated the definitive ideas about architectural plans, that would one day form the backdrop to world domination.[2] Drafts for central buildings, which, according to Albert Speer, were the corner-stones of his own plans for Berlin—probably had their origins in the years 1925 and 1926.[3] Two of these drafts were handed to Speer by Hitler in 1936 with the words "I made these drawings ten years ago. I have always held onto them, because I never doubted that one day I would build them. And now we want to make them happen."[4] In the years leading up to Hitler's takeover of power, he was obviously constantly busy organizing his architectural plans. Observations that come from his innermost circle show this. In addition to Putzi Hanfstaengl[5] and Heinrich Hoffmann,[6] both of whom had experienced Hitler's designs for monumental buildings before his imprisonment in Landsberg and both of whom were privy to similar information, Goebbels also reported in the summer of 1926 on Hitler's designs for "the future architectural landscape of the country."[7] In his diary, he noted that Hitler was "quite a master builder." Otto Dietrich[8] suspects that the plans for the construction of the party's huge convention buildings in Nuremberg stemmed from an idea that Hitler had while attending the party conventions of 1927 and 1929 in Nuremberg.

From the same time frame, there is a report from Otto Strasser,[9] who had stayed with his parents and Hitler in Dinkelsbühl after the Nuremberg Nazi party convention in 1927. During the evening of the first day of their visit, Hitler, using a map of Munich, developed his ideas for the renovation of the city: gigantic cuts through the city, wide avenues that met at the center in the form of a star, where, as Hitler suggested to his small audience, there would be an enormous monument.

After 1929 at the latest, Hitler was showing his plans to a much broader audience. There were much longer passages about art and architecture in his speeches at party gatherings,[10] as well as the acquisition of the Palais Barlow in the summer of 1930, which marked a change in his situation. At this time, one architect stood out during the transformation of the Palais Barlow into the "Brown House," an architect whose influence on Hitler's plans and the action he took in the building sector during the first years after his rise to power must considerably be taken into account.[11] Paul Ludwig Troost, whom Hitler had met through the Bruckmann family,[12] was not only Hitler's primary architect until his death in 1934, but continued to have an influence later on, in spite of his successor Speer. Hitler retained a sentimental devotion to Troost.[13] In 1941, he was still referring to him among close friends as the "greatest architect of our times,"[14] and he would mention the Führer Building in Munich as an exemplary edifice from which "all architects of the present and the future can learn."[15] Preliminary projects for this building came from Troost and were drafted in January and February 1932.[16] In 1932, Troost also reported to Nazi leaders about Hitler's tremendous building plans, which were to be commenced after the takeover.[17]

A speech by Hitler in April 1929 contains a typical passage on his policies concerning art and architecture, one in which he expounds on his aim of giving Germany a new face:

> Because a grandiose makeover of our way of thinking and feeling, our way of seeing the state and the world will be able to make this rebirth possible, we wish that this new state will survive over thousands of years through the representation of this third empire [Third Reich], which will not be an empire of department stores and numbers of tourists, of skyscrapers and hotels. We acknowledge our Third Reich must show documents of art and culture that will survive for thousands of years ... central points ... which

are of more value than department stores and hotels; common and uniting central points that humanity needs if it is not to fall into decay."[18]

Hitler compared these "central points" with medieval cathedrals, and based the justification of his ideas on their existence. He expressed himself in a similar way in November of that year, using a style akin to that of the "art speeches" he would give later, as he designed the architecture of a future Germany at the party conventions in Nuremberg: "The political rise also sweeps art along with it. I could not imagine a victory of the way we see the world unless it is embodied in monuments that last throughout time as proof of the victory of our conviction."[19] On that occasion, Munich was given a very prominent position in his plans. But he hadn't forgotten his plans for Berlin at that time either. Goebbels noted in February 1932: "The Führer spends hours musing with the draft for a new central party building as well as grandiose plans for the renovation of the capital. He has those plans completely finished, and it is continuously astounding how he deals with so many questions in such an expert manner."[20] What Hitler's motivation for such plans was, and why he was planning monumental buildings to last thousands of years, became clear in the aforementioned speech of April 29, 1929.[21] While making a comparison with France, he revealed his intentions: Napoleon I and Napoleon III built, according to Hitler, with the intention not only of making Paris the central point of France, "but rather to make it the shining central point of the whole world."[22]

Similar considerations can possibly be made with regard to Hitler's ideas on military policies and strategies. This is not connected in any way with an effort to prove Hitler's ultimate goals directly. It should be further pointed out that it is futile to analyze his possible plans based on the military potential that actually existed. Despite his verbal proclamations, Hitler speculated on the bluff that he could count on finding help, helpers, and support of a different kind, particularly in view of his ultimate global goals. To attain those individual goals was, under normal conditions, unthinkable, and the incredibly vast spectrum of plans and the game of pure chance involved were therefore very clear to him. In other words, besides the high amount of manpower and armament required, other capabilities would also be needed in order to win the game. Hitler's highly developed understanding of surprise tactics was already evident before 1933: Whether bluff or brutal attack, his masterful psychological warfare was intended, by way of the many bloodless conquests that preceded the war, to weaken the resistance of his military opponents along with that of the civilian population. Even if Hitler's thought processes cannot be followed back very far in depth, some comments on his ideas of how to deploy the navy, the air force, and the army are appropriate. Up to now, it has probably not been taken enough into account that Hitler's architectural drafts from the 1920's were also mixed in with his sketches of weapons and warships.[23] In other words, the monumentality of his ideas didn't stop at architecture, but was carried over into other areas. Therefore, within this study it must still be examined whether the Plan Z-Fleet,[24] which had been designed shortly before the outbreak of the war in 1939, could have for all intents and purposes been, in Hitler's view, a "sea-going monument" meant to show the flag of the new world power across the seven seas. The fleet had in that case no concrete function for Hitler, but was meant as an instrument of pressure, valued more for its demonstration of greatness than for the effectiveness of its weapons. There appear to be many points that indicate that Hitler was preoccupied with the symbolic meaning of this fleet even before 1933. In a similar way, it is assumed that Hitler's obvious interest in weapons for large ships and their firing capacity proves that by concerning himself with these technical details, he was already anticipating his long-term goals.[25] His close contacts with navy circles since 1928,[26] and his indirect contact with Admiral Raeder in the summer of 1931 regarding the question of arming small cruisers[27] all indicate Hitler's lively interest in this area of weaponry.

His reported conversations with experts from the Luftwaffe are also very similar. Without a doubt Hitler's most important partner in such affairs was Hermann Göring, who had returned to Germany in 1927 and who was working as the representative of large German airplane manufacturing companies.[28] Göring's contacts with Milch,[29] a Lufthansa director at that time, doubtlessly enabled Hitler to have a meeting with Milch in April 1932.[30] At that meeting, Hitler showed that he was very well informed. As an expert and supporter of Douhet's theories, his main area of interest was aerial bombing.[31] It remains unclear whether Milch had received exact orders from Hitler when he began to build a bomber fleet in 1933.[32] In an interview in 1939, Milch indicated that Hitler had explained his thoughts about the as yet nonexistent air force "long before 1933."[33] Hitler's interest in air force issues provides at least a hint at his knowledge of the possibilities of psychological warfare. Before the outbreak of war, he said to Milch: "Nobody asks me if I have bombs or how much ammunition I have. The only thing that is important is the number of planes and guns I have."[34]

The bluff and improvisational character of Hitler's war plans becomes even clearer when examining his thinking regarding the army, some of which might have originated with his personal experiences with trench warfare. A further development of new forms of war can clearly be seen.[35] Comments Hitler made in 1933 supply a "rough model of his techniques of aggression"[36]: "When I wage war, ... one day in the middle of peace I will have my troops march into Paris. And they will be wearing French uniforms." All key points will be taken over by these troops in broad daylight.

> The confusion will be unparalleled, but for a long time already, I have been in contact with men who are forming a new French government. A government that suits my purposes. We can find men of this sort. We find them in every country. We don't need to buy them. They come to us on their own. Ambition and illusion, party discord and arrogance drive them to us. We will have a peace agreement before the war even starts. ... Maginot line can hold us back. It is our strategy ... to destroy the enemy from within, to let him destroy himself."[37]

A few years later, Hitler could demonstrate his new type of warfare using Czechoslovakia as an example. The key to success was propaganda, as he explained to members of the press: "It became clear to me what it meant to take over a country with almost 2,000 km of fortified borders without firing a single shot. Gentlemen, we have in all truth this time won a country of 10 million people and over 100,000 square kilometers with propaganda at the service of an idea. That is something tremendous."[38]

Notes

1. Cf. page 25 note 3.
2. In addition, compare with the second part of the book on Hitler's buildings and building plans.
3. These drafts concern a dome and a hall of triumph, but can not be dated accurately. With regard to this: Fest, 1075 note 87. The drafts were certainly produced after 1923. In addition compare: Speer, 88, as well as spoken comments from Mr. Albert Speer from October 11, 1973, written comments from October 15, 1973. Further: W. Maser, *Hitlers Briefe und Notizen* (Düsseldorf-Vienna, 1973), 133, as well as pictures by Maser, *Briefe*, 134f; Speer, 160f; in addition compare the evidence by Dülffer, 218, Fest, 334f, and G. Wollstein, *Vom Weimarer Revistionismus zu Hitler* (Bonn, 1973), 6f.
4. Speer, 88.
5. E. Hanfstaengl, *Zwischen Weißem und Braunem Haus* (Munich, 1970), 80.
6. H. Hoffmann, *Hitler wie ich ihn sah* (Munich-Berlin, 1974), 156.
7. H. Heiber, ed., *Das Tagebuch von Joseph Goebbels 1925/26* (Stuttgart, 1960), 94. —entry from July 25, 1926.
8. O. Dietrich, *12 Jahre mit Hitler* (Munich, 1955), 173.
9. O. Strasser, *Mein Kampf* (Frankfurt am Main, 1969), 72.
10. Cf. the contents of BA NS 26/56.

11. In addition: A. Zoller, *Hitler privat* (Düsseldorf, 1949), 55; Speer, 53; K. Arndt, *Filmdokumente des Nationalsozialismus als Quellen für architekturgeschichtliche Forschungen* (Göttingen, 1970), 58f.
12. Speer, 54.
13. Details by Arndt, 59.
14. Reports of Dr. Werner Koeppen, 2. –entry from September 5, 1941.
15. Ibid.
16. Arndt, 46 note 18.
17. K. G. W. Ludecke, *I knew Hitler* (Plymouth, 1938), 464. –end of September 1932.
18. Speech from April 9, 1929, in the Löwenbräukeller. –*Völkischer Beobachter*, Southern German edition, April 10, 1929.
19. Speech from November 29, 1929 in the Löwenbräukeller. –*VB*, December 4, 1929.
20. Joseph Goebbels, *Vom Kaiserhof zur Reichskanzlei* (Munich, 1940), 38. –entry from February 3, 1932.
21. Cf. note 18.
22. BA NS 26/56, 144, –speech from April 9, 1929. –There are suspicions that the VB was censored internally during the twenties. Therefore, it is necessary to compare Hitler's speeches from documents in the main NSDAP archives with those printed in the VB. It seems that the VB did not publish important explanations regarding Hitler's goals in foreign policy.
23. Speer, 54. –pictures by Maser, *Briefe*, 140.
24. In addition: Dülffer, passim.
25. Ibid., 218.
26. Ibid., 216.
27. Ibid., 217f.
28. Hanfstaengl, 190; H. Fraenkel and R. Manvell, *Hermann Göring* (Hanover, 1964), 55.
29. Ibid.
30. D. Irving, *Die Tragödie der deutschen Luftwaffe* (Frankfurt am Main-Berlin-Vienna, 1970), 54f.
31. Ibid. –Also Milch's diaries, entry from April 28, 1932. Compare further: *Rede des Führers und Reichkanzlers Adolf Hitler vor dem Reichstag am 21. Mai 1935* (Berlin, 1935), 20f. Hitler gives detailed information about types of planes in this speech; BA R 43 II/1181, 62ff. –Hitler's visit to the Tempelhof airport on October 29, 1934.
33. H. Bongartz, *Luftmacht Deutschland* (Essen, 1939), 5.
34. Irving, *Luftwaffe*, 125.
35. H. Booms, „Der Ursprung des 2. Weltkrieges-Revision oder Expansion?" GWU 16 (1965), 329ff. The author rightfully draws attention to Hitler's tactic of indirect aggression. –332f.
36. Booms, 332, who uses this term in the quoted passage in the following footnote.
37. Rauschning, *Gespräche mit Hitler*, 13f. To verify the source, cf. 60 note 90.
38. W. Treue, "Hitler's speech to the German press. (November 10, 1938)." VfZG 6 (1958), 184.

Chapter 5

THE BEGINNINGS OF A POWER POLITICIAN
"Models" of Imperial Rule

When one reviews the early years, namely the period from 1920 to 1923, one notices that the question of more space for the German race was already on Hitler's mind in 1920.[1] He was displeased with the unfair division of the world and annoyed by the vastness of the British and Russian empires. In April 1920, he condemned British world rule by using a turn of phrase that he would use repeatedly in the opening of his speeches during WW II[2]: "England with her few million people rules one fifth of the world."[3] Hitler attributed this situation to three factors: nationalist feeling, racial unity in the colonies[4] and British genius.[5] At that point already, especially in view of the years to come, Hitler's statement must be kept in mind: "Small races" can, with certain characteristics and certain behavior, control and hold on to big parts of the world.[6]

A second issue during that particular year—and more important than has been thought—is Hitler's reading of "The Protocols of the Elders of Zion" and the influence the book had on him.[7] In light of this, the speech of August 13, 1920, in which Hitler's ideas are first recorded together in an orderly way, is of major importance. In the "reign of the Jews," Hitler sees the denationalization of races: They must decline in value … "because what the Jews need to be able to organize, to build up and maintain their world domination in a permanent way, is the lowering of the quality of other races so that they, as the only pure race, will be capable of ruling over all others in the end."[8] Even here, the "positive value" of the statement is to be noted: a "pure race" has the possibility of achieving world supremacy. According to Hitler, the vehicle for the attainment of this "Jewish goal" was Marxism. Once in power, this would cause the collapse of the local business world. International capital would then absorb the rubble in order to become lord and master of entire countries with very little effort, and would be able to erect the "Jewish world supremacy."[9]

Under no circumstances, however, does Hitler see the fight against "Judaism" as hopeless. In an article from January 1, 1921, in the daily "Völkischer Beobachter" on the theme of "the people's reflection and the party," he reached the conclusion that the ultimate Jewish goal was "the creation of the world state which Jehovah had prophesied"—which, in light of Germany's loss of political power, constituted a great danger. To counteract this, Hitler saw only one alternative: to awaken energies that "like all things of greatness, slumber within a minority." As a slogan, he used "the fight for the victory of our own race."[10] In an article that was published only a few weeks later in the same newspaper, the suspicion was confirmed that Hitler was accusing his opponents of seeking the same goals he himself was seeking. He discovered the same demands that had been put forward for his own "race" on his opponents' side, and claimed: "applying Jewish imperialist world supremacy plans" is possible "through the dictatorship of a ruthless minority."[11] Again, in the beginning of March 1921, he raised in a speech the problem he had outlined the previous year about the unfair division of the globe, in order to reduce the accusations of German imperialism. "That in Russia for every adult there is eighteen times more land available than in Germany, that England has fought forty-three wars so that today with a population of only 52 million it rules three fourths[12] of the world, these are things nobody wants to know."[13]

The fact that Great Britain held a special position as a world power despite a small population also occupied Hitler's thoughts in the following months. In a further article in the "Völkischer Beobachter," he once again wrote one of the "iron" observations that he would continue to give. He wrote: "In three hundred years of blood-drenched history, England has spread her rule over a quarter of the world's population and one fifth of its area of land."[14] England's three "global opponents,"[15] Spain, The Netherlands, and France, were defeated one after the other, and Germany was now being threatened by a similar development.[16] On the same day, the "Völkischer Beobachter" reported on a celebration in Rosenheim at which Hitler spoke in honor of the first anniversary of the local Nazi Party group.[17] Hitler's comments about the rise of Germany and the repulsion of its enemies are alarmingly clear. The "messiah-like tone" of his ideas cannot be overlooked. "The regeneration must come from us. We might be small, but once upon a time there stood a single man in Galilee, and now his message rules the whole world. I cannot imagine Christ as anything else but blond and blue-eyed, the devil only in the caricature of a Jew...."[18]

If Hitler was boasting about a "victory" of a "Teutonic empire of the Germanic nations" in 1921 in his newspaper article,[19] he went on to expand his ideas in global dimensions in 1922. In the fight with Bolshevism there are two possibilities: "Either victory for the Aryan side or their extermination and victory for the Jews."[20] In other speeches made that same year, he reiterated his claim of "the Jewish goal of world supremacy"[21] in order to strengthen the idea of Germany as a savior of the world from the dangers presented by Judaism. His claim to world supremacy was hidden behind the fight against the supposed striving of Jews for the same goal. National Socialism, according to Hitler, originated in Germany "as all great deeds originate from one point." Germany would in this way be an example to the world and would put truth to the saying that"the world shall be healed by the essence of the Germans."[22] The first decisive synthesis of race, state, and geopolitics had been reached, and Hitler had found an answer to the Jewish challenge.[23]

The source material of 1923 proves to be much broader, even in the respect that it offered a preliminary conclusion of his ideas. In a number of speeches in April, Hitler once again accused the Jews of striving for world supremacy,[24] of "destroying national states,"[25] and of attempting to "spread out their invisible state as the highest instance of spy tyranny throughout the world."[26] "The Jew," he continued in a speech from April 1923, "is therefore a subverter of nations. In order to make his rule over other races possible, it is necessary for him to work in two ways. Economically, he controls the races when he subjugates them politically and morally. Politically, he controls by propagating the fundamentals of democracy and the teachings of Marx, who turns the proletarians into terrorists on the inside and pacifists on the outside. He destroys the peoples in regard to both morals and religion," according to Hitler's vision of the universal enemy.[27]

As in earlier years, he evaluated the chances for a successful fight against "Judaism" as favorable, if a minority were to fight decisively. "Strength does not lie in the majority, but rather in the pureness of will to make sacrifices!"[28] The foundation for a conflict was the people. Even the symbols of battle again reflected the antagonism of the world for Hitler. The Soviet star—which for Hitler was identical to the Star of David, emblem of the synagogues—was "the symbol of one race ruling the world."[29] The only possible remedy would be the swastika banner.

Notes

1. It should be noticed that in one of Hitler's first speeches of which we have a record, he had already raised the question of living space, along with the question of whether it was right, "that a Russian has eighteen more times land available to him than a German?" –R.H. Phelps, "Hitler als Parteiredner im Jahre 1920," *VfZG* 11 (1963), 289.

2. In addition compare: Trevor-Roper, *Hitlers Kriegsziele*, 122; H. von Kotze and H. Krausnick eds., *„Es spricht der Führer". Sieben exemplarische* Hitler-Reden (Gütersloh, 1966), 221.

3. Phelps, 297, –speech from April 17, 1920.

4. By this, Hitler meant that there was no mingling of the British and the natives in the colonies.

5. Phelps, 297. Compare also Kuhn, 45f. Concerning Hitler's admiration of Great Britain, see Henke, 22f, 26.

6. Compare also the wording of the speech from April 17, 1920: "Is it 'right' that certain small races rule complete regions of the Earth?" –Phelps, 297.

7. Compare note 21 and Hildebrand's question of whether, at this early stage of power politics, Hitler had a clear idea of his program and whether anti-Semitism, anti-Bolshevism, and striving for new living space were just ideological backgrounds, or whether they dominated his thinking. In our opinion, the answer to the question must begin in 1920 and be followed through 1922. –Compare K. Hildebrand, „Hitlers *Mein Kampf*: Propaganda oder Programm?" *NPL* 14 (1969), 75; Kuhn part I.

8. R.H. Phelps, "Hitler's "'fundamental'" speech about anti-Semitism," *VfZG* 16 (1968), 411. –Cf., also 33 notes 24, 25.

9. BA NS 26/51, 15. –Hitler's speech from October 26, 1920, in the Kindlkeller. –VB October 31, 1920. It should be made clear that Hitler's speeches from 1920 on are based on references to the supposed Jewish goal of world domination. In addition: Maser, *Briefe*, 235, 239, 251, 253, 259: Jäckel, *Hitlers Weltanschauung*, passim; and finally: A. Tyrell, *Vom "Trommler" zum "Führer"* (Munich, 1975), 46ff, 169, 171, 215f note 280.

10. VB, January 1, 1921.

11. "Ist die Errichtung einer die breiten Massen erfassenden völkischen Zeitung eine nationale Notwendigkeit?" *VB*, July 27, 1921, and January 30, 1921. –BA NS 26/51, 37.

12. Probably a mistake in recording, since Hitler normally names other qualities of these nations.

13. BA NS 26/51, 78. –VB, March 10, 1921.

15. Ibid.

16. Ibid.

17. Ibid., 113.

18. Ibid.

19. VB, January 1, 1921.

20. E. Boepple, ed., *Adolf Hitlers Reden* (Munich,1933), 17. –speech from April 12, 1922.

21. Ibid., 30. –speech from July 28, 1922.

22. Speech in the Salvatorkeller on November 21, 1922. –VB, November 25, 1922.

23. Compare Hildebrand, *Weltreich*, 75.

24. Boepple, 49. –speech from April 13, 1923.

25. Ibid., 58. –speech from April 24, 1923.
26. Ibid., 55. –speech from April 20, 1923.
27. Ibid., 55.
28. Ibid., 86. –speech from September 5, 1923.
29. Ibid., 71. –speech from August 1, 1923.

Chapter 6

No Turning Back:

The Aftermath of September 14, 1930

Following his imprisonment in Landsberg and the completion of *Mein Kampf*, the theme of world supremacy hadn't been settled in any way for Hitler. A wealth of comments proves, on the contrary, that it was very much on his mind until 1933, especially given that he could have easily have kept silent on the subject after his victory in the elections of September 1930. Feeling overconfident in his ability to spread a message, he was repeatedly taken with the idea of announcing his long-term policy goals publicly. After 1931, however, he was increasingly of the opinion that he should speak of this only within his most trusted circles.

The amount of unknown, summarized, and scattered source material relating to Hitler's ultimate goals up to that point makes it necessary to paraphrase the texts and to discuss them quickly. The presentation of Hitler's thoughts and comments during the 1926–1933 period is very important. Their content is so explicit that it doesn't require extensive commentary. We shall continue to use the method of dealing with the questions posed during the analysis of *Mein Kampf*. The most important aim is, to show, using new source material, that *Mein Kampf* and the *Second Book* during the period from 1926 to 1936 were not the apex of his thinking, but were rather supported and confirmed by his statements in every year prior to his rise to power. At the same time, this can be viewed as proof of the continuity that existed in Hitler's plans for world supremacy. Even during these years, plans for world supremacy were clearly a definite objective for

Hitler. Hitler's comments relating to this point were not mere accidents, as one could assume following a cursory examination of both books, but were on the contrary placed both consciously and programmatically. It is of particular interest to consider the target groups of Hitler's speeches during the period up to early 1927, a time when he was forbidden to speak in public. One must also consider the public and non-public character of these speeches. The contents of these speeches, implicit or explicit, must be carefully taken into consideration with respect to the situation, especially from September 1930 onward. In the end, the ratio regarding the separation of the comments into those that refer to positive and negative goals will also be of interest. What was driving his plans? Did the "danger of Jewish world supremacy" dominate his thoughts, as in the early years before *Mein Kampf,* or were there other goals on his mind that had been developed more strongly and that stemmed from the exceedingly positive conclusions he came to regarding the supposedly "special value" of the German people in comparison to the other great peoples of the world?

With regard to 1926, the available sources to a large degree fail to yield any information. Even though Hitler was still working on the second volume of *Mein Kampf* at the beginning of the year, he was otherwise occupied with consolidating his own party.

The speech that Hitler gave to the leading representatives of trade and industry in Hamburg at the end of February of that year[1] is of key importance for the central question of the study. Throughout the entire speech, his paramount idea of defeating Marxism via a sort of copy of the same could only have been the result of Hitler's understanding of the fanaticism and tactics of his opponents. According to Hitler, this fight could only be fought with hordes of people possessed by a fanatical belief, "like there is on the other side today."[2] This was absolutely incomprehensible for his contemporaries at the time, and only days before the Hamburg speech, Hitler had expounded on the special role Germany had to play in the struggle against Judaism: "The latest goals of the Marxist world view are so radical that they could only be carried out by a totally fanatical raiding party."[3] This raging omnipresent fanaticism only had influence within Hitler's closest circles at that time. Goebbels, who shortly thereafter was sent to the "Berlin battleground" for the Nazi Party, made the following entry in his diary: "With this man, one can conquer the world. Let him loose, and he'll make the corrupt republic totter."[4]

As in 1923, Hitler called for a suitable war symbol, one that would at the same time strengthen the NSDAP's claims to leadership on a world-wide scale. "A uniform symbol must effectively counter the uniform symbol of the Soviet star, which has spread its influence across the globe.

The global plague of Bolshevism will not be conquered by countless small organizations with as many insignificant little banners."[5]

On a number of occasions in 1927, Hitler touched upon the main reason for the division of the globe according to the status quo. For him, the incident had occurred 300 years before, at a time when Germany was robbed of its chance to achieve world supremacy. The Thirty Years War, instead of helping Germany, had actually promoted England's interests, and Germany's power had been splintered off by emigration.[6] During a speech Hitler made in Munich in April, he spoke of Germany's division into many small states as having set Germany back. "Had Germany never degenerated into small states, had it never been ripped into 300 or more powerless entities, England wouldn't rule the world today, and we would be lords of the globe instead."[7] He felt that something must be done to counteract the consequences of this mishap of history. The division of the globe was a permanent fight,[8] one that could be started[9] with one hundred million Germans, only two thirds of whom were to be found in Germany. Two years later, Hitler referred to such a concentration of population of a particular "racial value" as a "danger for the world."[10]

For the first time, albeit in an indirect way, a picture of Hitler's vision for a future division of the world emerged. Almost word for word as he wrote[11] in *Mein Kampf* about "pacifism," he deemed it possible to develop world peace only "when a world power, i.e. the superior race, has gained unconditional and uncontested power. This power could deliver a type of global police and at the same time could make sure that the superior race was guaranteed the necessary living space. If this were not possible, then the inferior races would have to be limited."[12] What Hitler meant by the euphemistic description of "limitations" was to be experienced later on by the populations of the conquered Eastern territories during WWII. Over the course of many years, a limited public would hear endless monologues of his more expansive plans for the future of the East European populations after the successful outcome of the well-known Operation "Barbarossa."[13]

Over the course of 1927, Hitler clarified his ideas on the functional character of Great Britain, which he took as a model. As he saw it, Britain never did more than what was absolutely necessary to keep its colonies dependent, which for Hitler it meant controlling large territories beyond the home country. Great Britain, however,—again according to Hitler,—was prepared to use its power in an emergency at any time. "Behind the industrial spies lies the power of the sword. It is stupid to imagine that the English would not be ready to shed blood. … The English employ only what is absolutely necessary, not a drop too much nor a drop too little … whatever serves their purpose is correct, the protection of an enormous empire and its expansion."[14] In addition, one must keep this image in mind in order to understand Hitler's "revolutionary warfare," as well as his "*Blitzkrieg*" tactics as used up to 1941. Since Hitler not only wanted to inherit Great Britain, but also wanted his intention of ruling forever to be secured through the aid of the Aryan racial elite, he needed to have a suitable race. During a speech held on the occasion of a general membership meeting of the party, Hitler drew attention to his "people," commenting that to determine its value, one merely needed to cast an eye back upon history to see that "this people was the best that could be found on Earth."[15] In a secret brochure published in August 1927 and addressed to big business leaders, he disguised his long-term plans with such turns of phrase as the duty "to smooth the path into the far future for a single race … for the molding and highest development of its own existence." The phrase "The world shall be healed by the essence of the German people" would otherwise "make no sense at the present time."[16] There is no doubt that Hitler took this rather ordinary saying literally. In the previously mentioned brochure, he once again underlined the special role of the German people: there was no living people at that moment in time "that [had] produced more great people of importance than our German race."[17] With this race that "had written history for almost 2. 000 years,"[18] he wanted to illustrate the thought that "everything in this world made by man can just as well be destroyed by man and there exists no product of Satan that cannot be broken by a holy will. This, however, is what I believe."[19] Once more Hitler demonstrated his idea of the world as a "challenge cup" which Germany could win forever.

A speech held by Hitler in Landshut[20] in the summer of 1927 conveyed more specific information about his confused socio-Darwinian world of ideas. He saw the history of humanity as taking place in two great stages. In a first step, long ago, man conquered the world by battling with the animals. He had to be cruel and fight with all his energy. "And this law of struggle," as Hitler thought, "is a prerequisite to higher development."[21] Although he didn't explain this statement any further, it is very clear that he was referring to what he considered the special role of an "elite race," one whose sphere of rule is theoretically unlimited. "If man can call certain territories his own, this is due to his own efforts, and has nothing to do with a division of the Earth ordained by heaven."[22]

Hitler later communicated to a confidante why he did not publish his *Second Book*[23] written in 1928: "I thank my lucky stars that this volume was not published. Imagine the political problems this would cause for me right now … maybe later, when I am further ahead. Now it is impossible."[24] This historical document, which is, after *Mein Kampf*, the most important of the period before 1933, is to a large extent an exegesis of the "program" mapped out within *Mein Kampf*. In the forefront, there are Hitler's familiar comments regarding racial selection in the light of his popularized Darwinian principles and those of a permanent state of war. "We ... shall march into conflict; it doesn't matter whether we stop 10 or 1,000 kilometers behind the border lines of today. Then, wherever our success ends, it will always be the starting point of a new battle."[25] Policies about habitat and population are mutually dependent for Hitler and represent "a never-ending spiral."[26] Only the German people can be successful in the fight against the "Jews," whom, in his well-known words, he sees as subversives and profiteers rising up as "lords over a human kind which had been made leaderless."[27] Hitler also sees the German people as fulfilling its mission in a fight against the new enemy, the United States of America. No other European power possesses the racial quality value to weld the European continent together to oppose America.[28] Germany, as a leading power, would therefore consider coalitions only as being of a temporary nature, because it need not "tie itself to anything," on the contrary, it should "be able to decide on anything."[29]

This general comment by Hitler, which seems to have mysteriously disappeared into a corner somewhere, does not by any means represent all the source material for 1928. The threat presented by the Americans was one of Hitler's serious concerns, as he would express in a speech in September of that year.[30] He was criticizing German emigration, through which the best racial elements left the country, with the result that in the future other continents would determine the "fortunes of the world." He continued:

> We, in the entire European world, see today the American continent rising quickly, while over here they are still arguing about proletarian and bourgeois points of views. While they are fighting about stupid phrases, a great continent is lifting itself to become a global opponent and will inevitably assert its claims, insisting on better blood and stronger humans, which we have supplied ourselves. In this case we will not be able to say that we are fighting about global ideals. The fight of the American automobile industry is not a fight about global ideals but a fight about markets, and nothing else, and the weaker will be defeated. That continent has become the strongest."[31]

Hitler is here quite obviously primarily concerned with the leading position in setting up Aryan world supremacy. As opposed to the Soviet Union, who shall be eliminated in a "war of the races," an economic war against the United States to which he will also apply the typical socio-Darwinian formula is looming. At another point in this speech, the idea of Hitler's Aryan leadership becomes even clearer. "It is the Aryan who created the world as it is today. He has penetrated every corner of the Earth successfully. Even peoples of ancient culture such as the Chinese and Japanese are beginning to adapt themselves to Aryan culture, which in all reality represents the culture of the world today."[32] Hitler's concept of culture was narrowed by a bias towards technology, a word which for him, without a doubt, constituted a synonym for culture. He listed under "Aryan culture" airplanes, railways, automobiles, huge steam-powered machinery,[33] and large cities.[34] Again in this speech, he described the German people as the best in Europe; no other nation had more valuable personality characteristics than the Germans.[35] And shortly after this, his ranting intensified to state that the Germans were the most heroic people in the world, the most recent proof having been the First World War.[36] Above all, Germany had showed its true worth since the end of 1914. Hitler explained this at a party meeting in November 1928.[37] "With this, a new term has found its way into world history, so gigantic, bigger than anything previously known. A people becomes a fortification, surrounds itself with a protective shell, and sticks it out for four years. They retreat sometimes 1, 2, or 3 km, even 10 or 15, then they attack again, make sorties, and become an elastic line, moving constantly. An over-powerful enemy strikes and yet those attacked still find enough time, weapons, and strength to attack again every now and then."[38] It almost seemed that Hitler's illusions were rushing ahead toward his stubborn orders to stick it out in the Russian campaign, when the failure of "his war" became imminent.

On many other occasions, Hitler made direct connections with themes from previous years. In a speech at the beginning of 1928 in a small Swabian town, he renewed his missionary, global idea of the triumphal march of National Socialism with the following words. "By the way, every large oak grew from in a small acorn. And once there was single man in Palestine who fought against the world of his day and won. The idea of National Socialism will win…"[39] At another point, he complained about "the loss of world supremacy,"[40] which was caused by the splintering of Germany after 1648. For that reason, it was important for Hitler, instead of "regulating borders," to have policies that would ensure "the existence of the race for all eternity."[41] By holding to this, he indirectly rejected the "free interplay of forces," a metaphor he otherwise used quite often. Still insisting on the principle of an elite group, he explained on another occasion how he intended to create a "movement" using 600,000 to 800,000 men whom the masses would follow. "That is the number that is required. The rest will just march along with them when we step into marching formations. This principle of selection that takes place through perpetual struggle is the guarantor of the success of our movement. First we will drain the entire nation of their valuable human beings, and finally the international world as well. Those who remain after that will be simply the others who are not to be regarded as people but simply as numbers that go to the polling booth. They are the masses."[42] As well as demonstrating Hitler's cynicism and his disregard for people, although well known through other sources, this reference contains one of the few clues of Hitler's main ideas about the techniques he would use for spreading his rule.[43]

In a speech in Northern Germany, Hitler spoke more openly and clearly than on any other occasion during 1928. He discussed in depth the danger of a nation in decay "which could attain world supremacy."[44] To loud applause from the audience, he demanded a struggle for the "share of the world's rule that is rightfully ours. The free run of forces will continue to prevail in the lives of the people. In the end, the most competent race on Earth will rule. We don't know what race that will be, but we don't wish to eliminate our race from this competition."[45]

After the preceding exchange of ideas from March 1927 that was mentioned previously, the actual essence of what drove National Socialism was discussed once again in further correspondence between Rudolf Hess and Walter Hewel[46] in December 1928. "We are all really filled with great hope. I absolutely believe in our final victory." Hess went on to express himself in no uncertain terms about the policy of expansion: "This is the most important task of the movement—everything else is just preparation and means to the final goal."[47]

In a letter to the regional governor of Thuringia, Artur Dinter,[48] Hitler's fear of losing the path to power and not being able to reach all the way to his distant goals was already becoming obvious. In this letter Hitler developed the idea of having to realize his plans within twenty years.[49] "By dedicating myself to the fight of the present," he stated, "I believe I can gather the stones for a foundation which one day will be capable of supporting an universal edifice."[50]

Highlighting 1929 were two speeches Hitler delivered to party groups in which he dedicated himself to his visionary long-term goals. On the ninth anniversary of the movement, after reviewing the history of the party, he explained: "In 1920 the young movement began a work that is still carried out today uninterrupted, and will never be given up ... until the German people, also will have attained in the global wrestling match the position we wish it to have. We see the world as being a ball to play with[51] and we National Socialists will not miss a single moment to put our people into the world game of forces. We want to see the German people in the thick of this competition until the end of time itself."[52] Both here and in the following years, it can be observed that Hitler increasingly tended to use suggestive comparisons as a preparation of his policies, which become clear in the opening speech at the Nuremberg party convention. Here he took up a theme that he often used all the way to the war. According to Hitler, Germany in 1914 was the best nation in the world, its army the "best of all the countries on earth."[53] The German people had "more than proven its highest value throughout history. If the political leadership had been better in the many centuries past, the Germans would be ruling the world today on the strength of their achievements as well as by the virtue of our sacrifices."[54] Referring again to the role of a symbol for a war banner, Hitler spoke of "the miracle that the symbol of the Soviet star now stands face to face with the swastika."[55] He varied his theme a little when giving the closing speech of the convention: "The reorganization of the body of our nation is the most important mission of the National Socialist movement. Will it succeed? If you have seen the hundreds of thousands congregated here today, then I don't know if you could doubt our future success. When this type of democracy rules over our nation some day, and the broad masses, through a natural process, have chosen from their own the best blood as Führer, then global history will experience the one type with whom the German people outwardly assume those characteristics that give us the certainty that our history is the history of the world."[56]

Hitler came to talk about the special role of the "Aryan race" in view of the "global danger"[57] which the United States of America represented today, "not because they have a population of one hundred million but because of the value of that hundred million."[58] This was because of the human material that had been poured into the United States through a century of emigration of Germany's best blood.[59] In this speech Hitler's "agro-utopia" surfaced, stemming from his understanding of the Roman Empire, and it was not a coincidence to him "that the nation of the ancient world that produced the greatest thinkers was in essence a state of farmers."[60]

The year 1930 is remarkable, both within the framework of our considerations and in many other ways. It produced Hitler's most important comments regarding his ultimate goals, aside from his two books. Hitler discussed his goals mostly after the elections in September 1930.[61] This is the point in time that is generally accepted as the moment when the Nazi party changed its tactics and systematically[62] disguised its true objectives.[63]

However, the contrary is true. November 1930 offers clear evidence. Hitler's public appearances were striking, and, when considered together with the sources already known, must be treated as to be among the most important sources of information before the "seizure of power."

Of key importance was the speech that Hitler gave at Erlangen on November 13, 1930. The speech is especially significant because of what was going on there at the time. Erlangen was the first German university that already had an absolute majority of the National Socialist Student Association within the Academic Student Committee as of November 1929.[64] Despite the fact that it appeared to be a closed-door assembly of professors and students,[65] Hitler must have been well aware of the make-up of his audience, as well as of the publicity his remarks would receive. In spite of all this, he dedicated a large part of his speech to the last "stage" of his "program." Based on the partition of Germany after the Thirty Years War, which had prevented Germany's now well-known chance for world supremacy, "there was no other race that had as much a right ... to take part in ruling the world."[66] Hitler mentioned his fear that with the situation as it was at the time, Germany could lose its second and final chance completely, "even though we possess the highest entitlement not only to take part in this dividing of the globe that is once again taking place, but actually to play the most important part."[67] He justified this and heightened his ideas with the value of the race: "The German people has proved that, person for person, it is not only just as good, but superior to all other peoples."[68] According to Hitler, Germany lost the First World War only because the whole world was pitted against it. After the usual references to *Mein Kampf* about the relationship between population and land, Hitler reached new heights in a sort of creed and testament intended for his potential successors: "We know this much: every being strives to expand and every nation strives to rule the world. Only those who keep their eye on the latter goal will find the right path. A people that is too cowardly or no longer possesses the courage or the strength to meet this goal takes the second path, one of abdication and of personal surrender, which ends up in annihilation. There are only two paths, one path goes forward without interruption and can only be taken when certain insights lead a people, the second path leads downwards and is the result of a people being satisfied with false principles."[69] With this, Hitler made clear his understanding of the phrase "world supremacy or decline," and also what he understood "world supremacy" to be. His goal was nothing other than world domination or destruction.

Hitler was, during these days, on an election tour of Southern Germany that concentrated on Baden. The days leading up to this explanation of his foreign policy in Erlangen also point very clearly to his ultimate goals. On November 5, 1930, in Mannheim, he explained that, from 1648 onward, "no other nation had more entitlement to world supremacy than the Germans. We and no other nation should have that right."[70] This was greeted with wild applause. According to Hitler, capability and numbers had given the Germans the right "to claim this world supremacy."[71] A few days later in Offenburg, after he once again noted that "the German people at its average value was superior to all others," he posed the question: "When will a race be victorious in this world? I say: when it has a strong feeling for its own value, but secondly also when, in the construction of the state, it takes into consideration the principle that, just as peoples differ from each other in closed masses, so do individual people, and that a people must rise to the highest when its life is directed by the most capable individuals."[72]

Before the date of the Reichstag election, Hitler dealt with well-known topics in his campaign speeches. He claimed that the German people possessed "the best fundamental value," and that based on its 2,000 year history, Germany should take on a different position in the world. "Fate not only divided the surface of the earth into individual states but also placed humans there and let the forces free to play ... the Earth was divided and we lost a position of world supremacy that should have been ours by right."[73] On another occasion, he suggested to his audience, as he had in Erlangen, that Germany was the "most powerful and united body in the world"[74] during the First World War. But now, by contrast, Germany was only a leader as a nation of culture, since democracy had failed.[75]

To what extent the world supremacy of the "Aryan race" was a matter of concern to Hitler becomes evident in the argument he had with Otto Strasser in May 1930, which led to Strasser's withdrawal from the party. During the course of the dispute, Hitler made many blunt references to his foreign policy.[76] "The Nordic race," said Hitler, "has a right to rule the world and we must make this right the guiding star of our foreign policy."[77] Germany's interest demanded a coalition with England, because it was about establishing "a Nordic-Germanic reign over Europe and—in connection with a Nordic-Germanic America, over the world."[78] When the discussion continued the following day, Hitler did not depart from his ultimate goals. Again he emphasized "our task," "...to bring about a fabulous organization of the world, so that every country produces that which is most suitable, while the white race, the Nordic race takes care of the organization of this gigantic plan." "...Believe me," continued Hitler, "all of National Socialism would be worth nothing if it were limited only to Germany and if it didn't seal its rule over the whole world for this highly valuable race for at least one to two thousand years."[79] Hitler's vision of a 'Herrenvolk,' a race of overlords, became clear in these brutal sentences. In his understanding of the British in the eighteenth century, the Germans would control the flow of trade from offices, and the "rest of the world," would dwell as an uneducated mass, like helots, would only labor, and would be terrorized into submission as the need occurred.

Although the documents become more difficult to locate after 1931, there is enough that remains sufficiently expressive. These shifted more and more to the level of confidential dialogues, such as two conversations Hitler had with Richard Breiting, editor-in-chief of the Leipziger Neueste Nachrichten, who was close to the conservative right.[80] During the conversations, Hitler once again indicated the time pressure that controlled the sequence of events for his program in Europe,[81] but he also indicated his willingness, "in internationally favorable situations," to move the clocks forward.[82] By accelerating the alternatives of either victory or destruction, Hitler explained, "Either we succeed in ten years and that will be the end of war for all time, and I dedicate myself to construction and buildings, or we will spend another thousand years pouring our sweat out while forging cannons."[83] At these two meetings, he also put into more concrete terms his picture of the "core of the Aryan race" in the world which, according to him, could lead to a final, lasting situation: "The Nordic blood which is present in England, Northern France and in North America will, in the end, join us to bring about the radical change of the world."[84] But above all other considerations hung the concern of having to build up Germany's global position within a very short time, "before the Soviet Union becomes a world power, before the area of seven million square kilometers that belongs to the United States becomes the arsenal of worldwide Judaism. These monsters are still slumbering. When they awake" was Hitler's fear, "then it will be over with Germany."[85]

In a speech on the occasion of the Reichsführer congress of the Hitler Youth in November 1931 in Munich, Hitler demanded the "winning over of all heroic people of our nation" to be used in the principle of selection.

"These are the paths to supremacy and to the ultimate goal! Let us never give up our will to rule, otherwise Germany's history will come to an end and another nation will take its place. If we should succeed in producing the new political warrior, and I really believe we shall succeed, the world will experience a nation whose immense strength is invincible."[86] This speech must be seen as an example of how Hitler strategically rendered things harmless. In contrast to his speech in Erlangen of the year before, he excluded almost all explicit references to his goals of world supremacy. However, he achieved the same material results by suggestion, compared to his speeches from the previous years.[87]

The year 1932 proves to be more difficult regarding the search for and the choice of source material. During a campaign speech in July, Hitler referred to his intentions only very vaguely. "We have chosen our goal and we will defend it fanatically, ruthlessly to the grave."[88] Cheers of "Bravo" and of the applause of an audience that didn't really listen but was only reacting acoustically at that point—the recording that was handed down emphasizes Hitler's favorite words—already prevented, those few contemporaries who understood Hitler's message from articulating their warnings. In mid-September 1932, however, he openly confided his unchanged objectives to a comrade-in-arms from the early years of the "movement," who soon after became disloyal. It was his goal to develop Germany into the largest power in the world, Hitler said.[89]

Another problem for this year is represented by the memoirs of Hermann Rauschning. Despite justified doubts regarding the value of his "*Discussions with Hitler*"[90] as a source and despite frequent criticism of their use,[91] they cannot be completely dismissed. They remain a secondary source that provides evidence of the continuity of Hitler's ideas regarding his final objectives at the time of the "*Machtergreifung*" (seizure of power). Hitler's comments about a revolutionary type of warfare in the future,[92] and about the role of the German "core race" of 80–100 million people[93] as the "new ruling class of the world,"[94] have been sufficiently proven and secured through the evidence of the years before. All in all, they make it possible to reach the conclusion that, for the consideration of the present study, the year 1932 should be added to the previous years. Another indirect indication of the uninterrupted continuity of Hitler's ideas and plans is provided by a diary entry, one written by someone among his closest inner circle, according to which Hitler spent his hours of contemplation concerning himself with plans for "the grandiose reconstruction of the Reich capital." This project, according to the observer, was "ready to go."[95]

The scale of Hitler's projected goals was actually highlighted on the very day of the "Machtergreifung." In a small room next to the chancellor's reception chamber, Hitler happened to deliver, during the night, one of his endless monologues about his own role in world politics. His influence, he explained, "opened the final struggle of the white man, of the Aryan, for supremacy over the Earth." The non-Aryans, the colored, the Mongolians were already busy trying to grab power under the banner of Bolshevism. However, on this very day would start "the greatest Germanic revolution of races in the history of the world."[96] These visions overlapped with his architectural projects: On that same night, Hitler announced the rebuilding of the chancellery.[97]

Summary

In summary it can be said that the global scale of Hitler's "program," should already in 1920 be seen as a reaction to the supposed goals of Judaism to rule the world. This long-term goal is evidently present before the establishment of the short-term goals presented in *Mein Kampf*. Parallel to Hitler's reflections on short and medium-term goals in Europe, his visionary long-term plan also becomes quite concrete, expanded, anticipated, and accelerated in its time frame by his architectural plans. Stations along the way are 1922 (with its first complete synthesis of anti-Semitism, anti-Bolshevism and '*Lebensraum*'), the time during which *Mein Kampf* was written, and the last additions to the "*Second Book*" in 1928.

There is no long period of time during the years between 1920 and 1933 in which Hitler didn't speak—despite all the tactical coalition plans in Europe—about the program for conquering the world as the ultimate and only goal of the movement. Surprisingly enough, this holds true for the period immediately following the September elections in 1930 as well. These elections catapulted Hitler's party into the arena of power, but did not prevent him in any way from revealing his plans on different occasions, in more or less limited fashion, but quite clearly, to a public that was largely clueless.

Hitler's thoughts can be traced back in brief to the following source ideas:

1. The danger of Jewish world supremacy, related to the positive conclusions one could draw from Britain's position of world power: even small nations would have the chance, as long as they were of pure race, to become rulers over parts of the globe, or even of the whole globe, and to rule forever.
2. Germany may have possessed a chance to reach world supremacy in 1648, but missed it, and now faced the last opportunity to make use of it. Germany could have great hopes because it had a sufficiently large "core race," as well as a special value.
3. It could therefore be the "Aryan vanguard" for Europe and the whole world. First, the defeat of the Jewish Bolshevism would create the prerequisite for "the free interplay of natural forces," that would result in Germany's rise to world supremacy with Hitler as its leader. In this manner, Hitler's way of thinking can be seen as an escape towards the future as a defense against an imagined threat. He grabs the opportunity to become the "savior" of humanity. Through world supremacy, he wishes to give the "Aryan race" a biological final situation.
4. There can be no doubt that this "program," on the one hand, is still visionary, since there exist almost no dates by which specific elements of it should be completed. On the other hand, it shows the characteristics of a concrete utopia, and has to be seen as the ever-

present extension and driving force of the far more precisely detailed plan laid out for Europe (*"Lebensraum im Osten"*). It was also clear at this point that Hitler wanted to achieve at least the stage of "world supremacy" during his lifetime. An aspect that should not to be underestimated is that of his architectural plans, which anticipated the "world supremacy" stage and more, at a moment when the party had been reduced to a meaningless mob and Hitler's chances of ever coming to power had shrunk to almost zero.

Notes

1. W. Jochmann, *Im Kampf um die Macht. Hitlers Rede vor dem Hamburger Nationalklub von 1919* (Frankfurt am Main, 1960). The speech was given on February 28, 1926, ibid., 7.
2. Ibid., 106.
3. Ibid., 73.
4. Goebbels, *Diary 1925-1926*, 84. –entry from June 16, 1926. Goebbels was appointed as the Gauleiter (regional party head) of Berlin by Hitler in October 1926, after he had completely swung over to Hitler's side from the leftist wing of the NSDAP.
5. BA NS 26/54,103. –speech from August 12, 1926, in Passau.
6. Speech from March 6, 1927, in Vilsbiburg, –IfZ Archives in Munich, Fa 88 NSDAP main archive: Fasz. 59 2261/58.
7. Speech from April 6, 1927, in Zirkus Krone, –VB, from April 8, 1927.
8. H. Preiss, ed., *Adolf Hitler in Franken. o.O.o.J.*, 45, –speech from March 26, 1927 in Ansbach.
9. As was Hitler in several speeches in April, –VB, passim.
10. Cf. note 57.
11. Cf., 33 note 5.
12. IfZ Archives in Munich: PS-3753, Letter from Hess to Hewel from March 3, 1927, doc., 375, also in: A. Tyrell, ed., *Führer befiehl....Selbstzeugnisse aus der "Kampfzeit" der NSDAP* (Düsseldorf, 1969), 172. –Compare also 33 note 5.
13. Picker, 143f, –September 8 and 9, 1941, as an example.
14. Speech in Munich on May 16, 1927, –VB, May 18, 1927.
15. Speech from July 30, 1927 at the general meeting of members in Bürgerbräukeller, –VB, August 1 and 2, 1927 –also in Tyrell, 177.
16. Adolf Hitler, „Der Weg zum Wiederaufstieg," in Turner, Jr.., *Faschismus und Kapitalismus in Deutschland*, 51. Cf. also 43 note 22.
17. Turner, 54.
18. Ibid.
19. Ibid., 55.
20. BA NS 26/54,168 on the back, –speech from June 17, 1927, in Landshut.
21. Ibid.
22. Ibid.
23. *Hitler's Second Book. A document from 1928.* Introduction and notes by G.L. Weinberg (Stuttgart, 1961); English edition *Hitler's Second Book. The Unpublished Sequel*

to Mein Kampf (New York, 2003). Compare also Hillgruber, *Vorgeschichte*, 69f; Hildebrand, *Weltreich*, 86f; Hildebrand, *Außenpolitik*, 27; Dülffer, 211ff; Kuhn, 133ff; Jäckel, *Hitlers Weltanschauung*, 113ff; M. Broszat, „Betrachtungen zu „*Hitlers Zweitem Buch*," *VfZG* 9 (1961), 417ff.

24. Speer, 100.
25. *Second Book*, 77.
26. Broszat, *Betrachtungen Zweites Buch*, 423.
27. *Second Book*, 221.
28. Ibid., 130.
29. Ibid., 161.
30. BA NS 26/55, –speech from September 18, 1928, in Circus Sarrasani.
31. Ibid., 46.
32. Ibid., 41.
33. Compare Maser, *Briefe*, 139. –Instruction to the minister for transport, Dorpmüller, on December 3, 1938, to have the largest and fastest passenger ship in the world built by 1941/1942.
34. BA NS 26/55, 41.
35. Ibid., 49.
36. Ibid., 50.
37. BA NS 26/55, speech from November 9, 1928.
38. Ibid., 126.
39. BA NS 26/55, –speech in Memmingen from January 18, 1928, 3.
40. Speech from September 2, 1928, at the Führer conference in Munich, –VB, September 4, 1928.
41. Speech from May 23, 1928, Bürgerbräukeller –VB, May 25, 1928.
42. Speech from September 2, 1928. Cf. note 40.
43. Cf. 39 note 37.
44. Speech from October 18, 1928, in Oldenburg i.O., –IfZ Archives in Munich: MA 732, NSDAP-main archive, –cf. also Dülffer, 219 note 71.
45. Speech from October 18, 1928.
46. G.L. Weinberg, "National Socialist Organization and Foreign Policy Aims in 1927," *JMH* 36 (1964), 428ff.
47. Ibid., Hess –Hewel letter from December 8, 1928, 428f.
48. Hitler's letter to Dr. Dinter from July 25, 1928, –Tyrell, 205. –Dinter was Gauleiter for Thuringia from April 6, 1925 to September 30, 1927.
49. Ibid.
50. Ibid. –Compare a similar remark of Hitler's from 1932: "Indeed I cannot lose another single year. I have to gain power soon, in order to finish the gigantic tasks within the time left to me. I must! I must!" –A. Krebs, *Tendenzen und Gestalten der NSDAP* (Stuttgart, 1959), 137.
51. One should take note of Hitler's terms for the Earth: "toy ball," "challenge cup."
52. Speech from February 24, 1929 in the Hofbräuhaus, –VB, February 27, 1929.
53. VB, August 3, 1929.
54. BA NS 26/62,22. –Cf. also 44 note 29.
55. BA NS 26/62, 31.
56. Speech from August 4, 1929, –VB, August 6, 1929.
57. Preiss, 131, –speech from November 30, 1929, in Hersbruck. –Cf. 58 note 10.
58. Preiss, 131.
59. Ibid.
60. Ibid., 141.

61. The increase of NSDAP seats from 12 to 107 in the Reichstag election from September 14, 1930.
62. H.-A. Jacobsen, „Zur Programmatik und Struktur der nationalsozialistischen Außenpolitik 1919-1939." *Aus Politik und Zeitgeschichte. Beilage zum „Parlament."* B 50/67 (December 13, 1967), 6f.
63. Compare also Jäckel in the introduction to: Heuss, *Hitlers Weg,* xxxvi.
64. Fourteen out of twenty-five seats seats.
65. We are very well informed about the background of Hitler's appearance in Erlangen through Franze, *Erlanger Studentenschaft 1918–1945.* Here we can read the reactions to Hitler's speeches in the days that followed the November 13. –Cf. ibid., 130ff and 23 note 2.
66. Preiss, 165.
67. Ibid.
68. Ibid.
69. Ibid., 171f. –Cf. also Hillgruber, „„Endlösung' und Ostimperium," 135.
70. Speech from November 5, 1930, in Mannheim, –IfZ Archives MA 732, 3. Cf. also Dülffer, 219.
71. MA 732, 3.
72. Speech from November 8, 1930, in Offenburg, –IfZ Archives MA 732, 3.
73. Speech from August 31, 1930, in Kiel, –IfZ Archives MA 732.
74. Speech from August 12, 1930, in Munich, –VB, August 17–18, 1930.
75. Ibid.
76. Strasser, *Mein Kampf.* A reprint of "Ministersessel oder Revolution," 50ff.
77. Strasser, 57, –conversations with Hitler from May 21, 1930.
78. Ibid., 57f.
79. Ibid., 64, –conversation with Hitler from May 22, 1930.
80. Richard Breiting, chief editor of the "*Leipziger Neueste Nachrichten.*"
81. E. Calic, *Ohne Maske. Hitler-Breiting. Geheimgespräche 1931* (Frankfurt am Main, 1968), 31. –Authenticity of source questionable.
82. Ibid., 30.
83. Ibid., 86.
84. Ibid., 102.
85. Ibid., 71.
86. Speech from November 15, 1931, –VB, November 19, 1931.
87. Compare 53f.
88. F. Terveen, "From an election speech of Hitler's on July 27, 1932 in Eberswalde" *GWU* 10 (1959), 225.
89. Ludecke. 423.
90. T. Schieder, *Hermann Raschnings* Gespräche mit Hitler *als Geschichtsquelle* (Opladen, 1972), especially 62.
91. Jacobsen, *Außenpolitik,* 606 note 7; Hildebrand, *Weltreich,* 453f and note 36; Jäckel, *Hitlers Weltanschauung,* 14 note 22.
92. Rauschning, *Gespräche mit Hitler,* 13f. –Cf. also 37f in this chapter.
93. Rauschning, *Gespräche mit Hitler,* 42.
94. Ibid., 44f.
95. Goebbels, *Kaiserhof,* 38, –entry from February 3, 1932. –Cf. also 39 note 20.
96. Fest, 510. –Quote from H. Frank, *Im Angesicht des Galgens.* This eschatological passage does not appear in the published book.
97. Ibid.

Part II

HITLER AS ARCHITECT

Chapter 7

MEGALOMANIA AS POLICY

Albert Speer's "memoirs"[1] exposed the role architecture played in the way the Third Reich saw itself, a role played in particular at Hitler's great insistence and with his own input and personal interest. Therefore, the memoirs of his architect, who later became minister for armaments, are among the most important documents from one of the main characters of the Third Reich, not least because of the statements Speer makes about Hitler. However, historians' reactions to this book are conflicting.[2] One possible reason for this is that, while considering the catastrophe of 1945, historians prefer to avoid analyzing the content of a book relating to a secondary subject such as architecture, and they would prefer to let art historians formulate their critique. Or is it because almost none of Hitler's colossal plans ever came into being, and thus the plaster models of buildings and their blueprints can be discarded as utopian and non-historical, and therefore irrelevant?

At the same time, however, this topic has many connections to later history. In 1975, the provisional government of the West African country of Guinea-Bissau announced its intention to build a new capital in the middle of the country. More prominent examples were the new capitals of Brazil and Pakistan, Brasilia and Islamabad, which had also been moved inland several years prior. The list could go on.

Even if such decisions are primarily made for infrastructural reasons, it remains important not to overlook the political considerations attached to those decisions. In the search to establish an individual identity for a nation or a leader, one often sets up a neutral starting point, so to speak, which, free from any historical baggage, represent a symbol of the country's seemingly open road to a future that still has to be shaped.

Such happenings are in no way limited to our century. Throughout history, architecture has embodied political ideas and was both the sponsor and mediator of human communication. Therefore, for many scientific disciplines it goes without saying that, in addition to written documents, architecture and symbols of rule must be regarded as the self-expression of an era and also of the people who shaped that era. It also should be included as the main object of study and as a complementary subject in the area of historical sources.[3] History is full of uninterrupted attempts by both secular and religious rulers who tried to use art to document their importance and to reiterate their demands on the people.[4] The pyramids in Egypt, the architecture of the highly developed cultures of the land of the two rivers, the Tigris and the Euphrates (today's Iraq), and other examples from further throughout history: a vast wealth of structures by rulers and popes all testify to aspirations to power and claims to eternity.

In the twentieth century, thanks to the advances brought about by the Industrial Revolution, totalitarian states find themselves a special temptation to use art and architecture to manipulate and influence. In the Third Reich, the process of erosion and the radical estrangement of art from its earlier relatively autonomous position is clearly evident.

The artist and architect are both used as instruments of propaganda to publicize political ideas in their own specialties. There are many related works that take as their theme the way in which art illustrates the changing relationship between the politics and the artistic expression of an epoch.[5] Architecture, especially, is in a position to be misused, as it gives the propaganda of a totalitarian regime the chance to develop a very permanent form of demonstration, no one can erase the presence of public buildings. Such attempts, therefore, represent the amplification of propaganda in film, sound, and the written word. Architecture enlarges and completes the area of constant influence.

It is therefore surprising that in the research dedicated to the Third Reich, even in our times, the impression prevails that Hitler's long-term plans or final goals were "so far beyond all the planning of the present that he felt no compulsion to slowly start realizing these plans in a concrete way."[6] Many monographs both about internal and external affairs came to the conclusion that Hitler's role in decision making was not necessarily dominant during the first years following the "seizure of power," and for that reason there was no long-term setting of goals that was obvious within the system.[7] Both of these statements are wrong and have been corrected partially by the Speer memoirs. However, apart from a few studies that examine certain aspects of Speer and what he had planned in Hitler's name, there has been no detailed analysis of his memoirs, and most importantly no pursuit of the issues discussed in the book, regardless of its failings and reservations.[8] Joachim Fest is the only author who has looked into this in more detail in his biography of Hitler.[9] There was, however, a relatively early biography of Hitler that indicated the importance of architecture in the Third Reich.[10] The comments Hitler made during his conversations with Rausching[11] also indicated paths for research, but important above all was the publication of *Hitler's Table Talk*,[12] where Hitler until the end of 1941 had frequently offered his opinion about architecture. Several passages in a 1948 study about journalism in the Third Reich have had somewhat of a pioneering effect.[13] This can also be said of the most important contributions to architecture from closely related fields, most especially from art history.

An item of great value is the 1950 study by A. Dehlinger,[14] which unfortunately only exists in typescript at the present time. The author was able to analyze previously unknown material from the archives of the planning authorities responsible at the time, and in questioning witnesses, he filled an information gap that otherwise would have remained empty. Apart from a few contributions after this[15] and the too strongly psychological study by H. Lehmann-Haupt,[16] a new series of studies on art history was not published until the beginning of the sixties, although the important documentation in the volumes by J. Wulf[17] and A. Teut[18] as well as the fundamental monographs by H. Brenner[19] and B. Miller Lane,[20] must be mentioned. Although all these studies have indeed evaluated the enormous body of material that constitutes the huge official printed stock of sources, until today here has been no thorough development and evaluation of the archives of Koblenz,[21] Nuremberg,[22] or Berlin.[23] This is also true of the essay by K. Arndt,[24] which nonetheless opens up another avenue of source material for studies about architecture in the Third Reich through film documentaries. The institute for scientific films in Göttingen has been working on the scientific evaluation of Nazi documentary films for several years and has published booklets about its work.[25]

Finally, the work by A.M. Vogt[26] must be mentioned, which deals more with theoretical questions than practical ones. As much as the initiative to present art of the Third Reich to a broader public by way of an exhibition is welcomed,[27] it is unlikely that this might be of use in the field of architecture. Apart from the number of inaccuracies, the presentation remains weak and the meaning of the architecture unclear. Hitler's role is completely misunderstood due to the one-sided selection of literature and commentary. However, the pictures in the catalog and the references open a door. Also, the 1974 work by R.R. Taylor[28] is very unsatisfactory.

The author is undecided regarding Hitler's role in the architectural policies of the Third Reich,[29] and because he fails to ask key questions and practically ignores the relationship to political history, he reaches unsatisfactory conclusions.[30]

The general weakness of studies in art history of the Third Reich is their undervaluing of the "Hitler factor." His important role becomes clear in a different set of source material, memoirs and diaries. They contain an amazing amount of indications of Hitler's plans, and they are for once an exception, and remain important as source material. In all other apologia, where personalities of the Third Reich were marked by the lack of understanding of the nature and direction of the Nazi regime, the importance of Hitler as a master architect is generally not properly evaluated and is treated accordingly. Therefore, observations regarding this matter are interpreted as marginalia, anecdotes, or in the most extreme cases as proof of Hitler's demonic nature, rather than as a subject of inquiry that should not be supressed. Despite how widespread these sources are: military,[31] diplomatic,[32] artistic, and architectural,[33] as well as people from Hitler's most intimate political[34] and personal[35] circles, for the most part, the majority of statements concur. There is no doubt as to their truthfulness.

Speer reports that while acting as Hitler's architect, he referred to models of the architecture of the French Revolution.[36] There are indeed striking similarities between the drafts of Etienne-Louis Boullée and Claude Nicolas Ledoux, with their domes and military buildings and monuments, and Speer's drafts[37] (coincidentally, like most of Speer's plans, the French architects never got beyond the blueprint stages). Just as the connection between rule and architecture has a long history, so does that of architectural utopia: models for society articulated through revolutionary architectural projects. Most importantly, plans for ideal cities and ideal states have existed since the early Italian Renaissance (e.g. *Sforzinda* by the architectural theorist Filarete, Thomas Morus's *Utopia*, and Thomas Campanella's *City of the Sun*.) While Hitler was intent on setting world records with his architecture, as is still to be demonstrated individually, the megalomania of the end of the eighteenth century was legitimized exclusively by the argument of natural science. For architects like Boullée, it was about coping with and assimilating the revolutionary findings of his age: it was about the vastness of the universe. The enormity of these architects' buildings stemmed from a background in astronomical and natural sciences, and was not connected to political greatness.[38] However, soon after Boullée, a sudden change took place, that led into a neoclassicism, not only in France but also in Europe and North America.[39] Completely different political systems during the twentieth century preferred classicism as the predominant architecture of the time in the moment when those systems were beginning to acquire authoritarian features.[40] In Russia, after a short period of revolutionary architecture around 1917, there was a radical change which led to a neoclassicism of a Stalinist character.[41] Given all the differences individually, the architecture of Fascist Italy and the style of buildings during the Third Reich also belong to this development. There is indeed no doubt that these building projects all contained the main elements of classical architecture (i.e., columns, arches, high podiums, and triangular gables), even if these were perverted in their dimensions.[42]

But it seems questionable whether the vantage point from the field of art history, which is predominantly aesthetic, possesses enough evidential value and knowledge when it classifies the architecture of the avant-garde at the time of the French and Russian revolutions as the architecture of hope,[43] work that expresses social utopia, while at the same time viewing the neoclassical revival in Europe and North America as an architecture of nostalgia which recalls Mediterranean Greek and Roman culture.[44]

Proof of why the architecture of the Third Reich, a style tailor-made to the most significant buildings, was not an architecture of nostalgia, but rather the trade-mark of triumphant National Socialism, a device used to overcome capitalistic industrial society in order to realize a social utopia that Hitler assumed resembled antiquity, but which had also begun with him. It will have to be shown that a connection between politics and architecture existed in Hitler's conscious thought.[45] Architectural planning was not a substitute for political helplessness, which required diverting and neutralizing superfluous energy, but rather the conscious anticipation of expansion policies that were later planned and carried out.

After this short digression into the realms of art history, which will also touch upon the question of classification amidst greater connections, it also must be asked: what role did Hitler play in the architectural intentions of the Third Reich (meaning, essentially, the large buildings)? Was he the determining factor? What relationship existed between architecture and Hitler's understanding of history and art? These questions call attention to the central issue regarding the role architecture played in the Third Reich, namely: Can Hitler's political goals be read to a certain extent from his architectural ideas? At the same time, it will be of great importance to observe Hitler's behavior after his seizure of power. At what point did he actively begin to concern himself with the relevant questions? Through the examples of several large building projects of the Third Reich, their functions will be examined with a view to the role each would play in the coming empire, in order to finally examine the effect architecture had on the economic and social history of the Third Reich.

Notes

1. In contrast to the memoirs published in 1969, the Spandau Diaries contain hardly anything about the building policy of the Third Reich.
2. For example: K.D. Bracher, „Die Speer-Legende." *NPL* 15 (1970), 429ff; K.-H. Ludwig, „Die wohlreflektierten ‚Erinnerungen' des Albert Speer." *GWU* 21 (1970), 695–708.
3. For an example from the Middle Ages, see P.E. Schramm, *Kaiser Friedrichs II Herrschaftszeichen* (Göttingen, 1955).
4. In addition: G. Hellack, „Architektur und bildende Kunst als Mittel nationalsozialistischer Propaganda," *Publizistik* 5 (1960), 77ff.
5. As an example: A. Speer, *„Die Bauten des Führers,"* in a propaganda book: A. Hitler, *Bilder aus dem Leben des Führers* (Hamburg-Bahrenfeld-Leipzig, 1936), 72ff.
6. The last: Petersen, 179.
7. As an example: H. Mommsen, *Beamtentum im Dritten Reich. Mit ausgewählten Quellen zur nationalsozialistischen Beamtenpolitik* (Stuttgart, 1966); Broszat, *Soziale Motivation und Führer-Bindung des Nationalsozialismus*, 392ff.
8. Short references in: Hillgruber, „„Endlösung' und Ostimperium," 135 note 8; Dülfer, 218; Wollstein, 6f; Reinhardt, *Wende vor Moskau*, 31; Hildebrand, *Außenpolitik*, 27 note 38; Hildebrand, „Hitlers Ort," 589 note 21; C. Cross, *Adolf Hitler* (London, 1974), 280f, W. Maser, *Adolf Hitler. Legende, Mythos, Wirklichkeit* (Munich-Esslingen, 1972), 100, 111f; Maser, *Briefe*, 130ff. From the areas of social and technical history, the following should be mentioned: G. Hortleder, *Das Gesellschaftsbild des Ingenieurs. Zum politischen Verhalten der Technischen Intelligenz in Deutschland* (Frankfurt, 1970), 121ff; already published before Speer: G. Jansen, *Das Ministerium Speer. Deutschlands Rüstung im Krieg* (Berlin-Frankfurt am Main-Vienna, 1968), 34 ff; finally: K. H. Ludwig, *Technik und Ingenieure im Dritten Reich* (Düsseldorf, 1974).
9. Fest, 334, 526f, 706, 723ff, 943.
10. W. Görlitz and H.A. Quint, *Adolf Hitler. Eine Biographie* (Stuttgart, 1952), 475f, 561.
11. Rauschning, *Gespräche mit Hitler*, 34, 190, 265.
12. Picker, *Tischgespräche;* A. Hitler, *Libres Propos sur la Guerre et la Paix, Recueillis sur l'ordre de M. Bormann,* preface by R. d'Harcourt (Paris, 1952); also see *Hitler's Table Talk 1941-1944,* with an introductory essay on *"The Mind of Adolf Hitler"* by H.R. Trevor-Roper, trans. N. Cameron and R.H. Stevens (London, 1953).
13. W. Hagemann, *Publizistik im Dritten Reich. Ein Beitrag zur Methodik der Massenführung* (Hamburg, 1948), 66ff.
14. A. Dehlinger, *Architektur der Superlative. Eine kritische Betrachtung der NS-Bauprogramme von München und Nürnberg.* –Two vols. IfZ MS 8/1 (a), MS 8/2 (a).
15. Cf. 68 note 4.
16. H. Lehmann-Haupt, *Art under a Dictatorship* (New York, 1954).
17. J. Wulf, *Die Bildenden Künste im Dritten Reich. Eine Dokumentation* (Gütersloh, 1963), 235ff; Wulf, *Theater und Film im Dritten Reich. Eine Dokumentation* (Gütersloh, 1964), 169ff.
18. A Teut, *Architektur in Dritten Reich 1933–1945* (Berlin-Frankfurt am Main-Vienna, 1967).
19. H. Brenner, *Die Kunstpolitik des Nationalsozialismus* (Reinbek, 1963), 121ff, 154ff, 276f.
20. B. Miller Lane, *Architecture and Politics in Germany 1918–1945* (Cambridge, Mass., 1968).
21. For the chapter at hand, items from the *Reichskanzlei* (Chancellery) R 43 II and R 120 general building inspector were used for the German capital.

22. City Archives Nuremberg –party congress buildings. (Also available in the Federal archives in Koblenz).

23. Bauhaus Archives, Archives of the Akademie der Künste, State Archives.

24. K. Arndt, „Filmdokumente des Nationalsozialismus als Quellen für architekturgeschichtliche Forschungen." Zeitgeschichte in Film und Tondokument. 17 historische, pädagogische und sozialwissentschaftliche Beiträge, ed. G. Moltmann and K. F. Reimers (Göttingen, 1970) 39ff.

25. As an example, the publications that accompany the twenty minute film "Das Wort aus Stein" from K. Arndt and H. Döhl. The film shows a series of model buildings for Munich, Augsburg, Berlin, and the "Hohe Schule der NSDAP" on the banks of Chiemsee. A thorough, but unfortunately rather unsuccessful interview of the institute with Speer should also be named.

26. A.M. Vogt, „Revolutionsarchitektur und Nazi-Klassizismus," Argo. FS für K. Badt, ed. M. Gosenbruch and L. Dittmann (Cologne, 1970), 354ff; Vogt, Russische und französische Revolutions-Architektur 1917/1789. Zur Einwirkung des Marxismus und des Newtonismus auf die Bauweise (Cologne, 1974).

27. In addition: Exhibition catalog of Art in the Third Reich. Dokumente der Unterwerfung. ed. Frankfurter Kunstverein (Frankfurt am Main,1974).

28. R.R. Taylor, The World in Stone. The role of Architecture in the National Socialist Ideology (Berkeley-Los Angeles-London, 1974).

29. Ibid., 30, 36, 56, 259f.

30. Ibid., 271.

31. M. von Faber du Faur, Macht und Ohnmacht. Erinnerungen eines alten Offiziers (Stuttgart, 1953), 206; B. von Loßberg, Im Wehrmachtführungsstab. Bericht eines Generalstabsoffiziers (Hamburg, 1949), 85f, 126; G. Thomas, Geschichte der deutschen Wehr- und Rüstungswirtschaft (1918–1943/45), ed. W. Birkenfeld (Boppard, 1966), 172, 197.

32. O. Abetz, Das offene Problem. Ein Rückblick auf zwei Jahrzehnte deutscher Frankreichpolitik (Cologne, 1951), 81; Francois-Poncet, Botschafter in Berlin, 268; P. Stehlin, Auftrag in Berlin (Berlin, 1965), 160ff.

33. Speer, Spandauer Tagebücher; P. Bonatz, Leben und Bauen (Stuttgart, 1950), 168, 178ff; A. Breker, Paris, Hitler et moi (Paris, 1970), 84ff.

34. Dietrich, 163ff; H. Frank, Im Angesicht des Galgens. Deutung Hitlers und seiner Zeit auf Grund eigener Erlebnisse und Erkenntnisse (Munich, 1953), 130, 320; Schacht, 40, 52f; F.C. Prinz zu Schaumburg-Lippe, Als die goldne Abendsonne. Aus meinen Tagebüchern der Jahre 1933–1937 (Wiesbaden, 1971), 29f; L. Graf Schwerin von Krosigk, Es geschah in Deutschland. Menschenbilder unseres Jahrhunderts (Tübingen-Stutgart, 1951), 200f; Strasser, 52, 72; U. von Hassell, Vom andern Deutschland. Aus den nachgelassenen Tagebüchern 1938–1944, with commentary by H. Rothfels (Frankfurt am Main-Hamburg, 1964), 55; Das politische Tagebuch Alfred Rosenbergs aus den Jahren 1934/35 und 1939/40, ed with commentary H.G. Seraphim (Göttingen, 1956), 110f, 124; Tagebuch von C.V. Krogman 1933 bis 1945—Forschungsstelle für die Geschichte des Nationalsozialismus in Hamburg; K. von Schuschnigg, Ein Requiem in Rot-Weiß-Rot, „Aufzeichnungen des Häftlings Dr. Auster" (Zurich, 1946), 45; Weizsäcker-Papiere, 252.

35. Hoffmann, 156, 161, 169; Hanfstaengl, 80; A. Kubizek, Adolf Hitler. Mein Jugendfreund (Graz-Göttingen, 1953), 116ff, F. Thyssen, I Paid Hitler (London, 1941), 171ff; F. Wiedemann, Der Mann, der Feldherr werden wollte. Erlebnisse und Erfahrungen des Vorgesetzten Hitlers im 1. Weltkrieg und seines späteren Persönlichen Adjutanten (Velbert und Kettwig, 1964), 87f, 139, 220f; Zoller, 55f; H. Kehrl, Krisenmanager im Dritten Reich. 6 Jahre Frieden-6 Jahre Krieg. Erinnerungen (Düsseldorf, 1973), 186.

36. Speer, 174f. Cf. also Vogt, *Nazi-Klassizismus*, 354. Along with Speer, one should also consider: Speer, *Die Bauten des Führers*; *"Die Bürde werde ich nicht mehr los,"* interview with A. Speer about *Adolf Hitler and the Third Reich*, SPIEGEL 46 (November 7, 1966), 48ff; R. Wolters, *Albert Speer* (Oldenburg, 1943); Film-Interview Göttingen.

37. In addition: Ausstellungskatalog *Revolutionsarchitektur. Boullée, Ledoux, Lequeu*. ed. Staatliche Kunsthalle Baden-Baden und Gesellschaft der Freunde junger Kunst e.V. (1971). The interior architecture of the congress hall in Nuremberg especially shows striking parallels to Ledoux's draft for the theatre in Besançon –Dehlinger, 66.

38. Vogt, *Nazi-Klassizismus*, 357ff.

39. Ibid., 361f.

40. Ibid.

41. Vogt, *„Revolutionsarchitektur 1917/1789,"* 243.

42. Vogt, *Nazi-Klassizismus*, 354; Hellack, 90; Arndt, 42.

43. Vogt, *„Revolutionsarchitektur 1917/1789,"* 232.

44. Ibid.

45. Cf. Speer, *Spandauer Tagebücher*, 202.

Chapter 8

HITLER'S VIEWS ON ARCHITECTURE, HISTORY AND ART

From his early youth in Vienna, Hitler showed great interest in archi-tecture.[1] In *Mein Kampf,* he tells us of a trip to Vienna, the metropolis on the Danube, when he was fifteen. He explains how impressed he was by the important buildings of the city. Above all, he was taken with the opera house, the parliament buildings, and the Ringstrasse.[2] Despite fail-ing the entrance examination for the Academy of Fine Arts, Hitler, ac-cording to his recollections in *Mein Kampf,* decided to become a master builder.[3] Sketches from this period still exist that eloquently demonstrate his emotional imagination and vividly show the untiring enthusiasm of the sketch artist.[4] In 1941, Hitler still recalled that part of his life with the following words: "At the time I [fantasized about] living in palaces and it was exactly then that I thought up my plans for a new Berlin."[5] Even if one has to doubt the stated goal behind this information, one can accept that long before the drafting and establishment of Hitler's politi-cal ideas, a "program" existed in the form of drawings that demonstrated, in the context of his failed career, his detachment from reality and his propensity for daydreaming, although it remained apparently stable in the contures. Hitler's wish to become a master builder could very well have been a form of compensation syndrome. The large buildings were to be tangible proof of his personal greatness and were meant to counteract his lack of self confidence.[6] This type of psychological interpretation cannot, however, fully explain the teleology that can be found in Hitler's architectural plans from 1924–1926 onwards. While writing Mein Kampf, Hitler seems to channel his architectural drafts, giving them a political function, something for which there had been no evidence up to that point. At that time, Hitler was not only drafting the sketches that in later years he would give to Speer for him to execute as projects.[7] Hitler also developed his ideas about remodelling the architecture of public buildings in Mein Kampf[8] and these precise ideas later become the central theme of some of his "cultural" speeches to the political assemblies of the Nuremberg party conventions. Particularly noteworthy is the mythical-archaic vision of architecture whereby he states a confused historical fantasy, claiming that "the geopolitical importance of a central point for a political movement … cannot be overestimated." "Only when this central point exists, surrounded by the enchanting magic of a place like Mecca or Rome, can it grant a political movement the energy which is founded on the inner unity and the recognition of a leader on top who represents this unity."[9] Important information in these speeches regarding the role of architecture, already reminiscent of the quoted passage from Mein Kampf, could present Hitler's understanding of history, from which an account of his thoughts on the purpose of art and its function might be pursued.

In the preceding chapter, it was explained that Hitler often spoke about the role of art,[10] and more specifically that of architecture. From the time he became chancellor, he had significantly more opportunities to do so, and the following occasions would produce a great deal of important information:

1. Speeches on art at the Nazi party conventions in 1933–1938.[11]
2. The laying of corner-stones for buildings.
3. Inaugural speeches at exhibitions.

These speeches on art can be viewed as a substitute for political speeches. For Hitler, however, they were quite clearly seen as politically harmless and incapable of giving any insight into his real goals. Neither did he think that a critical observer might be able to "decipher" a hidden message in his words. An analysis of these speeches is therefore automatically beyond his calculating consciousness. Hitler was more open and programmatic than usual, so that his statements about long-term goals are clearer than in his official political statements. As previously shown in other problem areas, it is also evident in Hitler's ideas on architecture, in which there were hardly any changes for over twenty years, that constant expansion and enlargement ran parallel with the political development. In order to grasp some of Hitler's ideas out of this stable pattern of thought, it seems necessary to delve into his abstruse way of seeing the world and partly to accept his premises in order to find concrete strands of thought that do indeed form a chain, in spite of this jungle of irrationality, half truths, skewed historical comparisons, and proliferating images of race.

The question of whether there was a historical model according to which Hitler may have established his intentions and plans is especially important. As somebody from "inside Germany" who came from the old protected area behind the *limes*, he greatly admired the Mediterranean culture.[12] Hitler's historical model was Rome.[13] It was only to the Roman Empire that Hitler granted the attribute of true world supremacy: "The Roman Empire was the only true world supremacy that ever existed."[14] It was "incomparable," because it "ruled the whole world."[15] Even the ambitiously spread out Great Britain, whom Hitler since 1923 had credited with positive characteristics according to his ideas of "racial value," never was on par with Rome in his eyes because Rome, in contrast to the United Kingdom, "had been founded on the blood of Roman citizens."[16] In other words, Hitler considered Rome as a state that had developed according to socio-Darwinian principles. Opponents who got in the way of its rising or expansion were eliminated until Rome was unchallenged in its supremacy of the world at that time. Hitler traced Rome's successes from the alleged fact that the ancient ruler of the world "basically was a farmer state."[17]

Hitler's agrarian utopia—the defense of the "soil" with "one's own blood," and the holding on to agrarian life even within an immense growth of power—is visible in these speculations about Roman history. Certainly this comparison of history also touches on the central point of the issue regarding this study. The model of Rome allows one to speculate on the role that Hitler had foreseen for the Third Reich. Clearly he didn't want to share rule equally with any other power.

The second decisive step in our understanding of Hitler's concept is that he considered ancient Rome and the history of the Germanic tribes to be almost identical. In this way, he creates a 2,000-year-old German history of global culture and supremacy from which he can draw. According to Hitler, the Germanic tribes came into contact with "surely the most natural, energetic, and admirable empire the world had ever seen,"[18] and only Christianity had prevented the Roman Empire from developing even further under the aegis of Germanic culture, theoretically working toward a position of global supremacy, by reaching out and conquering the "New World."[19] This construction of history consequently allows Hitler to continue his thinking, leading to the third step in our determining the connection between his understanding of history and art.

If one accepts this "link" between the Romans and the Germanic tribes, then the racist element, the ground upon which Hitler's wishful thinking was doubtlessly based, becomes apparent. Hitler is of the opinion that the entire culture of the white race is built upon the ancient Greek and Roman world.[20] All other conclusions regarding the foundation of an imperial tradition are consistent: Greeks and Romans were united with Germanic tribes in a "core race," and therefore their example is decisive for all culture.[21] This Greek and Roman art culture which Hitler discusses thus conveys not only a cultural ideal "from one of the most beautiful periods of human development,"[22] but also—and this is decisive with regard to Hitler's building projects in the Third Reich—the idea that there is an "eternal" form of art: the Greek-Nordic type.[23] "There is no new culture in this world, no more than there is a new language or a new race. The culture of a nation is the mass of cultural creations that have been collected over thousands of years."[24] Culture must go back to "that immense imperial power of antiquity," which, despite the fact it was killed off one and a half thousand years ago as a real phenomenon, still lives on as "an unreal force in the imagination, and still has an effect."[25] Hitler therefore consistently rejects the idea of a period of style or a national style of art. Instead, he promotes the Gothic cathedrals of "our Germanic imperial royal families,"[26] as he calls them on another occasion, to the status of timeless style.[27] When building a theater, it would be foolish, Hitler explained in his first cultural speech in 1933, to want to outwardly deny "that we are merely renovators that are continuing an institution that has substantially existed for thousands of years. ... It is therefore completely wrong to speak of trying to find a 'new style.'"[28] "For there is no art established in time but rather only in nations." There is therefore "also no standard of yesterday and today, of modern and not modern, there is only the scale of 'unworthy' or 'worthy' and with that, 'eternal' or 'temporary.' And this eternity lives in the very existence of the peoples, as long as they also are permanent, which means that they exist."[29] According to Hitler's view, it is therefore essential "to return to the elements of form" "that in the past were discovered by races of similar status either to develop further or simply to refine or be regarded as indispensable syllables in the language of architecture."[30] Hitler's purely superficial, primitive, and sensory way of considering Greek sculpture and certain forms of painting also fit into this picture. For Hitler, every "beautiful body" necessarily comes from the ancient world, and therefore is Nordic and National Socialist.[31] "In this way, ancient Greek art," according to Hitler, "is not only a formal reproduction of the Greek way of life or of the Greek countryside and its people, but a proclamation of the Greek body and spirit in and of itself."[32] And from this point, it is a short mental journey, according to Hitler's petit bourgeois view of history, to wanting to breed humans according to specific models in order to preserve the phenotype of the ancient warriors.

Beyond Hitler's architectural vision based on Greek and Roman antiquity, there is another important component that must be considered: the question of the "value of ruins." Already in *Mein Kampf*, Hitler is preoccupied by the fact that the only remains from the ancient world are those of large public buildings.

> The character of an ancient city was not to be found in its private buildings, but in the public monuments which didn't seem to be meant for the moment, but for eternity. They were to reflect not the richness of one individual owner, but rather the greatness and importance of the general public. If one compares the proportions of ancient public buildings to those of private dwellings of the same period, only then does one understand the paramount power and force of the emphasis given to the principle of allocating the first priority to public works ... the temples, the spas, stadiums, circuses, aqueducts and basilicas.[33]

According to Hitler, this also held true in the Middle Ages. "What was expressed in the Pantheon or the Acropolis now wrapped itself in the forms of Gothic cathedrals. Like giants these enormous constructions towered over the tiny crowded buildings of medieval cities" as "the visual expression of a view of life which basically only corresponded to that found in the ancient world."[34] Hitler's understanding of art was in reality only oriented to proportional size, and the aggressive vocabulary he uses allows us to forecast his future plans: force, power, and enormous monumental buildings. Against this look back upon centuries of German history, he places a countermovement, which according to him began in the nineteenth century[35] and which led to the fact that private capitalist buildings dominated the skyline in, for example, 1925 Berlin. "Our descendants will one day have to admire the department stores of some Jews and the hotels of some companies as the characteristic expression of the culture of our era."[36] Equivalent comments about Berlin and Munich demonstrate that in 1924 he was already busy with renovation plans for both of these cities. On many occasions after 1933 he was critical of the capitalist building style, and he rejected skyscrapers for Germany, although this did not prevent him from contracting a 250-meter-high skyscraper to be built in Hamburg as "Gateway to the World."[37]

Hitler planned the architecture of the Third Reich along the lines of his ancient models and he even demanded sketches of the buildings rendered in a state of ruin.[38] He chose granite as the building material for eternity and implied a magical fate for his buildings, akin to a magic spell.

This is what he said at the laying of the cornerstone for the Congress Hall in Nuremberg. "If the movement should ever be silent then this witness will still speak after thousands of years. Here in the midst of a hallowed grove of ancient oaks, people will come and admire with reverent amazement this first giant among the buildings of the Third Reich."[39] A few years later, he already set the buildings he had just begun on par with their ancient models: "The gigantic works, as a sign of the cultural reconstruction of the Third Reich, will one day belong to the permanent cultural heritage of the occident, just as the great works of the ancient world are today." They ensued a breakthrough of German culture "in one of the most tremendous political changes in history … our people will care with proud respect for the monuments that we place today in the eternal treasury of art."[40]

When travelling abroad, Hitler was especially interested in visiting comparisons with his plans for Germany.[41] Rome above all was his great model. It is reported that during his official visit to Italy in 1938, he stood on the ground of the Colosseum for hours and that his impressions found their expression in the corrections he made to the already named Congress Hall in Nuremberg, a building which was meant to be larger than the Colosseum in its dimensions.[42] The Congress Hall was finally built and is still the biggest hall in Germany. Also, Hitler's visit to the government buildings in Rome resulted in as many suggestions for projects in Berlin.[43]

Similar to the way he was using ancient Rome as a model, Hitler's ideas also moved in the direction of following in the footsteps of the designers and builders of Roman military roads in Eastern and Northern Europe. The runways or roads that were being planned in Russia for the rapid movement of troops,[44] fit in with Hitler's idea that in contrast to the railway, which connects points, only roads can truly open up the land,[45] an idea that found expression in his plans to build motorways through the European "core country" all the way up to Trondheim in occupied Norway and the Crimea. After the war, the German people would need the opportunity to personally travel on these roads and visit the conquered territories in their Volkswagens so that they could be ready to defend them in an emergency.[46] But even with illusions such as these, Hitler did not remain consistent with his own thinking. In the spring of 1942, he indulged himself in the idea of having a split level railway of the future going from Upper Silesia to the Donez coal basin on a four meter-gauge track.[47] Each of these huge cars was to carry 600 people at a speed of 200 km per hour.[48] The Munich section of German Railways gave in reluctantly. The already gigantic plan for the new train station in Munich was once again expanded to accommodate the huge train.[49]

It is clear that Hitler's ideas were based on a European "*tabula rasa.*" His willingness to take these intellectual daydreams literally is shocking. This was "planning" according to a distorted picture of history. Things that fit his vision were reinterpreted, added on, and placed into the perspective of the future great Germanic Empire that never came into being. Even today, a film of the model buildings that were part of the plans can,[50] through subtle camera work that makes the models appear real, actually create nightmares. The lines of a poem by Erich Kästner become very relevant. "If we had won the war—lucky that we didn't."

Notes

1. Kubizek, 116ff; F. Heer, *Der Glaube des Adolf Hitlers. Anatomie einer politischen Religiosität* (Munich-Esslingen, 1968), 34f; Nolte, *Faschismus*, 358.
2. *Mein Kampf*, 18. Cf. Heer, 55f, 153f, 160; Speer, 89.
3. *Mein Kampf*, 19f.
4. Speer, 94 and elsewhere Fest, 728f.
5. *Libres Propos*, 46 –entry from September 27–28, 1941; compare also Hitler's opening speech for the architecture exhibition on December 10, 1938: Hamburger Forschungsstelle Geschichte NS, Slg. Hitler-Reden I.
6. W.C. Langer, *Das Adolf-Hitler-Psychogramm*, foreword by F. Hacker (Vienna-Munich-Zurich, 1973), 221f. –An analysis of his personality and behavior, written in 1943 for US psychological warfare. Cf. also Lehmann-Haupt, 47.
7. Cf. chapter four, this volume, 32f.
8. *Mein Kampf*, 288ff.
9. Ibid., p. 381. Arndt, 50 interprets this quote wrongly as being about Munich.
10. Compare 35ff, this book.
11. With regard to this: A. Fryksén, „*Hitlers Reden zur Kultur: kunstpolitische Taktik oder Ideologie?*" *Probleme deutscher Zeitgeschichte*, ed. G. Rystad and S. Tägil. Lund Studies in International History 2 (Stockholm, 1971), 235ff.
12. Schramm rightfully refers to this in the introduction to the *Tischgespräche*, 33.
13. In addition see Nolte, *Faschismus*, 500; Heer, 56.
14. Hewel Diary –entry from June 8, 1941.
15. *Libres propos*, 110 –November 2–3, 1941.
16. Cf. note 14.
17. Preiss, 141.
18. Jacobsen/Jochmann, *Hitler's speech in the Chancellery to the officer cadets who graduated in 1938 on January 25, 1939*; Picker, 174 –February 4, 1942.
19. *Libres propos*, 5 –July 11–12, 1941.
20. Cf. note 18.
21. A. Hitler, *Die Reden Hitlers am Reichsparteitag 1933* (Munich, 1934), 26f. –The Greeks were Dorians according to Hitler and therefore Germanic; in addition Speer, 110.
22. Hamburger Forschungsstelle Geschichte NS –Sammlung Hitler Reden II –September 6, 1938.

23. Strasser, 52.
24. A. Hitler, *Ausgewählte Reden des Führers 1938. Rede des GFM H. Göring auf dem Parteitag Großdeutschlands. Sonderausgabe für die Luftwaffe* (Berlin, 1938), 26.
25. Ibid., 28.
26. A. Hitler, *Die Reden Hitlers am Parteitag der Freiheit 1935* (Munich, 1935), 32.
27. Strasser, 52.
28. Hitler, *Reden Reichparteitag 1933*, 28.
29. Domarus, 705f –July 19, 1937, speech at the opening of „Haus der Deutschen Kunst" in Munich.
30. Hitler, *Reden Parteitag 1935*, 40.
31. Dehlinger, 33 –also cf. Speer, 110.
32. Hitler, *Ausgewählte Reden 1938*, 24.
33. Mein Kampf, 290.
34. Ibid., 291.
35. Ibid., 288.
36. Ibid., 291.
37. In addition see this book, 81; for criticism of capitalism see also *Parteitag 1935*, 39ff, and Domarus, 528f.
38. Frank, 312; Fest, *Gesicht des Dritten Reiches*, 278.
39. Domarus, 527 –September 11, 1935.
40. Hamburger Forschungsstelle Geschichte NS –Slg. Hitler-Reden II –September 6, 1938.
41. For the Paris visit 1940: Breker, 94ff; Speer, 186ff.
42. Wiedemann, 87f –Wiedemann Papers, 68f.
43. Wiedemann, 139.
44. Examples of this: Picker, 143 –September 8–10, 1941; 418 –June 27, 1942; 458 –July 18, 1942.
45. Koeppen Reports, 20 –September 19, 1941.
46. Ibid.
47. Picker, 299 –April 27, 1942.
48. Bonatz, 179f; Speer, *Spandauer Tagebücher*, 239f.
49. Bonatz, 180; Dehlinger, 107f.
50. *"Das Wort aus Stein."* –Cf. This book, 69 note 25.

Chapter 9

BUILDINGS AND THEIR FUNCTIONS

Hitler's ideas focused on buildings that were to last forever. All government buildings were to be built in granite so that they could be expected
to last from three to four thousand years.[1] In case Europe didn't suffer
the same fate as Atlantis, then "these buildings would most likely still
be standing … just the way they are, in 10,000 years."[2] Hitler said this at
the end of October 1941, a few weeks before the failure of his blitzkrieg
attack on the Soviet Union robbed him of his last chance to complete his
architectural projects that had been restarted in 1940 after having been
dropped at the beginning of WW II. The absolute brutality of his plans
can be seen in a note in the official minutes of a viewing of the model
for a newly designed Hamburg: "You should also not overlook that what
we are building is unique for two to three generations," Hitler explained,
considerably scaling back all other projections of time. "Later generations
can come who will be happy to be able to switch the location of a drain or
move a gas chandelier from one side to the other."[3] It was Hitler's stated
goal, with the help of architecture, to pre-program future developments
as far as one could think and prevent any change right from the very
beginning. This intention is not only evident in large buildings but also
in city planning. The church was to be replaced with the political party
building, as well as the great assembly hall, the square, and the big avenue
for parades. This architectural planning represented "a future already set
in stone."[4] Hitler explicitly stated it once when he gave his reasons why
Berlin and not Vienna should have two hundred meter high monuments:

"My actions are always based on a political way of thinking."[5] If Hitler was thinking in such time frames, namely buildings of granite that would last for thousands of years, then it is necessary to question the political function of these buildings. What was their role in an empire that would have to stand in particular relation to its representative architecture? The main reasons behind Hitler's architectural plans are the following:

1. The breakdown of the supposed German inferiority complex—the German people is the world's master race.
2. Buildings to strengthen the image and authority of the political movement, the NSDAP.
3. The planning of architectural projects as a substitute for aggression at times when political power was reduced—for the preparation and definition of his expansion goals.
4. Buildings to act as a Trojan horse: demonstrating a willingness for peace.
5. Buildings to act as a catalyst to achieve Hitler's ultimate goals more quickly.

In a heretofore unknown speech that was given on February 10, 1939, in front of army troop commanders in Berlin,[6] Hitler spoke of the German people as "the strongest people not only in Europe, but—and some of you may be surprised—practically in the world."[7] He made that statement in connection with a theme that, according to the knowledge of well-known sources at the time, cannot be found in any other comparable document. In answer to the criticism of his buildings, streets and bridges as possibly being too gigantic,[8] Hitler repeated his theory from the beginning of the speech that the German nation is the "strongest" people "in existence today."[9] With regard to his architectural plans, he then continued:

> In my view, this does not take place out of a craving for status, but rather based upon the coldest calculation that only with such monstrous constructions can a nation be given self-confidence. Among other methods as well, as this is not to be the only attempt to raise the self-confidence, but it is rather simply a means of slowly persuading the nation in many areas that it is not of a second class value, but that it is equal to all other nations in the world, even to America.[10] For this reason, for example, I am having this big bridge built in Hamburg. One may ask me: Why don't you build a tunnel? I don't think a tunnel would be very effective. But even if I thought, subjectively, that a tunnel were very effective, I would still put up the biggest bridge in the world to Hamburg[11] so that a German returning from abroad or going abroad, or a German who has the opportunity to compare Germany with other countries, will have the confidence to say "What's

the big deal with America and its bridges? We can do exactly the same thing. That's why I am having skyscrapers built there with the same dimensions of the big American ones. That's why I am having Berlin expanded into a colossal capital. That's why these gigantic parks are being created in Nuremberg, and in Munich. That's also why these enormous motorways are to run throughout Germany. Not just because of traffic needs, but also additionally out of the conviction that it is necessary to give the German people, that earlier had been broken down, the confidence it has a right to and requires as a nation of eighty million people and which it needs."[12]

Apart from the inferiority complex of the Germans, which Hitler had already identified in the twenties, this speech clearly shows the scope of Hitler's plans. Although he emphasizes that he only strives to be the equal of America—Great Britain is no longer mentioned—he makes no secret of his true ambitions: the German nation is stronger than America, and that's why the buildings must be bigger. That's why he didn't want a bridge for Hamburg to be patterned after those in America, but on the contrary to be the largest bridge in the world. Already in the planning stages, this proved itself to be a difficult task. As it became clear that, due to the ground structure, the self-supporting surfaces between the pillars could not be longer than those in the Golden Gate Bridge in San Francisco,[13] Hitler demanded that at least the area of the roadway surface of the Hamburg elevated bridge over the Elbe should be larger than that of its Californian model. A skyscraper which was planned for Hamburg and intended, it was reported, to be taller than its American counterparts,[14] had to be reduced in size during planning because of subsoil difficulties that did not exist, in New York. As a solution to make up for this loss, Hitler referred back to the East-West highway that was being built in Berlin, and told Speer to make it wider than the one in Buenos Aires, which was the widest roadway in the world at the time.[15] In addition to this, according to Hitler's wishes, the biggest stadium in the world for four hundred thousand spectators was to be built in Nuremberg,[16] the biggest airport,[17] and the biggest hall in Berlin,[18] the most gigantic sea resort,"[19] (whose ruins still can be seen) in Rügen—and the largest, and fastest ship in the world.[20] The largest and most powerful transmitter in the world was to be built in Herzberg in the area of Lower Lusatia south of Berlin.[21] The list of examples could go on and on.

Hitler's efforts to outdo the existing buildings in every realm everwhere in the world with a project in Germany is clear, and the suggestion of size as a replacement for power, (and later as an expansion of it) is consistently identifiable in his speeches. These inferences became very transparent in the autumn weeks of 1941, before the apparently imminent end of the campaign in Russia. At this time, Hitler told his listeners of his vision of the future Berlin, long before the actual date when the buildings were to be completed. "Berlin will one day be the capital of the world."[22] "When one enters the Imperial Chancellery, one should feel that one is visiting the lord of the world. One will approach the buildings across broad elegant avenues," stated Hitler, who had sat for many hours in the model rooms surveying the "Führer buildings" in the five "Führer cities," Berlin, Munich, Nuremberg, Hamburg, and Linz.[23] "With an arch of triumph, the military Pantheon, and the square of the people—things that will take your breath away, we will now be able to outdo our only rival in the world, Rome. It shall be built according to such dimensions that St. Peter's and the square in front of it will seem like toys by comparison."[24] The new Berlin would be seen as one of the wonders of the world, as he told one of his employees during those years.[25]

Hitler's 1937 cultural speech showed that he also saw a more immediate purpose for his buildings: to help the difficult beginnings of the new Reich, as it were. He saw them as a way of strengthening the authority of the National Socialist movement.[26] "Therefore these buildings should not be thought of as something for 1940, nor for the year 2,000, but they should stretch for thousands of years into the future like the cathedrals of our past."[27] The buildings will help "our people politically to unite and become strong. For society, they will become an element of pride and a feeling of belonging together for the German people. On a social level they will underline how ridiculous the other earthly differences are compared to these gigantic witnesses of our unity."[28] Hitler's efforts to "give a people a strong internal sense of security,"[29] through buildings was already obvious in the early years following the "seizure of power," when he prescribed large building projects as a remedy for bad times. This would serve to show that the temporary suffering was just a passing moment compared with the creative powers of the nation.[30] In the official proclamation for the implementation of the Enabling Act, he had already explained his views clearly enough, although in restricted and tactful language suited to the specific situation: "Blood and race will once again become the source of artistic intuition. It is the duty of the government, especially in times of limited political power, to ensure that the nation's internal value of life and will to live, finds an even more powerful cultural expression. This decision obliges us to have a grateful admiration of our glorious past." Hitler, interestingly enough, did not clarify what this meant. He continued, "In all areas of our historical and cultural lives we must build a bridge from this past to the future."[31]

Hitler's declarations that he sought peace could well be served by his thoughts on architecture. In this spirit, he presented the argument at one of his public meetings in 1936 that the erection of his monument (meaning his building plans) would be "better suited to peace than for war."[32] General Bodenschatz did not want to shut out such argumentation. At the beginning of 1939, as he explained to a foreigner: "Hitler needs peace in order to carry out the gigantic tasks that are to bear witness to the greatness of the National Socialist order for the coming generations." Most specifically. the domed hall in Berlin was "according to Hitler, worth more than three victorious wars."[33] Still, at the May Day rally in the Lustgarten in Berlin in 1939, Hitler assured his audience: "And so many of these buildings need ten or even twenty years to complete. I have therefore good reason to wish for peace."[34]

Aside from the fact that Germany was without a doubt the most powerful country in the world, Hitler hoped to gain additional centripetal forces from his buildings. "Foreign countries will see the most convincing proof of Germanic genius and strength in these buildings. They will bow down in awe before such works—and march with Germany!"[35] In Europe, there was only one city that could possibly be Europe's capital, namely Berlin. "The capital of Europe must become the most colossal city on earth. In this way the capital would also be the magnet it should be as the center of a New Europe."[36]

Notes

1. Koeppen Reports, 6 –September 6, 1941; Speer, *Spandauer Tagebücher*, 88.
2. *Libres propos*, 81, October 21–22, 1941.
3. Protokoll Senatssyndikus Eiffe –Krogmann Diary –entry from January 21, 1939.
4. Interview with Speer from October 11, 1973; Speer, *Spandauer Tagebücher*, 31.
5. *Libres propos*, 82 –October 21–22, 1941.
6. BA NS 11/28, 86ff. –Compare the reference to the speech: H. Groscurth, *Tagebücher eines Abwehroffiziers 1938-1940*, ed. H. Krausnick et al. (Stuttgart, 1970), 166f. With more documents about the military opposition to Hitler. See also chapter 13 this work with one further passage of the speech, 116ff.
7. BA NS 11/28, 88f.
8. Ibid., 96.
9. Ibid.
10. Compare the very similar passage in Hitler's speech from April 24, 1936, at Crössinsee: "I also am convinced that our German race is really the best in the world. ... I believe we must give our race the task of establishing a prominent new culture. The buildings for which we are laying the foundations and setting the corner stones, they must be unique." –IfZ Archives, Fa 88, Fasz. 52.
11. In addition compare Speer, 96; Schuschnigg, 45.
12. BA NS 11/28, 97f.
13. Wiedemann, 221; Domarus, 779. –A picture of the model in: *Bauten der Bewegung*, 1,76.

14. Wiedemann, 221.
15. Ibid.
16. Dehlinger, 72.
17. BA R 43 II/1181, 62, back of the page.
18. Speer, 175.
19. von Kotze and Krausnick, *"Es spricht der Führer,"* 214 –Hitler's speech to construction workers on May 20, 1937, Photo: *Bauten der Bewegung*, 1, 110.
20. Maser, *Briefe*, 139.
21. PRO FO 371 C 4942/5/18 –24 380.
22. *Libres propos*, 82 –October 17, 1941; Speer, *Spandauer Tagebücher*, 84, with a corresponding comment from Hitler from the late autumn of 1940.
23. This was the language of the Third Reich. –In addition, a letter from RFM von Krosigk to Lammers on January 29, 1941 –BA R 43 II/1012 a.
24. *Libres propos*, 81.
25. Dietrich, 242.
26. Domarus, 19; cf. Also, Speer, *Spandauer Tagebücher*, 201f.
27. Domarus, 719.
28. Ibid.
29. Hitler, *Reden Parteitag 1935*, 40f.
30. Ibid., 32.
31. A. Hitler, *Die Reden Hitlers als Kanzler. Das junge Deutschland will Arbeit und Frieden* (Munich, 1934), 18.
32. A. Hitler, *Des Führers Kampf um den Weltfrieden*, (Munich, 1936) 38 –Speech in Karlsruhe on March 12, 1936.
33. Stehlin, 161f.
34. Domarus, 1185.
35. Stehlin, 161f.
36. Weizsäcker-Papiere, 252 –May 1, 1941 (note from Hewel).

Chapter 10

HITLER AND HIS PLANS AFTER 1933

On the same night of his appointment as chancellor of the Reich, Hitler announced his decision to rebuild[1] the Chancellery, and began a whole series of activities that indicate plans already completed before 1933.[2] Here the question arises as to what role Hitler personally played in the huge building projects. Of course, a certain influence of Troost, Hitler's first architect in the twenties, can be assumed. Troost, however, who had made a name for himself as the interior designer of the Hapag-Llyod luxury liners,[3] was principally an interior designer and was noticed by Hitler as a furniture designer.[4] Also, Hitler's early sketches and his insistence on carrying out old plans support the notion of an independent vision of architecture that Hitler tried to realize in concrete projects as soon as he came to power. Hitler therefore must be regarded as the decisive factor in the development and planning of large buildings in the Third Reich. It was only in this area of architecture that he showed continual interest.[5] Perhaps here, as in no other area, his insistence and his amateur dabbling shows his role as the decisive force in promoting his vision.

Despite the haste and the pressure under which Hitler enacted his "program" from the middle of the thirties, planning sequences can still be determined:

1. Rebuilding and renovation of existing buildings: the Brown House, plans for rebuilding the Chancellery made before 1933.

2. Buildings that involved moderate planning: Königsplatz in Munich, Haus der Deutschen Kunst (House of German Art), the "Führer Building," the new Chancellery.
3. Large buildings of the future: primarily in Berlin, Munich, Nuremberg, Hamburg, and Linz (the Fuhrerstadt)—sketches and models, some of them made before 1933.[6]

In the same way, a well laid out plan can be determined that considers "buildings for eternity":

1. Careful choice of architects according to Hitler's taste.
2. Hitler's sketches that have been further outlined by architects and corrected by Hitler.
3. Tests of models and building materials.[7]
4. Building sections in order to see the full-scale effect.

Evidence of Hitler's exceptionally strong interest in architecture can be observed right up to 1945.[8] On journeys when he visited Munich and Nuremberg, his first visits were to the halls where the city models were kept. Also, his routes of travel between North and South Germany always touched on places which were of architectural interest to him.[9]

Hitler, whose influence on the formal and technical planning of the buildings was decisive, was definitely the initiator of the large building projects.[10] Things were only built with his permission and only after numerous inspections. Decisions were irrevocable and had the character of commands. The "real architect of the Third Reich"[11] preferred to be on the Obersalzberg when planning because in Berlin, he could never "really reflect on such plans properly." For this, he "needed to be in his mountains," as he explained in 1935 to local Berlin politicians. "Perhaps he would invite the gentlemen to a meeting in the mountains about this."[12]

Hitler's decisive role becomes extremely clear during the meeting mentioned above regarding Berlin, when a state official asked him to call together a committee that Hitler himself had instigated, "because the plans for the city of Berlin indeed depend on the grandiose ideas the Führer had offered for its rebuilding."[13] With vivid criticism of an architect who was working on the soon-to-be Olympic Games sites of 1936, Hitler claimed: "that he did not yet know of the right architect for the job. Professor Troost, actually would have been the right man, but he was dead, and whether the architect Speer was adequate remained to be seen."[14]

Officials from the cities that were listed for large building projects were constantly on call for Hitler. With one phone call from Speer, the models were loaded into trucks and transported overnight to Berlin. The following day, the city council was ordered to follow by plane in order to confer with Hitler. He was always well informed of the details, assessed the state of development, and made the decisions he deemed necessary.[15]

After 1933, Hitler's architectural interests were clearly known to all, especially within his inner circle. At a social function held by Goebbels, Hitler passed around photos of models that depicted new buildings in Munich as "an eternal monument of our time,"[16] which one of the guests recorded in his diary. On that evening, Hitler gave him the impression of being a man "who enjoyed being involved in such projects" and who couldn't wait until "he [was] at last in a position to turn words into deeds."[17] Hitler was in his element during that evening, quoting figures, making sketches, and praising Troost as the greatest architect Germany had known, who "would never be kitschy, but always generous."[18] The finance minister found him in a similar mood at a lecture on budget issues, standing over blueprints for Berlin that were spread out on the floor. Hitler grabbed the bull by the horns and discussed plans and financing issues. "He didn't know if he would live to be very old, but he did want to see the rebuilding of Berlin completed."[19]

After 1933, Hitler also announced his intentions at much more official events. After his careful comments about his plans on the occasion of the governmental declaration of the Enabling Act at the end of March, he was much more explicit a few weeks later at a speech in Munich: "The movement has taken on two thousand years of German history and culture. It will become the carrier of German history and future German culture. It will make sure that new, unforgettable documents are created that will continue to place our people among the great civilizations of world history. We do not work for the moment, but for the judgment of the millennia."[20]

Hitler's announcements on October 15, 1933, at the laying of the cornerstone for the "Haus der Deutschen Kunst" (The House of German Art) were more precise, he explained that he could not imagine "another rise of the German nation without a renaissance of the German culture and, primarily of the German art."[21] Berlin as capital of the Reich, Hamburg and Bremen as capitals of sea-going transport, Leipzig and Cologne as metropolitan centers of trade, Essen and Chemnitz as their industrial counterparts, and Munich as the capital of German art were all listed as projects, to which Nuremberg was also added, after Hitler made the decision to always hold future party conventions there.[22] On a bronze plate at the "House of German Art," Hitler's motto from the first party convention after the takeover of power was forever inscribed: "Art is a lofty mission that requires fanaticism."[23]

A decisive factor that supports the thesis that Hitler had fixed ideas and a series of specific plans on architecture when he became the chancellor, is confirmed by meetings with Berlin officials in the years between 1933 and 1935. Not only do they prove that Hitler, beginning with his first year in office, went about carrying out his plans from the years 1924–1926, but also provides additional evidence of Hitler as a cunning tactician, who knew how to cleverly stage himself without embarrassment. Shortly after the party convention in Nuremberg, a meeting took place on September 19, 1933, between Hitler and top officials of the Berlin city council and high officials of the Reichsbahn (German Railways).[24] Hitler had been called in as arbitrator in a dispute between the two parties to decide how three railway stations in Berlin would be connected. The parties had not been able to reach an agreement. He used the situation cleverly to focus on transport questions of the future and thus made a link to his personal aims. By strongly criticizing the last centuries of civic planning in Berlin, and by claiming that the last spacious sites had been built in 1650, he justified his demand to make up for lost time and "do now what had been neglected in the past." Berlin was to be able to "compete with all the capitals of the world" and "take on any form of competition with other cities, for example, London, Paris, and Vienna."[25] In a letter of thanks to the head of the Cancellery, Hans Lammers, on the same day, the Berlin city council welcomed the fact that Hitler had "laid out major plans for the rebuilding of Berlin that are suitable to lead to an undreamt-of development and that will help make the capital be and look like the noblest metropolis."[26]

Hitler had achieved what he wanted. At the very least, from this day on Hitler had become the deciding authority as far as Berlin officials were concerned. They now made every effort to have their ideas carried out as though they were decisions coming from the Führer. At the same time, Hitler had been successful in presenting his own wishes to the right people in an uncomplicated and easygoing manner. There was no longer such a rush for future meetings, although the Chancellery was flooded with requests for such meetings.[27]

At another meeting in the Chancellery on March 29, 1934,[28] Hitler was therefore able to present old plans from the "time of his struggle"— nothing in his plans had changed since that time. While discussing the location and dimensions of the North-South and the East-West broadway, he already demanded the huge triumphal arch[29] and an assembly hall large enough to hold 250,000 people,[30] which were plans that Speer was to carry out later on. It was already part of his set plans to build larger governmental buildings, new buildings for the three branches of the armed forces, monumental party convention buildings, museums, and building complexes for science.[31] Hitler was both critical and in agreement with the slightest changes in Berlin, as noted in the minutes of a meeting that was very similar to another one held on July 5, 1934.[32] At that time, he once again demanded the construction of a triumphal arch at the crossing point of the broadways "for the unconquered army, in order to remove, once and for all, the pernicious thought from a courageous folk that Germany supposedly lost the First World War on all fronts and in all other aspects."[33]

On that occasion, he also announced setting aside twenty million Reichsmark (RM) per year in the government budget, 1.2 billion RM in all, "for the rebuilding of Berlin, in order to make it a worthy capital and a significant world city."[34] Even though a committee was to reach a preliminary decision as to how the money should be spent, Hitler said that he himself "would retain final power of decision on all major issues.[35]

On October 29, 1934, Hitler landed at Tempelhof airport in Berlin, returning from a trip, in order to meet with the administration there about work to enlarge the airport before continuing on to the Chancellery.[36] As always, he showed strong interest in the plans for the extension of the airport, and connected them to his own plans. "In planning the North-South axis, he imagined himself in the year 2,000 and offered his sketch for the airport, the dimensions he planned were nothing special. If a Prussian king had had the courage to build the street known as "Unter den Linden" sixty five meters wide, back when Berlin was a city of forty thousand, that would have called for much more courage than it did now for Hitler to build a North-South axis one hundred thirty five meters wide and tripling the size of Tempelhof airport for a Berlin of four and one half million people. The airport at Tempelhof will have to be the biggest and most beautiful of all civilian airports in the world."[37]

Hitler's plans for Nuremberg probably go back as far as 1927–1929, when the Nazi Party had its first party convention there.[38] Even before 1933, Troost had drafted plans for the Nuremberg party convention complex[39] according to Hitler's instructions. Speer continued with this work after Troost's death, when his task became the complete planning and implementation of the creation of "a stylistically developmental document of tremendous proportions," as Hitler outlined in his cultural speech of September 9, 1936.[40] The completion of the buildings was planned for 1942.[41] The drafting and construction of a hall that would hold 60,000 people, was not to be directed by Speer; the plans dated back to 1928 drafts.[42] Professor Ludwig Ruff, whom Hitler had met through Gauleiter Julius Streicher,[43] was to build a hall inspired by the Colosseum in Rome, but it was to be 1.3 times longer and 1.7 times wider.[44] In 1938, after his visit to Italy and intense study of the Colosseum, Hitler had the draft corrected.[45] The hall was still under construction in 1942–1943 and it was the one building of all the large building projects of the Third Reich that came nearest to completion.[46] It was Hitler's intention to maintain the record set by this building for the next eight hundred years.[47] It was designed "to gather the cream of the crop of the National Socialist Reich between its walls each year for centuries to come," as he expressed it while laying the corner stone on September 11, 1935.[48]

The party convention complex, which in 1936 already gave one observer the impression of a "Greco-Roman, if not indeed Babylonian-Assyrian building style,"[49] measured ten thousand meters by six thousand meters[50] in the final plans and was to have a one hundred meter wide road that functioned as the connecting element. The gigantic assembly halls, the Luitpold grove, the Zeppelin field, and the March Field were not only there to serve functionally, offering masses of people enough space, but they also had an emotional function. The party buildings were designed to force people who gathered there to integrate and at the same time to give them the feeling that as an individual they were members of the group by their own free will. Effects like the Speer light dome increased this feeling even more. [51]

At the same time, Nuremberg had a deep significance for foreign policy. It was an "army show" meant to demonstrate the togetherness of the nation and to act as a deterrent.[52] The important point, both in Nuremberg and other places,[53] was Hitler's pseudo-religious role: despite the enormous dimensions, the architecture always emphasized the spot where Hitler would be. The attempt to create the aura of the "Übermensch," the superior human, for himself by using architecture and technical advances is apparent in one specific detail: a hidden drainpipe was to be connected to a canopy above the speech podium in order to prevent rain from gathering on the canvas.[54]

Of all the plans that were drawn up for the party convention complex, the design for the stadium was the most gigantic. Hitler confided to a friend in 1938 that he wanted to build it so big "that even the pyramids would take a step back compared with the masses of concrete and gigantic stone. I am building for eternity because … we are the final Germany."[55] The stadium fulfilled at least the physical criteria.[56] Planned to accommodate four hundred and five thousand spectators, the stadium was to make the Olympic games redundant. After the 1936 Olympics, Hitler announced: "Berlin was the last international Olympics in which Germany took part. In the future we will hold the most magnificent sport events in the world and the greatest sports competitions that ever took place under our own direction, for ourselves, in Nuremberg."[57] At the end of November 1936, an order was signed regarding the future "National Socialist Games," which, according to Hitler's wishes, were to be organized under the patronage of the SA and which were to be a sort of continuation or replacement of the international Olympics.[58] In the spring of 1937, Speer informed Hitler of the non-Olympian dimensions of the playing field, and even he was instructed: "Completely unimportant. In 1940 the Olympic Games will once again take place in Tokyo. But after that the Olympics will always take place in Germany, here, in this stadium. And it will be our decision as to what measurements the playing field shall be."[59]

The "German Stadium" for which Hitler laid the corner stone on September 9, 1937, with the words that this shall be an "eternal witness" to a nation united in National Socialism and to a powerful empire,[60] surpassed all known dimensions.[61] The front façade, according to the draft, consisted of two towers that were each one hundred thirty meters high,[62] the length, measured 605 meters without the front court,[63] and 264 elevators with a capacity of 32,000 persons were to handle the logistics smoothly.[64] If one were to make a comparison with the Olympic stadium in Berlin, then Nuremberg was planned to be twice as wide and five times as high.[65] Since the highest tiers were set to be at a height of ninety-two meters, they presented a virtually unmanageable distance to the field, and therefore, supplying special binoculars for the spectators was taken into consideration.[66] In order to study the effect, Hitler had a complete section of the stadium built to full scale in the Franconian Jura near Nuremberg.[67] When the war started, the excavation work for the stadium had almost been finished. Construction was halted in September, 1939.[68]

As in the case of Munich, there are indications that Hitler had very specific ideas for the renovation of the city as early as 1924,[69] and at the very latest by 1927.[70] Plans drawn up by Troost[71] had already been finished in the "capital of German art"[72] from 1933 on, as Hitler said about Munich on October 15, 1933, while laying the corner stone for the House of German Art.[73] After the city was named as one of the main sites of rebuilding, and on the occasion of Speer being named general building inspector for Berlin,[74] Hitler announced the completion of his plans at a speech in Munich at the beginning of April, 1939.[75] The details were only given to the press weeks later.[76] Hitler's architect for Munich was Professor Hermann Giesler,[77] who took his position shortly before the end of 1938. His importance during the Third Reich has been overlooked up to this point. A few days before the rebuilding directive was issued for Munich,[78] following the one issued for Berlin, Giesler was named "general municipal architect for the capital of the movement."[79] This occurred after he, was temporarily to be placed on the same level as Speer,[80] as general building inspector. Hitler thus put an end to the undesirable situation in Munich, where plans had not been progressed as much as was wanted under Gerhard Wagner and the chief municipal architect in Munich, Professor Alker.[81] There are many indications that Hitler had created a sort of double occupation and competition for Speer, which was typical in many areas of National Socialism.[82] As far as the number of projects given to him was concerned, Giesler was just a good as Speer. He was responsible not only for Munich, but also for the rebuilding of Augsburg, Weimar,[83] the so-called "Supreme School of the National Socialist Party" on the banks of Chiemsee, and later also for Linz.[84] Towards the end of the war, Hitler was only interested in plans for Linz, where he wanted to be buried one day. In the bunker of the Chancellery, he was still looking over drafts for that project.[85] Long after there was no more activity on the building sites, Giesler was still travelling through Italy to negotiate purchases of stone and marble.[86] In the course of his activities, he gave the impression of being a radical and blindly devoted follower of the Führer[87] in his attempts to hurry up plans for Munich, "a city whose generous dimensions make it worthy of the task of becoming the center of European culture."[88] In detail, the following monumental constructions were planned for Munich:[89] first, a road 6.6 km long and 120 m wide, which was to be an East-West axis.[90] Along this road, Hitler and Giesler planned to build an opera house, a theater for light opera, an enormous swimming pool, a hall of ballrooms and hotel suites, two skyscrapers, the Eher publishing house that printed Hitler's *Mein Kampf*, a KdF hotel, and other hotels, as well as a monument to the party.[91] At the center of the axis, Giesler planned, on Hitler's orders, a huge railway station which was to have the biggest steel skeleton dome in the world,[92] so big that it would outdo the "Grosse Halle" in Berlin. Extensive suburbs to the north and south would become necessary because the axis[93] would have huge gateways at the city limits, behind which would be the SS barracks as a kind of fortification.[94]

From the plans for Munich, which was also to become the European fashion capital after Paris had been made redundant,[95] several ideas must also be presented in detail to make the scope of the project clearer. The new Munich opera house, which Hitler had drafted by hand shortly after the end of the French campaign,[96] required an area three times as big as the Royal Court Opera House in Vienna and the Grand Opera in Paris.[97] The main railway station, which was continually revised and enlarged by Hitler,[98] was in its final draft version 378m wide, with a dome of 270m in diameter and a height of 136m.[99] According to Hitler's wishes, there was to be a four-meter-wide track laid from the train station to Rostov-on-Don in Russia.[100] The dimensions of these blueprints were larger than can be imagined, and they become clear only when compared to St. Peter's and its square in Rome: the Munich railway station would have been six times its size.[101]

Relevant to the question of Hitler's ultimate goals are his plans for the "victory monument to the party"[102] in Munich, which, next to the station, was one of the few projects that was planned and calculated in detail. In Hitler's view, construction was to begin at the end of 1946, and completion was planned for January 1950,[103] a date when the other plans in Munich and Berlin were also to be completed.[104] The column of the monument, with a height of 214.5 meters, would have stood 2.2 times higher than the Frauenkirche. The column had a diameter of 25.5 meters in places and was to be crowned by an eagle whose wing span would have been 33 meters wide. On the base, a gigantic frieze 11 meters high (the frieze of the Parthenon is 92 centimeters high) would show scenes from the "period of the party's struggle."[105] It was Hitler himself who drew the blueprint for the column and made it to scale using an angle and a slide rule,[106] which attests to his intense interest. The question of what the years 1946–1950 meant to Hitler with respect to his political plans and why victory parades and a world exhibition[107] were planned for 1950 will be have to be dealt with elsewhere.[108]

Hitler's plans to turn Berlin into the central point of his political movement, one that had "the magical charm of Mecca or Rome,"[109] is already stated in *Mein Kampf*. The drafts for a triumphal arch and a huge domed hall[110] that Hitler presented to Berlin officials[111] shortly after he came to power, as well as observations from people close to him in the "years of struggle,"[112] lead to the conclusion that Hitler had been in a sort of initial planning phase since 1924–1926. Immediately after he took office as chancellor, the initial planning phase intensified, and plans thus became decisions.

The plans for Berlin only began in a big way in 1936, when Hitler assigned Speer to supervise and begin the planning of the individual projects.[113] As was to happen in Munich a few years later, Hitler was obviously no longer satisfied with the Berlin city council's way of carrying out his plans.[114] In January 1937, Speer was officially entrusted with the task and named "General building inspector for the rebuilding of the capital."[115] In that very same year, construction began on some of the first projects in Berlin. At the laying of the first corner-stone for the technical military faculty on November 27, 1937,[116] Hitler explained: "These construction projects should not be measured according to the needs of 1937, 1938, 1939, or even 1940. For this purpose, over the next twenty years we will ignore the criticism of the present work to be performed in Berlin, and leave it to the judgment of all the generations that come after us." He made a similar statement at the opening of the first "German architecture and craft industry Exhibition," a show which "to this extent, humanity has not yet seen."[117] Hitler justified his policies of secrecy by appealing to the idea that" it is a deep rooted principle of National Socialism," not to parade before the public with difficult problems and have them discussed, but to have plans mature completely and then present them to the people. There are certain things that cannot be discussed, for example all the eternal values."[118]

The technical military faculty alongside Heerstraße came near completion, and is lying today under the debris of the destroyed Berlin, which was brought there to form a hill. In 1938, a wave of preparatory activities started for Berlin, a city which was planned to accommodate ten million people:[119] the purchase of property,[120] demolitions,[121] the construction of living quarters for builders,[122] and commissions for individual buildings given to a number of prestigious architects besides Speer.[123] Even before the outbreak of the war, a critical observer had the impression that the city was "the capital of a global empire. There wasn't a lot left reminiscent of Prussia."[124] The new Reich Chancellery, finished within several months at the beginning of 1939, was regarded by Hitler as a temporary building that he planned to leave in 1950.[125]

The core of the new plans for Berlin was a North-South axis which was to be over six kilometers in length, two and a half times the size of the Champs-Elysées in Paris.[126] Along this axis, about forty separate projects were planned: government buildings,[127] and military administrative complexes.[128] The Supreme Command of the Air Force building, in later to become the German Ministry of Finance, had already become too small for Göring.[129] Plans included buildings for national organizations and for the party and all its various subsections.[130] The size of the separate blocks were planned to be between 150m and 500m long.[131] Two huge railway stations were to form the boundaries at both the North and South ends of the axis. The main station in the South would have been larger than Grand Central Station in New York. The forecourt of the station was to be one thousand meters by three hundred thirty meters and was planned to be surrounded by captured foreign weapons, the spoils of war.[132] A complete re-organization of all kinds of transportation, as had also been planned for Munich, would be covered in order "to have peace for the next five hundred to one thousand years."[133] There were also museums,[134] a film city in Babelsberg,[135] a university city in Charlottenburg,[136] and the planned construction of six hundred and fifty thousand apartments,[137] all by 1950. Smaller representative buildings for prominent figures, a house for Hitler (to be built on a plot in Schwanenwerder peninsula which had already been bought),[138] a residence for Goebbels,[139] and the redesigning of Grunewald park[140] in Berlin were the other projects that completed the plans. However, these plans were surpassed by three particular projects.

Hitler had plans to build a triumphal arch, which was doubtlessly modeled on its Paris counterpart,[141] and he meant this to be a sort of "anti-Versailles demonstration."[142] It was to tower above the Paris arch by more than twice the height.[143] The arch itself was planned to be one hundred seventy meters wide, one hundred nineteen meters deep, and one hundred seventeen meters high.[144] Behind the eighty-meter high opening, according to the plans, there was to be another huge building visible at a distance of five kilometers, the biggest assembly hall in the world, which would accommodate one hundred eighty thousand people.[145] Hitler was planning to use this hall to practice a form of direct "democracy." At the second German architecture and craft industry exhibition in 1938,[146] he criticized the lack of capacity of the churches in democratic regimes. The Protestant cathedral in Berlin had only 2.450 seats for 3.5 million worshipers. "But people will understand that we, who are indeed truly a people's movement, have to build with the people in mind, and that our halls have to be built to hold one hundred fifty or two hundred thousand people. This means that we will build as big as today's technical advances allow and that we will build for eternity!"[147] The Berlin Hall was to have a diameter of 250m, the bottom of the dome would have been 220m above the ground and would have created a space below that was seventeen times the size of the interior of St. Peter's in Rome.[148] Hitler's place was to be under a huge golden royal eagle, and it was from here that he would send his messages throughout his new gigantic empire.[149]

In the early summer of 1939, Hitler demanded that Speer correct the German eagle which was to crown the building at 290m above ground: "This will be changed. The eagle will no longer stand above the swastika, it should reign over the globe. The crowning feature of this largest of buildings must be the eagle on top of the globe."[150] In a Führer palace which was to be built next to the hall, Hitler planned to live in a residence of two million square meters.[151] The diplomats' path to the "Lord of the World"[152] was to be half a kilometer long. But the buildings on the North-South axis were also planned to "take the breath away"[153] for visitors coming to Berlin after leaving the South station. "Berlin as capital of the world" would only have been comparable to ancient Egypt, Babylon, or Rome.[154]

The "claim to world supremacy" was made by Hitler "long before he even dared to mention it within his closest circle,"[155] wrote Speer in his memoirs. The globe on top of the dome was "not just a symbol"[156] of Hitler's ambitions, but much more, continued the chief architect for Berlin: "(I) took part in a war which we, in our innermost circle, were never allowed to doubt that it was being waged in order to gain world supremacy."[157]

Notes

1. Fest, 510.
2. Compare with chapter 4, 34ff.
3. Brenner, 121.
4. Speer, 55.
5. Ibid., 93. –See also: BA R 43 II/1016, 76. –A letter from Speer to Lammers from August 30, 1940.
6. Compare also Langer, 221f.
7. Dehlinger reports that for the Nuremberg stadium alone ninety-three wagon loads of samples of hard stone were transported before the contract was actually given. –Dehlinger, 152.
8. Speer, 147f. –A vivid picture: H. Hofmann, ed., *Hitler abseits vom Alltag. 100 Bilddokumente aus der Umgebung des Führers* (Berlin, 1937).
9. E.g, Weimar. Cf. Dietrich, 163.
10. Dehlinger, 13f; Hagemann, 68; Wiedemann, 204; Arndt, 60.
11. Wiedemann, Private Papers, 68.
12. BA R 43 II/1181, 89, –written record of a meeting from June 28, 1935.
13. Ibid., 88.
14. Ibid.; compare also Speer, *Spandauer Tagebücher*, 404, 634. Speer reflects the possibility of only having been an aid to fulfillment. The architect who was criticized was probably Werner March, who had built the Reichssportfeld in Berlin. (1934–36).
15. The Krogmann Diary gives a clear picture of Hamburg at this time. Entry from March 14, 1937, –Hamburger Forschungsstelle FS Geschichte NS; compare also Speer, 93; Lehmann-Haupt, 56ff, with a report of a visit of several hours Hitler made to the building models on March 15, 1941.
16. Schaumburg-Lippe, 29, –entry from November 28, 1933.
17. Ibid., 30.
18. Ibid.
19. Schwerin von Krosigk, 200f.
20. Domarus, 257, –Führer congress of the NSDAP on April 22, 1933, –VB, April 24, 1933. Further information about Hitler's activities in 1933: Domarus, 448, –Hitler's speech from September 5, 1934.
21. Hamburger Forschungsstelle Geschichte NS –Slg. Hitler-Reden II.
23. Ibid., 29.
24. BA R 43 II/1181, 74ff, –minutes of the meeting with the following participants: OB Dr. Sahm, State Commissioner Dr. Lippert, Engel, Dr. Maretzky, Head Architect Zangemeister. –From German Railways: General Director Dorpmüller, General Director Kleinmann, Privy Councillor Kreft.
25. Ibid., 75.
26. BA R 43 II/1028, 33f, –letter Maretzky/Lippert.
27. Cf. BA R 43 II/1181.
28. BA R 43 II/1181 a, 2ff.
29. Ibid., 2.
30. Ibid., 3.
31. Ibid., 2f.
32. Ibid., 4ff. –Participants: Hitler, Funk, Lippert, Sahm, Dorpmüller, Head Civil Architect Kühn, Director Röbe (German Railways).
33. Ibid., 7.

34. Ibid., 9.
35. Ibid.
36. BA R 43 II/1181, 62ff. –Participants: Oberführer Schaub, Oberführer Baur, Major a. D. Carganico, District Leader Schlenstedt, Major a. D. Böttger.
37. Ibid., 62, back of the page.
38. Dietrich,173.
39. Brenner, 121. –Speer denies this, cf. Janssen, 35.
40. Domarus, 639. Cf. Speer, 80ff.
41. A. Hitler, *Reden des Führers am Parteitag der Ehre 1936* (Munich, 1936), 9. –September 8, 1936.
42. Dehlinger, 64. It is not clear here whether Hitler had already initiated the building.
43. Ibid.
44. Ibid., 65.
45. Wiedemann, 87f.
46. Dehlinger, 60. –In total 208 million Reichsmark were used for the building of the convention hall. –Ibid., 68.
47. Wiedemann, 87; Wiedemann, Private Papers, 69; Speer, *Spandauer Tagebücher*, 403.
48. Domarus, 527.
49. Abetz, 81.
50. Dehlinger, 62.
51. Compare Hellack, 86f.
52. Ibid.
53. For example, Hitler's place within the domed hall in Berlin. Another example is the tower of the NSDAP supreme school, which was planned to be built on the banks of Chiemsee, and from which Hitler was to speak to the world from a powerful transmitter. An observatory was to provide the connection to space. –Dehlinger, 39 and the January edition 1939 of "*Die Kunst im Dritten Reich*," 2ff. (Essay by H. Giesler).
54. Dehlinger, 56f.
55. Frank, 320.
56. Compare the figures given by Speer, 81. –Photos in: *Bauten der Bewegung*, 1: 48ff.
57. Dietrich, 175f.
58. Domarus, 657, –November 27, 1936; *VB*, December 1, 1936. Compare also Görlitz and Quint, 475.
59. Speer, 84.
60. A. Hitler, *Reden des Führers am Parteitag der Arbeit 1937* (Munich, 1938), 52.
61. The cost of building would have amounted to 500 million Reichsmark. –Dehlinger, 170.
62. Ibid., 71.
63. Ibid., 73.
64. Ibid.
65. Ibid., 68f.
66. Ibid., 70; Görlitz and Quint, 476.
67. Dehlinger, 70, picture by Speer in photo section after 112.
68. Görlitz and Quint, 75; Jansen, 37.
69. *Mein Kampf*, 289f. Hitler criticizes the modern building policies of Munich.
70. Strasser, 72; Dehlinger, 75. See also chapter four, this volume. 32f.
71. Compare fourth chapter, 35; Arndt, 39ff.
72. Compare Arndt, 44ff.
73. Hamburger Forschungsstelle Geschichte NS, Slg. Hitler Reden II.

74. Domarus, 674.
75. BA R 43 II/1179 a, 8ff.
76. Ibid. –Compare also Dehlinger, 82.
77. Giesler, born in 1898, died in 1990. The brother of Munich's Gauleiter, was unfortunately not willing to give personal information or information about his work. Speer treats him as marginal, in the same way as he treats all the Munich plans. Speer's incorrect and changing ways of spelling his name is symptomatic of this. Compare 158, 185f, 209, 310. The relationship between the two was strained, although Speer showed a very cooperative spirit in 1938. In addition: Janssen, 349 note 32; Speer, 209.
78. BA R 43 II/1020 a, 65 –RGBl. I, 1891.
79. BA R 43 II/1180, 76.
80. Ibid., 73. The reasons for this decision could not be determined. Apparently it happened under pressure from Hitler.
81. BA R 43 II/1180, 76.
82. In addition: Jabobsen, *Außenpolitik;* Broszat, *Staat Hitlers*. Speer also indicated this possibility –*Spandauer Tagebücher,* 217.
83. Weimar represented the furthest developed city with regard to rebuilding projects of the Third Reich. –Dehlinger, 39. Photos in *Bauten der Bewegung,* 4: 70.
84. Regarding Giesler's argument with the head planner for Linz, Professor Roderich Fick, compare BA R 43 II/1019, 1019a.
85. Fest, 44; Speer, 310.
86. PA AA Handakte Hewel, –Hewel's letter to ambassador von Mackensen from October 21, 1942.
87. Details from Dehlinger, 90f, 93. –Giesler as an architect was self-taught, just like Hitler. – Cf. Speer, 158; Dehlinger, 10.
88. This was Giesler's impression from speeches given by Hitler. –BA R II/1020, 33, –Giesler's letter to Lammers from April 23, 1941.
89. An estimate of the costs came to six billion Reichsmark. –Dehlinger, 88. –See also Görlitz and Quint, 561.
90. Dehlinger, 94.
91. Ibid., 83.
92. Ibid., 94.
93. Ibid., 89, 177.
94. Ibid., 120f.
95. Speer, 158; Hagemann, 69.
96. Dehlinger, 102f. –Hand-drawn sketch from July 9, 1940. –The Milan Scala, compared to the Opera House in Munich, would have had one-ninth of the area.
97. Ibid.
98. This stands as an example against Maser, *Briefe,* 133f, that claims that Speer extended Hitler's plans.
99. Dehlinger, 106; Bonatz, 180.
100. Dehlinger, 107, 161; Bonatz, 179.
101. Dehlinger, 104.
102. With regard to the details compare Dehlinger, 100ff.
103. Ibid., 100.
104. BA R 43 II/1185, 38.
105. Dehlinger, 95, 101 –Photo by H.Picker and H. Hoffmann, *Hitlers Tischgespräche im Bild,* ed., J. von Lang (Oldenburg-Hamburg, 1969), 169.

106. Dehlinger, 101; Speer, 158, –also a picture after 160. It is unfortunately not possible to date it exactly.
107. Speer, 156, 189.
108. Ibid., cf. chapter 22, 200 and elsewhere.
109. *Mein Kampf*, 81. –Cf. also Speer, 87.
110. Speer, 88, 94, 170; Hoffmann, 161.
111. Compare also 87ff. Speer assumes that the talks began from 1936 on, ibid., 167 and is corrected with this.
112. See chapter four, this volume 32ff.
113. Speer, 87.
114. Ibid.
115. Ibid., 90; Dehlinger, 76f; Domarus, 674, –January 30, 1937. –GBl. I, 103.
116. Domarus, 765; Keesings Archiv der Gegenwart, 3315.
117. Domarus, 778, –January 22, 1938. –Compare also Austellungskatalog.
118. Domarus, 779. –With regard to Hitler's policy of secrecy with his building projects, see also Speer, 154.
119. Janssen, 36; Brenner, 126; Keesings Archiv, 3395, –January 25, 1938, and 3599, –June 14, 1938.
120. BA R 43 II/1013 a, 12 f; R 43 II/1182 a.
121. BA R 43 II/1183, 1f.
122. Ibid.
123. Birkenholz, Bonatz, Gall, Giesler, Härter, Klotz, Kreis, J. Krüger, W. Krüger, L. Ruff, F. Ruff, Sagebiel, G. Troost.
124. Faber du Faur, 206.
125. Speer, 152; Domarus, 1035; A. Hitler in the monthly magazine „*Die Kunst im Dritten Reich*" (July, 1939).
126. Speer, 90, 153.
127. Ibid., 150ff with regard to the separate projects.
128. Speer, 159; Bonatz, 178f.
129. Speer, 150f.
130. Ibid. 156.
131. Ibid., 149, 152.
132. Ibid., 149.
133. Domarus, 865, –speech from May 22, 1938.
134. BA R 43 II/1184, 40.
135. BA R 43 II/1182b, 63.
136. BA R 43 II/1183 b, 116; 1176 a, 180.
137. BA R 43 II/1185a, 130.
138. BA R 43 II/1184, 2ff.
139. BA R 43 II/1184, 63.
140. BA R 43 II/1184a, 140.
141. Breker, 103.
142. In addition see this volume, 87.
143. Speer, 149f.
144. Ibid., 150.
145. Ibid., 167.
146. Domarus, 983. –December 10, 1938.
147. Ibid.
148. Speer, 167f.

149. Ibid., 168.
150. Ibid., 175.
151. Ibid., 171.
152. Ibid., Libres propos, 81, –October 21–22, 1941.
153. Libres propos.
154. Ibid., 82, 350, –March 11–12, 1942.
155. Speer, 83.
156. Ibid., 525.
157. Ibid., epilogue.

Chapter 11

ARCHITECTURE AND THE THIRD REICH

The issue of Hitler's relationship to architecture, even with the knowledge that he was the main individual responsible for planning large buildings, cannot be closed without considering several consequences of that relationship for the structure of the Third Reich. Many new questions have come to light because the problems of architecture include a problem similar to that of the confessions, namely that the new plans for cities no longer provided for the construction of new churches. This chapter may also show that a scientific positivist approach, limited to the determination of capacity and actual size, is unable to adequately grasp the National Socialist system. The utopia, the attempt to achieve the impossible, is not just a constant to be observed, within the study of Hitler, but rather distinguishes the Nazi system in its totality.

If the construction projects are quantified and the end of 1941 is taken as the time frame, there is a list of fifty German cities which were to be extensively rebuilt, that included practically all the large German cities.[1] In addition to that, there were the enormous projects in the five "Führer cities," and the extension of German harbors, with Trondheim in occupied Norway to be the largest German naval port of the future.[2] Plans for war memorials and mausoleums at the borders of the new "Germanic Empire"[3] must also be included, as well as the unknown needs inside the conquered territories of the Soviet Union. Even with all of this, however, only the tip of the iceberg has been recorded, because all the way down to the level of the Gauleiter and mayors, the Nazis were under the influence of a frenetic construction mania during the first years of the war.[4] The Gauleiter were dreaming of an embassy in Berlin,[5] and the regional capitals wanted a public square that followed the example of Berlin, with huge halls and parade grounds.[6] But the private residential sector must also be mentioned here, as must the streets and motorways in the hoped-for empire, as well as Thingstätten,[7] the common use buildings for military and paramilitary purposes in a new society where the term "civilian" was no longer used. A huge KdF fleet[8] was to give the new Germanic global citizen a permanent Nuremberg experience at sea, and the global resort Prora on Rügen island, as well as other spas,[9] were meant to do the same on land. At the same time, a strong automobile industry would allow for tourist trips to the Crimea.[10] But life in the country was waiting for thorough changes and for a new meaning for the term "Lebensraum." Long before the completion of the large building projects, which was to take place by 1950, by the middle of the 1940's the re-armament of the three branches of the military was to be complete, because in addition to the operation in the East, preparations were also taking place for tasks in the future colonies.[11]

The reality of the situation was quite different, with a shortage of skilled workers and a general shortage of manpower before the war started,[12] as well as bottlenecks for building materials and a considerable array of problems involving payment. The shipyards weren't the only place where there was disquiet among the workers before the outbreak of war in 1939.[13] In Nuremberg, there was a revolt on the building site of the party political complex due to the high speed required of the workers, who didn't even stop on Sundays.[14] There were still the working-class residences planned for thirty thousand workers[15] in Munich, but even to keep to the deadline for the impressive boulevard and the railway station alone, thirty six thousand workers would have been needed.[16]

Just as serious was the shortage of materials. Even the largest European deposits of travertine, marble, and filling material were not enough for the main building sites in the Third Reich.[17] Just for the buildings planned in Nuremberg and Munich alone, four times the annual production of granite from Denmark, France, Italy, and Sweden would have been needed.[18] Even in 1941, a transport of hard stone, paid for in hard currency, still arrived from Scandinavia on a fleet that had been built especially for it.[19] Hitler ignored frequent warnings from the authorities responsible for such transactions and forbade a calculation of the total costs.[20] His mentality as a conqueror and plunderer provided him with a simple rationale for his behavior: the national deficit, according to his plan, would be balanced by gains in territory and the use of foreign labor.[21]

In this light the observation that in 1937–1938, the time when the avalanche of city renovation directives began, the SS founded the German Earth and Stone Plants (DEST),especially to satisfy the needs of Hitler's architectural plans.[22] The security personnel at the concentration camps, the Death's Head Units, were practically doubled within the year.[23] The top priority up to that point, which was fighting political opponents, suddenly took a back seat. Concentration camps were now being built for economic reasons, reasons that had the potential to break open the whole system.[24] New camps were set up near natural deposits of quality stone,[25] abandoned quarries that were put back into operation, and large brick factories.[26] This idea of building concentration camps for economic purposes may or may not have originated with Hitler, but whatever the case may have been, he was in full agreement with the policy.[27] It was planned that after the end of 1941, the prisoners—armies of slaves—that would have been deported from the Soviet Union would be used heavily in constructing the large buildings.[28] For the conquered territories in the East, Hitler planned to use three to five million prisoners as workers over a period of twenty years.[29] The concept that the involvement in architecture also signaled an enormous increase in power for the SS, does not seem exaggerated. With a working force at almost zero cost, as the biggest producer of building material, the SS would have controlled one the biggest "growth branches" of industry, a possibility with unimaginable consequences, and not just for the economy.[30] Slavery and death would have been the consequence for the European Jews and the East European nations.

Many of the architects and engineers who worked on these projects must ask themselves about the role they played in this endeavor. Already on a scale model or a draft on paper, the Nazi penchant for gigantic things is absolutely clear.[31] In city planning offices, many of them worked until the end of the war in an unreal world: the fronts of the war came nearer, but the planning went on right until the end.[32] The question does not involve Speer alone, but all leading German architects. It seems that the only thing, done in huge workplaces with hundreds of employees was to draw up plans.[33] We know little or nothing about the financing aspect, the forced donations for building projects,[34] the plundering of Jewish assets,[35] or whether anyone simply posed the question of why and for what purpose all this was being done.

Speer probably answered the question for each one of them when, shortly after his liberation from Spandau prison in 1966, he admitted that he'd imagined that "after the war all my buildings would have been completed."[36] There are also other insights into that mindset. For example, after a victorious war, Fritz Todt found inspiration and a model in the memorials of the Incas,[37] and hoped to be able to build on a scale similar to them. He spoke of the roads of the future stretching from Trondheim to Klagenfurt and from Calais to Warsaw.[38] At the end of September 1939, four weeks after the beginning of the war, Speer was rushing to complete plans for the Führer buildings after "the end of the conflict" (like most Germans he believed in a short military campaign)"[39] In contrast to most of his colleagues, he can be granted some sense of reality. In 1940, he forecast that it would take Germany's best architects ten years just to produce drafts for the five Führer cities.[40]

For a long time, though, an unbelievable rash of amateur planning was taking place. The Gauleiter were setting up their own town planning committees,[41] aside from the municipal positions, plans that began with demolitions and encroached on city budgets themselves. Directives for the rebuilding of cities were encouraging them. The new heads of the city planning departments constituted a special authority within the city's administration: they received guidelines from Hitler and could give official orders to the cities.[42]

It almost seemed as if a certain shift in power and therefore in responsibility had to take place within the higher levels of decision making of the Third Reich's hierarchy. To what extent did the de-politicized specialization of a young technical elite, within the Nazi system, become a factor in the loss of perspective and the loss of political and moral integrity of the old guard, for example within the military? Were these architectural plans not a confirmation for Hitler of his role, giving him warrant to force the high civil servants and the military to follow him and to win in the end also the wavering individuals? In the end—one has to say—great parts of the German nation seem to have been in a mood of awakening, comparable to the Germanic tribes which invaded and destroyed the Roman Empire.

Notes

1. This number points to BA R 43. –Cf. Breker, 84f.
2. Ibid., 131.
3. Brenner, 128f. –BA R 43 II/1306, 14.
4. BA R 120/892, 14ff.
5. BA R 43 II/1185, 87.
6. Speer, 157.
7. Wulf, *Theater und Film im Dritten Reich*, 169ff.
8. Keesings Archiv, 2474 –March 21, 1936.

9. Ibid.
10. This volume, 74.
11. See also 134ff.
12. D. Petzina, „Die Mobilisierung deutscher Arbeitskräfte vor und während des Zweiten Welt-krieges." VfZG 18 (1970), 443ff.
13. Dülffer, 559f.
14. Dehlinger, 45. –With regard to criticism of the speed of construction on new motor-ways: Bonatz, 168.
15. Dehlinger, 166. –Cf. BA R 43 II/1183, 1f.
16. Dehlinger, 166.
17. Ibid., 152.
18. Ibid., 166.
19. Speer, 196.
20. BA R 43 II/1177, 25.
21. Picker, 311f. –May 4, 1942.
22. With regard to the following: E. Georg, Die wirtschaftlichen Unternehmungen der SS (Stuttgart, 1963), 42f.
23. Ibid., 144 –December 31, 1937: 4, 833 men; December 31, 1938: 8, 484 men.
24. Ibid., 42f.
25. Ibid., 42f, 44. –Flossenbürg, Natzweiler, Groß-Rosen, Mauthausen.
26. Ibid., 47, 49f. –(e.g., Neuengamme).
27. Ibid. 42f, 111.
28. BA R 43 II/1180b, 84.
29. Koeppen Reports, 64. –October 17, 1941.
30. In addition: Georg, 90, 145f; A.S. Milward, Die deutsche Kriegswirtschaft 1939–1945 (Stuttgart, 1966), 140.
31. Apart from Speer, Giesler and Bonatz were the only ones to have written memoirs.
32. In addition: Krogmann-Tagebuch –entry from August 31, 1944 –Hamburger For-schungsstelle Geschichte NS.
33. Dehlinger gives the unbelievable number of 700 employees for the the civil engi-neering department of Munich, 88. –See also Wulf, Bildende Künste im Dritten Reich, 238f.
34. von Hassell, 55.
35. Krogmann-Tagebuch –entry from November 29, 1938 –Eiffe report.
36. SPIEGEL interview, 56.
37. BA NS 26/1188.
38. Ibid.
39. BA R 43 II/1021, 36 –Speer to Lammers, September 28, 1939.
40. BA R 43 II/1021 76f –Speer to Lammers, August 30, 1940.
41. BA R 120/892, 14ff. –See also Jansen, 36 note 20.
42. For Berlin: Brenner, 125f; for Munich: Dehlinger, 85, 88.

Chapter 12

Summary

From the beginning of his chancellorship in 1933, Hitler turned his architectural ideas of the "years of struggle" into reality and actively adapted them into his "program." At the same time, his architecture of supremacy, despite all its similarities to the other neoclassical European architecture that typified the totalitarian regimes of the twentieth century, was in fact tailor-made for National Socialism and should be viewed as a rupture. His architecture was not a simple architecture of memory in its aesthetic or nostalgic form, but an expression of the social utopian driving force behind the ideology of National Socialism.

With a short head start for Nuremberg, from 1937 onward enormous construction and planning activity began which would only be completely stopped in 1945. Many building sites were closed during the war, but were reopened in the years of high hope with regard to the war's outcome. Plans were made right up to the very end of the war. All large public projects—and Hitler was only interested in these, as his ideas were based heavily on the history and architectural culture of antiquity—pointed toward his goal: these buildings were to set the scene for a Germany that would rule the world. Berlin was to be the capital of the world, and the stadium in Nuremberg was to be the venue of the new Olympic Games. Buildings were designed to last forever: the figure of a thousand years was simply a euphemism for the length of time that Hitler considered while planning buildings, one which he wanted to use as a sort of "totem" in order to swear in the masses to unity and a fighting spirit.

The unbelievably short planning phases of a building boom, in which public buildings were to be completed as early as 1950, was indirectly an indication of the need for war with the Soviet Union for plunder. The building program could not have been realized with the material resources and manpower of central Europe alone.

The change in National Socialist foreign policy that took place from 1936 to 1938—after the occupation of the Rhineland and following Great Britain's position towards Italy regarding the conflict in Abyssinia, which Hitler found "weak,"—finds parallels in Hitler's architectural policies and in changes within the social organization and power structure of the Third Reich, with the rise of the SS as an industrial factor. After the planning phase, the aggressive phase began. The study of the role architecture played in the context of Hitler's goals proves that starting with 1933, he decided on course bent on expansion. This is when the necessary long-term planning for the construction projects began. In all its aspects, architecture offered Hitler an instrument of hitherto unbelievable leverage for internal and external politics: before 1936, architecture functioned as a substitute for aggression, and afterwards as a "Trojan Horse" that could be used to show his desire for peace.

Hitler's retreat from politics to be an "artist" didn't begin during the war years. This powerful "under-current" existed from the start of his political career. His passion for architecture, which was already obvious during his youth, had been coupled with his political sense of mission as early as 1924.

Part III

HITLER AND MILITARY ISSUES
From Whale Bay to Lake Erie

Chapter 13

HITLER'S ADDRESSES TO GERMAN OFFICERS

New research results indicate that until war broke out in 1939, Hitler was not simply involved with the realignment of the borders of the Third Reich, but had also added more steps of his "program" to his agenda.[1] Up to that point, however, there had been a gap for the years between 1933 and 1936 due to a lack of resources. This gap could not adequately refute the opinion that Hitler's foreign policy was opportunistic and without a set direction.[2] A variation of this impression is the notion that an aggressive change followed the policy of so-called "peace" that had lasted until 1938.[3]

By examining Hitler's architectural plans and by following a certain number of decisions taking place just beneath the political level, it was possible to show how the continuity of his thoughts and plans was carried forward through January 30, 1933, and further, without a break. One must then ask again whether the political "distortion" prevents an understanding of Hitler's ultimate political goals even past this secondary area. Can the thesis still be supported that as of 1933, Hitler, in contrast to his "years of struggle," never again mentioned his long term plans?

Once again, for our purposes, the subject must remain his long-term plans. It will not suffice to simply concentrate on Hitler, but rather, after examining the role of architecture in Hitler's long-term plans, to return to the more "classical" areas, in which the instrumental character of foreign policy becomes clear: by the separate military branches of the army, navy, and air force.

With the question of the degree of importance the armed forces played in Hitler's considerations, it should be checked whether he planned to use them to achieve not only his short and medium-term plans, but also his ultimate political goals. How did the military react to this from its vantage point, and how much power did they think Germany should actually have?

What were the underlying political assumptions behind the armaments programs? Did they include a potential extension to non-European expansion plans? The issue of divergence from the intended goals, requires examination of the areas where the interests of Hitler and the military became connected. Attention should also be paid to the change in political views among leading officers, as well as to the formation of groups within one branch of the armed forces,[4] and the separate branches, as the army, the navy, and the air force cannot all be seen as having a uniform attitude towards National Socialism.[5]

With regard to Hitler, a difference must be made between:

1. His "political" influence of the armed forces through guidelines and speeches, and
2. His direct intervention in military fields of activity such as armament plans.

Already on February 3, 1933, Hitler discussed aspects of his multi-staged plans during an address to the supreme commanders of the army and the navy, in which he described "the conquest of new Lebensraum in the East and its merciless Germanization"[6] as a possible goal of German foreign policy. At the end of February 1934, in view of the escalating crisis between the SA and the army, he justified his vote to create a new professional army within eight years before the representatives of both groups by appealing to the idea of an aggressive war that would use short, decisive strikes to create "Lebensraum" in the West and then in the East.[7] These two pieces of evidence, which show that Hitler still kept to the central idea in *Mein Kampf* directly after the seizure of power, are relatively isolated if Rauschning's discussions with Hitler are not taken into consideration. The contents of these discussions only correspond in part to Hitler's comments in front of the officers, but prove much greater detail for certain other aspects.[8] Despite concerns as to the reliability of the source, Rauschning's notes must still be viewed, however, as an indication of the atmosphere of continuity of Hitler's objectives in 1933–1934.[9]

It was only in 1936 that Hitler began to realize his "program" in a way that could be interpreted from outside. His successful Rhineland coup at the beginning of March, 1936,[10] which elicited no reaction from the

Western powers, particularly Great Britain, strengthened his idea that the United Kingdom was "weak," especially given that, a few months before during the outbreak of the Abyssinian war, Great Britain had only made a show of its Mediterranean fleet against the aggressor, Italy.[11] Hitler's demand for colonies at the same time showed a change in course in his politics toward Great Britain.[12]

A few weeks later, at the opening of the Ordensburg Crössinsee in Pomerania, surrounded by trusted party supporters, Hitler made it clear how the occupation of the Rhineland fit into his political concept: "I am of the opinion, and a very proud opinion that has truly been confirmed for me in the last three months, that there isn't a nation on Earth better than the Germans. And furthermore I am of the opinion that our German people really is the best in the world.... Where is the nation that could stand up to us on its own?"[13] This people, continued Hitler, should be given "first class tasks," "purposely chosen because they are tremendous," tasks that would be "unique." Should those tasks be realized, they would lift this nation to a level above other peoples. The creation of the best army in the world should be part of it.

Despite several missing details that will be supplied in the course of the description, the suggested formula that Hitler had already used on his listeners in the 1920s is identifiable:

1. The German nation is the strongest (i.e. = greatest) people in the world.
2. Because of this, the German nation is militarily superior to all others (including the United States).
3. German politics must therefore strive for goals that would have to guarantee a "Lebensraum" corresponding to the size of the people.

It is obvious from these comments that it was Hitler's aim to attract a fanatically determined entourage that was prepared to follow the theoretically limitless goals of his foreign policy blindly.

Already at the beginning of 1936, Hitler made his ambitions very clear to another target group of his, in as far as it is possible to classify his favorite target groups at this stage. Besides the heads of the army, since 1933 he had been targeting all military and paramilitary youth groups, who according to Hitler's expectations were to embody the heroic type of human after an initial phase of indoctrination. These included officer cadets, members of the party schools and the educational system, and students, as well as leaders of the party and SS.

At a rally to celebrate the tenth anniversary of the National Socialist Party at the Circus Krone in Munich, with help of a historical outline of the colonial policies of Great Britain, Spain, and the Netherlands, he explained that the "organization drive of the white race" was an expression of a natural conviction "that the white race has been called to rule the other parts of the world and to dominate them."[14] Hitler further stated that the world supremacy would be lost "when Europe and the white race forgot or lost the basic rules upon which their world supremacy was built."[15]

Hitler's comments resulted in an extensive wave of protest throughout Asia. Countries like India and Japan called for a trade boycott against Germany. The Foreign Office requested from the Chancellery a retraction of the corresponding passages in Hitler's speech.[16]

As Hitler had addressed the colonialism carried out by the white race in his January speech, without touching on the division of power and the agreements among the existing world powers, he was more precise about Germany's task in an August 1936 memorandum about the four-year plan. In addition to demands that the German army be prepared for action within four years and, at the same time, to secure the German economy to a point that it could support a war,[17] demands that Hitler frequently made at the end of his explanations, he also demanded in another mostly unnoticed part of the memorandum that the German army should be developed into the "best army in the world" to be used as an instrument in the fight against Bolshevism.[18] "Since Marxism, through its victory in Russia, has created one of the largest empires in the world from which to carry out further operations," wrote Hitler, "this issue has become a threatening one. A unified authoritarian power with an ideologically well-grounded will to fight is standing up against an ideologically disunited world."[19] This image of the enemy had already been described during the "years of struggle" and corresponded to the solutions that Hitler offered in his memorandum. "The German people, impeccably led in politics, ideologically steadfast, and militarily well-organized, is certainly the most high quality factor of resistance the world has at its disposal."[20] Here again the pattern appeared that was often used in the 1920s: an Aryan raiding party, representing the rest of the world, at war with Marxism. At this point, another viewpoint should be noted: global powers such as the Soviet Union that already represented world empires were not dormant, according to Hitler's socio-Darwinian theories, but planned further incursions into other countries' spheres of power.

In a similar way, but coming from a different starting point in his thinking and political plans, Hitler seized the problem of ultimate goals in a speech given one year later to district leaders at the Ordensburg Vogelsang in the Eifel mountains, not far from Cologne. The confrontation with democracy would be inevitable. "We must simply hope that this conflict will not happen today, but that it will take years before it comes. The later the better."[21] With that, Hitler had within a few months hinted at the global concept of his political goals: firstly against Bolshevism, with the active help of other democracies or with sympathetic neutrality, and after that the destruction of these democracies as the early political form of Bolshevism, as it has become more than familiar to us from Hitler's plans during his "years of struggle." The details were still missing. But the relative density of his comments starting in 1937,[22] which corresponds in time with the beginning of the "national construction project," allows the conclusion that Hitler was now considering further steps of his "program." The conclusion of the centrally important revisionist foreign policy was being increasingly eclipsed, for the time being, by these considerations. This can be proven with regard to his colonial plans from 1937 onwards.[23]

The information and ideas found in the minutes of the Hossbach meeting (named after the writer of the minutes, a general) were still concerned with continental objectives. But already there is a correspondence between Hitler's intention of finishing his continental program by 1943–1945 and his later intention to begin constructing war memorials.[24] Two months later, however, Hitler returned to his great theme at another address in front of officers. This would be a theme that he wouldn't give up until 1945. With the worsening prospects of the war, the gaps between moments when expressing his ideas became longer, but Hitler kept to this theme in principal until his end in the Chancellery bunker. In a speech to the generals on January 22, 1938,[25] he explained, in connection with the national food supply, that it was necessary "to acquire a new living space by force.... One insight leads me to believe that the situation for the German people is nonetheless hopeful. If we observe the ruling peoples of the world, the British, the French, the Americans, statistics indicate that only an insignificant number, 40–50 million, of pure blooded members of the leading country rule over millions of other peoples and huge areas of the world. There is only one people on Earth that in great unity, having the same racial background, speaking the same language, lives herded together in the heart of Europe. That is the German people with its 110 million people in central Europe. This comparison makes me hopeful and this unified block in central Europe will one day own the world."[26]

Hitler's scenario for the division of the world, which remained the same up until the end of the war, was almost complete. As we know, since at least 1919 the imbalance between the population and surface expansion of Great Britain had bothered Hitler. His vision of a division of the world rivaling that was complete in the formulations he used in the 1920s. For tactical reasons, he had for some time stopped using that formulation.

But now it had emerged from the woodwork, unchanged. Hitler gave his final thoughts on the subject to the German press[27] at the end of 1938, when he maintained that the quality and number of people were decisive factors in "global history." "The quality of the German people is incomparable. I will never be persuaded that another nation is more valuable. I am convinced that our people, especially today, with its gradual racial improvement, represents the highest quality that exists on Earth at this time."[28] Hitler demonstrated German superiority by using the following figures. Although America had a population of 125 million, after removing the immigrants and the inferior racial elements, there were less than 60 million Anglo-Saxons left. In Russia, according to Hitler's grotesque numbers games, there were only 55 million real Russians; in the British Empire only about 46 million Englishmen, in France with her colonies about 37 million "real Frenchmen." "But in Germany," Hitler continued triumphantly, "from the year 1940 onward, there are 80 million people of one race, and surrounding us another eight million who from a racial point of view belong to us.... I believe unconditionally in this future."[29]

The high point of all of these more or less very similar speeches—and at the same time a more direct turn to the subject of the chapter—are the speeches Hitler gave to the officers in 1939. Of the twenty or so speeches to officers known at this point and given between 1939–1945,[30] the addresses of 1939 are the decisive ones, not only because of their number.[31] Their content could be an important indication of whether Hitler had other plans for the completion of his "program" before the outbreak of war, plans that he just gave up after the unexpected quick victories in the West in 1940. This would at any rate make his hasty, optimistic evaluation of the overall situation far more comprehensible.

To address this question, we shall place at the center of our observations a speech made to army troop commanders in Berlin[32] on February 10, 1939. This speech was previously unknown. Its character as a key document into Hitler's thinking and plans, justifies a closer examination of its content:

"The year 1938 was possibly not completely understood by most of the German people from the very beginning as one would have expected. Also some circles within the army certainly viewed some of the events if not skeptically, then at least with apprehension. It wasn't understood that at one moment, because German foreign policy could look back on many successes, while on the other hand, the instrument of foreign policy was still being established, it wasn't understood that at such a time one could make more risky decisions, the outcome of which were, to say the very least, very much in doubt. ..."

The year 1938 has indeed ended with an overwhelming success. That alone should be reason enough for us to understand the need for actions taken this year, because one will be able to draw valid conclusions for similar cases in the future. I find it especially important that the officer corps be knowledgeable of the train of thought that moved me, not only in 1938 but in general for many, many years. It had to lead, especially in 1938, to quite pressing conclusions and decisions."[33]

After this, Hitler outlined the duties of an officer with respect to politics and the need to defend a cause to the death. But he also outlined the reasons underlying his speech. A general has to know the basic thoughts and principles behind his policies, because thanks to this knowledge, he would understand the actions of the politician, "and because I believe," continued Hitler:

"that in the end, one can only audaciously and energetically represent that which one understands.

I have decided therefore to do the following in a series of lectures:

1. Explain the basic principles of National Socialism to the top generals of the German army in a way which, for obvious reasons, cannot be done publicly."[34]

2. Explain certain procedures and the reasons that led to them, and to draw conclusions that arise for the future.

"The year 1938 with all its events is only a consistent continuation of decisions which originated in 1933. It is not as if 1938 would, let us say, represent a special action that had previously gone unnoticed. On the contrary, all the individual decisions that had been taken since 1933 are not the result of immediate considerations, but rather the implementation of an existing plan, only perhaps not exactly in keeping with precise dates. It was, for example, not clear to me in 1933 when we would leave the League of Nations. But that this had to be the first step to rebuilding Germany was clear, and that we should pick the first suitable moment was also clear. The next step then became national rearmament, and that had been planned from the beginning without the agreement of any foreign powers, only the pace could naturally not be set right away, and also the extent of the rearmament could not be quite exactly, shall we say, assessed. It was also clear that after a certain development, after a certain time of this rearmament, Germany, at great risk, would have to proclaim to the rest of the world that she was free to rearm. The moment of this step was naturally not foreseeable. It finally became clear that any further steps would result in the remilitarization of the Rhineland. Here again the date was actually planned for a year later; I didn't think of carrying this out until 1937. Conditions at the time made it appear sensible to take this step earlier in 1936. It was also quite clear that in order to strengthen Germany's political and especially military position, it was necessary to solve the Austrian and Czechoslovakian problem. In the beginning I wasn't quite sure whether both problems had to be or could be tackled at the same time, or whether to take on Czechoslovakia first or Austria first. There was no doubt that these problems had to be solved. So all these decisions, therefore, were not just ideas that were realized on the spur of the moment, but were the result of long-range plans, which I was determined to realize the moment I believed the general conditions were suitable.

If 1938 goes down in our most recent history as one of the greatest success, then it is, of course, just a single step on a long path, gentlemen, that is laid out for us, and the inevitability of which I would now like to briefly explain.[35]

…The demise took place in 1918 and the strongest nation in Europe numerically lost its position of power and with it the possibility of asserting its most important and most natural interests by any means and under any circumstances. This is really about the strongest people not only in Europe, but rather—some of you may be surprised—practically in the entire world."[36]

At another part of the speech, Hitler underlined the role of the German people as a supreme world leader,[37] only to continue with his already well-known comparison of the "core peoples" of the world powers.

He justified the haste of his "program" by saying it was the duty "of all to represent the interests of our people as if the fate of our race for centuries to come were placed exclusively in our hands today. We cannot free ourselves from the responsibility of acting as if the entire future of Germany were now actually being shaped exclusively by our hands."[38] Although he was talking about the future of Germany, the term "the fate of our race" betrayed Hitler's true categories of thought, as is also proven in another passage of the speech: "The next struggle will be a purely ideological war, in other words a conscious war of peoples and races."[39]

In speaking about his own role in German politics, Hitler uttered some revealing words: "In recent years I have climbed the steepest and most dizzying path that a person ever had to climb. I also think it is something unique in world history when a man in 1919, that is twenty years ago, embarks on a political career, a man who was in my position, with my prerequisites, and twenty years later achieves *the* goal."[40]

"We have to catch up on things that have been neglected for three hundred years." One could take this as being another main theme of the speech and as a return to a theme of the early 1920s. "Since the treaty of Westphalia our nation has taken a path that lead us away from world power[41] and more and more to impoverishment and political powerlessness." Six years have gone by since the restoration, Hitler continued. "We cannot suppose that our path has ended here. On the contrary, gentlemen, this is where our path starts. And we all have the duty to follow this path, cool and determined to make use of every opportunity that presents itself."[42]

Hitler in no way laid his cards on the table here, even if the words "our path starts" gives enough away. Five years later, he spoke about things that he had not yet dared clearly express at the time of 1939. In a two-hour address in front of field marshals and generals on January 27, 1944, at the "Wolfsschanze," Hitler regretted the German religious war in connection with the last 300 years, and said: "The only people that without doubt was predestined to rule the world lost its chance for global supremacy."[43] The second chance, which Hitler had continually referred to since the 1920s and with which he had courted his generals in the February 1939 speech, was no longer part of the talk given in 1944.

He referred once again to his own special historical role at the end of his presentation to the troop commanders at the Kroll Opera House in 1939 as he announced the solution to the problem of more living space for the Germans and promised "in our generation to realize everything that can be realized."[44] In the next one hundred years, no one would have more authority than the Führer. The theoretically limitless program laid out by Hitler and his socio-Darwinian understanding of foreign policy surfaced in his last sentences:

> I believe ... that we must continue to stay on the enemy's heels, we shouldn't allow him any time to rest at all. The respect and prestige that we have won can best be kept if we constantly use every single opportunity, no matter how small, to immediately achieve a new success. In this way we will all become used, I would like to say, to the enemy, and the enemy will slowly get used to the idea of resigning himself to the strength of the German people.
>
> Therefore you should not be surprised, if in the coming years every opportunity is taken to try to achieve some German goal or other and then I ask of you, please, to trust me deeply and stand behind me. Be above all assured that I have previously given these problems much thought, that I always consider everything. Be assured that once I have announced the decision to carry out this or that action, then this decision is irrevocable, that I will carry out my decision against all odds, and secondly that it is a decision which has been most thoroughly thought through and finally that the realization of my goal will only be made easier if we all, each in his own job, work together towards the same goal."[45]

Even if one removes Hitler's obvious euphoria at his successes in 1938, the value of the document's statement about Hitler's "basic plan"[46] cannot be doubted. Even the necessary cutbacks in the situation—Hitler, in front of his officers, had to slip into the role of the politician who acted according to long-term and well-thought-out plans—change nothing of the intrinsic value of the document. The coincidence between the content of the speech and actual action taken is striking. The very fact that his speech was basically a prologue to more addresses gives his statements a fundamental value. With that in mind, it becomes possible to interpret Hitler's addresses to the supreme commanders in 1939 as a sort of cycle of speeches, one which was calculated to provide comprehensive and complete instructions to the army about his final intentions. This cycle of speeches, a new key document in the framework of the most important source material about Hitler, must—after recognition of the speech of February 10, 1939, in its entirety—be viewed at the same time as proof that Hitler, after 1933, announced his ultimate goals in connection with one another. Historians do not have to rely solely on reconstructions. The spectrum of his goals, and his personal conviction of his "mission" caused Hitler to share his ideas beyond his innermost circle. Statements about world supremacy were therefore not, as the judgment dismissively reads from time to time, "spur of the moment" inspirations, "madness," or something out of "The Twilight of the Gods," but rather consciously placed contemplations. The problem is to record the consequences of Hitler's statements in quantity as well as quality. Hitler's choice of causes was unique, not solely in terms of what his ultimate goals were, but in terms of the way they were formulated. The records known as of now, the minutes from 1937–1939, can be verified by the existence of this speech as a text. It has to be doubted, however, if the minutes really do justice to Hitler's statements about his ultimate goals. It would seem as though the authors of the minutes and other notations that summarized these eschatological passages in Hitler's speeches didn't find the passages particularly important. This might be because they saw things from the different vantage point of the day-to-day German realities, or maybe they had been too accustomed through over-repetition to even notice what Hitler was actually saying. Writings by the counter-intelligence officer Helmuth Groscurth, however, show that critical listeners were well able to grasp the true consequences of Hitler's remarks related to this theme. We will come back to this.

From the many facts that can be drawn from Hitler's speech, we shall consider only the following for our deliberation: in the speech of February 10, 1939, it becomes clear as never before that Hitler acted according to a multi-stage plan after 1933. Although there was a certain variability with regard to deadlines, overall it was concise and almost deterministically calculated. As with the question of South Tyrol in 1922,[47] it is clear that

Hitler was aiming for a result that was qualitatively completely different than a revisionist policy. For Hitler, the *"Anschluß"* of Austria or the annexation of the Sudetenland was not an issue of irredentism, but rather the problem of regaining neutral territory for military expansion.[48] At the moment when the majority of Germans regarded the German nation-state as almost complete, Hitler announced to his generals that they were on the brink of a series of wars of expansion, which were no longer to be conventional European wars, as they were viewed by Ernst Nolte, but rather ideological and racial issues. The Soviet Union was considered as a target, but also the United States, because its "core population" "with regard to numbers" would be smaller than that of the coming European Empire. The constant repetition of these number games also appears to have been for Hitler an effort to overcome the psychological defense mechanism against being the aggressor in a war. In all his remarks, it is obvious that he made an effort to try to present his case when justifying his struggle for more "Lebensraum" for the largest population in the world, which also meant the right to the theoretically largest number of square kilometers in the world. The task of bringing about this goal was first given to the army, since the armament of the other two branches of the armed services would only be completed in time for the non-European phase of Hitler's "program." This also explains the high number of speeches given to army officers during this period. Hitler intended, as is revealed in his speeches, to use the military solely as an instrument. Every political decision was to be carried out by the Führer's "instrument of aggression" without prior information and without questions. The fight for the primacy of politics, if one thinks about the conflict between Bismarck and Moltke during the war in 1870–1871, was forcefully escalated by Hitler to the point of perverting its content. In place of the ideal of the Prussian officer, however that ideal was understood, Hitler had offered the model of the ideological "fighter," a trusting functionary who would always obey the party in military questions and who would always be ready to follow his Führer.[49]

Also on January 18, 1939, during the address to the youngest officers in the army in Berlin,[50] the speech was dominated by images that Europe would be offered of the strongest people in the world, and most of all the value of that race. Hitler also used this occasion to confirm his intention to develop the German army into the most powerful in the world, not as a "parade decoration" but for "immediate deployment."[51]

A few days later, in a speech given to his supreme army commanders,[52] Hitler sketched the meaning of the Roman Empire for the white race and announced that one day the Aryans would conquer the world.

In a speech to graduating cadets of the military academies on March 11, 1939 in Berlin,[53] Hitler underlined the decisive racial quality that the

Germans possessed when compared with all other nations in the world, and answered his own question, as to whether the Germans would be capable of "fulfilling a decisive mission in this world"[54] with a clear "yes." The things that supported this conclusion were, in Hitler' words:

"1. the intrinsic quality of our race.
2. the strength in numbers of our race.
3. the absolute proven fighting ability of our race."[55]

If one compares the speeches of February 10, 1939, and March 11, 1939, with the remarks of November 5, 1937, and the notes from the meetings on May 23, 1939,[56] August 22, 1939,[57] and November 23, 1939,[58] it seems that there are no great differences in the description of Hitler's long-term plans. Hitler also addressed the problem of Lebensraum here, although not to the detailed extent of his speech of February 10, 1939. But what did his statement actually mean when, on November 5, 1937, he pointed out that Germany possessed the most united racial core in the world and as such had more of a right to greater living space than other nations?[59] What led him to make the comment on May 23, 1939, when speaking about the British Empire not just as a physical but also as a worldwide psychological entity, that the quality of the German race at the same time was on average superior to that of the British?[60]

It must be stressed that Hitler once again spoke explicitly about the direction of his expansion plans after 1936. The exact targets and time frames for areas outside Europe were still missing at this stage, but from 1937 on, it seems that Hitler's intention of informing the army commanders of his global expansion program and of preparing them for it was clear. Also, the absolute need for urgency for the planned measures becomes obvious. Hitler, who took on an almost messianic role, basically wanted to see his entire "program" fulfilled before his death. One could think that the images he used years later, namely that he, like Moses, would only see the promised land from afar,[61] were only a tactical ruse.

In the reported version of Hitler's speech to his supreme commanders given on November 23, 1939, in the Chancellery—a version which was probably provided by Groscurth—confirms the contents of the speech of February 10, 1939. Once again, the theme was the violent expansion of Lebensraum. "A racial war has started about who will rule over Europe and thus over the world."[62]

"One can do anything with a German soldier,"[63] said Hitler at another point, and he once again demanded fanatic, blind allegiance from his officers. The dominating image of his long-term plans made him to repeat once again: "It has to be determined who will dominate Europe and thus the world."[64] These writings of Groscurth also support the previously-given idea that Groscuth's records are more precise about Hitler's ultimate goals than those of the generals Hossbach or Schmundt. All of Hitler's speeches to officers that are known in their entirety contain passages about world supremacy or hint at the notion. It is therefore improbable that Hitler would fail to express himself clearly on this subject in the speeches that are only available in summary form.

Even after the outbreak of war, Hitler spoke to officers about the matters of greatest concern to him in at least ten speeches up to the end of 1944.[65] In 1940, in three speeches to officer candidates,[66] he referred to the unique racial quality of the German people[67] and forecast a German victory. "The Earth is there for whoever will take it for his own."[68] "The Earth is a challenge cup that is snatched from those who become weak."[69] In a speech on December 18, 1940,[70] when discussing the problem of living space, Hitler addressed an argument that he tended to overuse at that time, named that Germany would possess only 600,000 square kilometers, while Great Britain on the other hand would control forty million square kilometers, Russia nineteen million, the United States nine and one half million, and France ten million. These apparently meaningless statistical comparisons, which Hitler presented just as often as he did the comparison of populations, were obviously not an unwise approach, as they appeared plausible at first glance and impressed the people around him. An air force general spoke a style identical to Hitler's when he defended German foreign policy to a member of the French embassy in the following words: "All we demand is our natural right, nothing else, and we won't accept that a country which rules over three fifths of the globe challenges us this basic right."[71]

The problem of living space was brought up unchanged by Hitler, in the years to come. It is impossible to think of a better source than the speeches to officers to demonstrate how Hitler's ideas had not changed since 1919. Even as the course of the war was already pointing toward total defeat, Hitler was still philosophizing to his generals about Germany's lost opportunity at "world supremacy."[72] Also in the Platterhof speech at the end of June 1944[73] and in a speech to division commanders at the end of 1944 about the January 1945 offensive to take place in southern Alsace,[74] the dictator who had lost all sense of the world outside his headquarters stated that "still today without a doubt German forces are the strongest in the world."[75] Any other military power could be handled in the "twinkling of an eye," but the strength of the German nation would lie in its people. He ended his speech with: "A people cannot be any better than our German people."[76] In front of all those present, Field Marshal von Rundstedt ceremoniously vowed to do everything that was necessary for the success of the Alsace offensive.

In a series of monographs on the role of the army in the Third Reich, the phase of "partial fascism" has been especially studied in recent years.[77] The interaction of a leading political and social group, namely, the military elite and National Socialism, has mostly been attributed to the collapse of the German Empire in 1918 and the subsequent loss of identity for the army. Under this interpretation, the Weimar Republic only represented a transitional period for most of the officers, a period which they spent waiting, and ready for the return of a strong national state. More recent research, however, shows that already before 1933, a deep change of attitude towards the state was noticeable within the army. The experiences of the First World War, with its clash of massive armies and its economy based on total war, led a group of reformers to replace the notion of a distinct imperial army with the complete militarization of society, at which point there was only a slight difference between a cold and a hot war.[78]

The officer corps experienced a much broader transition from the Weimar Republic to Hitler, contrary to what has long been assumed, and the attempt to keep the military away from society made by the generals von Blomberg and von Reichenau was doomed to fail from the very beginning. The growth of the officer corps from 4,000 to 24,000 men[79] by 1939, a factor of six was bound to have brought a substantial shift in the political spectrum, as the increase in new members at least partially included the age group that had been involved in the Nazi Party organizations. There is little to be found in the way of source material on this subject, since apart from a few pilot heroes,[80] these groups never wrote any memoirs about the war.

The chief of staff, General Beck provides a good example of the dilemma felt by conservative and nation-minded officers who thought within the boundaries of a power state. Even an exception such as Beck, who worked out the consequences of Hitler's policies at a very early stage, was much too close in his own phraseology and goals to Hitler's pseudo-revisionist course from the early years of Nazi foreign policy. This led superficially to a convergence of interests between Beck and Hitler's first initiatives in foreign affairs.[81] Although, for example, in one statement of May 29, 1938, Beck refuted point by point Hitler's speech of the day before to the leaders of the state, party, and military, he also emphasized on the other hand the point on which he and Hitler agreed: Germany would need more living space both in Europe and in the form of colonies.[82] Even if Beck did not share Hitler's primitive and overcharged social-Darwinist geopolitics, this example shows that some of the leading minds among officers, even in the twentieth century, saw wars in central Europe as a political instrument, and from the very beginning they did not reject violence in the dealings among states. Their patterns of thought were those of the nineteenth century. Their difference with Hitler during the phase of redrawing the borders of central Europe, apart from the qualitatively different initial starting point, was that Beck wanted to carry out German power politics more intelligently and with a more reasonable understanding between Germany and the other great powers, compared with what had happened during the era of Kaiser Wilhelm II.[83]

This temporary convergence of goals was threatened during the Sudetenland crisis, but already by the end of 1938 the mood among the generals had completely changed,[84] precluding any form of opposition.[85] The next decisive blow was the successful campaign in the West in 1940.[86] Even these officers who had previously doubted now abandoned their skepticism, since they had only predicted that Germany would gain a position of world power in the distant future.[87]

By the end of 1938, the army had started making plans for colonies in Africa.[88] In June 1940, preparations for the establishment of colonial troops began.[89] A few weeks later, the chief of staff of the army, General Halder, learned from his supreme commander, Field Marshal von Brauchitsch, that it had been ordered that a new colonial regiment be formed in Bergen, in occupied Norway. At the same time, a staff was to be formed within the General Army Office to deal with colonial matters.[90] An order was also given during this time to gather information from experiments on how to use motorized vehicles in the tropics.[91] A series of meetings took place during the months that followed between von Brauchitsch, Halder, and General Buhle, the chief of the organizational department of the general staff.[92] In an organizational request issued in April 1941 for the army subdivision after the completion of the Russian campaign, thirty-three divisions were planned for deployment in the tropics.[93] The number of operational troops that, from the fall of 1941, were planned to be at war in Spain and Morocco, North Africa (Egypt), Anatolia, and Afghanistan was even higher. Without even counting air and land transport units, these troops alone numbered forty-six divisions.[94]

These plans didn't consider any lapse of time following "victory." As had happened in the plans for the campaign against Russia, there were an extravagant number of objectives and Halder was puzzled by the end of September 1940 about the political direction Germany had chosen.[95] The war with Great Britain alone had placed the German armed forces in a conflict all around the Mediterranean just two years after the army was still trying to work out transport problems relating to the distances between Dresden and Prague or Passau and Vienna. According to Halder, in view of the overextended German forces and despite the diminished military capacity, it could be concluded that General Rommel—who had

been through the Haushofer school of thought,[96]—had planned "too many
… world conquering tasks."[97]

But the euphoria surrounding the pseudo-victories even took hold of
men like Halder[98] in the first weeks of the Russian campaign, and even at
the beginning of October 1941, the chief of the armed forces command
at the OKW, General Jodl, emphasized that, in having successfully established the encircled area of Melitopol, Briansk, and Vyasma, "finally and
without exaggeration the war had been won."[99]

Already after the campaign in France, the army's propaganda machine
took a new course and began to school German soldiers in their "attitude" for imminent future tasks. The "Mitteilungen für die Truppe" (official announcements for the army), in calling for an "imperial attitude,"
demanded that the bearing of Germans "within, and more importantly
outside the borders of Germany, must reflect the distance, the size, the
importance, and the style of a global empire."[100] In the spring of 1941, the
publishers of the troop magazine became bolder and wrote: "The Führer's
revolution which was at first meant to be a revolution of the German
people has become a European revolution and is about to become a global
revolution."[101] With this, the direction of things to come was clear. The
German armed forces were to carry the National Socialist banner in the
coming global revolution.

Hitler's army adjutant, Engel, tried as 1940 was giving way to 1941 to
assuage a less optimistic comrade's concerns with the tip that there would
be many tasks for the army after victory. He wrote: "Believe me, there will
so many jobs to protect our greater German living space. The fighting
spirit of our soldiers will be kept going by the confusion and the eternal
changing of postings that will be needed to secure our greater German
living space. Just think of all the regions and places where the German
soldier will stand guard in the future. It will go from all the way up to
Kirkenes, Lublin, the coast of Flanders, and not to forget the colonies
to which each German division will be sent for approximately one year.
So you see, after the war we soldiers will not become boared and we will
always have lots of work, so that in the future we will also be able to fulfill
what our Führer demands of us."[102]

It seems hardly possible to prove Hitler's or the military's long-term
plans through examining armament production for the army. Weapons
developed for the tropics could theoretically have been used in any area
anywhere in the world, and therefore escape an exact interpretation.

It might, however, be of interest to examine a short outline of Hitler's
giant-tank project, which shows certain parallels to the plan for the rearmament of the navy and to the architectural ideas. Obviously impressed
by the heavy Russian tanks that had appeared on the Eastern front, Hitler

ordered the development of giant tanks to outdo their Russian counter-parts.[103] Since he had taken over as factual army chief at the end of 1941, his existing interest in weapons development, especially in tanks, had increased.[104] Without the input of the general staff, Hitler started the development of the tank called "Maus,"[105] with the actual construction of the tank to begin early in 1943.[106] Hitler was convinced that the tanks of the future would weigh over one hundred tons, although the heaviest Russian tanks only weighted fifty-two tons.[107] At the end of 1944, two experimental tanks started their test drives. Despite its frontal armor plating of 250 mm, this largest tank in the world, weighting in at 188 tons, was no longer able to sufficiently protect against hollow shells. During the planned deployment on the Eastern front at the end of March 1945, one vehicle had to be abandoned and blown up before it reached its destination.[108]

The blueprints for a large tank that had been developed in the summer of 1942 under Hitler's orders by leading technicians at the Steyr plants turned out to be even more gigantic.[109] According to the blueprints, it was to weigh 1,500 tons and to be equipped with an 80cm gun and two backward turrets with 15cm guns. The frontal armor plating was also to be 250 mm thick, and this monster vehicle was to be powered by four submarine diesel engines.[110]

Even in a marginal issue like the development of these tanks, which was a complete failure, Hitler's obsession with all things big and his desire to set records are both evident. Completely misjudging the demands put on tanks in action, he saw them as a psychological fighting instrument, the *furor teutonicus*[111] of WWI's Eastern front. It is obvious that Hitler's outstanding contribution in the development of the German tank was a dead end. But the generals went along with it.

Notes

1. These are the theses for the area of colonial and navy policies put forward by Hildebrand, *Weltreich*, and Dülffer.
2. And finally: Rich, *Hitler's War Aims* I, xv.
3. This version seems to be the result of military memoirs, and as such they found their way into this study. Compare F. Hossbach, *Zwischen Wehrmacht und Hitler 1934–1938* (Göttingen, 1965), 30f, 163.
4. K.J. Müller, „Ludwig Beck—Ein General zwischen Wihelminismus und Nationalsozialismus," *Deutschland in der Weltpolitik des 19. und 20. Jahrhunderts. FS for F.Fischer*, ed., I. Geiss and B.J. Wendt (Düsseldorf, 1973), 516.
5. M. Messerschmidt, *Die Wehrmacht im NS-Staat. Zeit der Indoktrination* (Hamburg, 1969), 9.

6. T. Vogelsang, „Neue Dokumente zur Geschichte der Reichswehr 1930–1933." VfZG (1954), 435. With regard to the reactions of those present, see K.J. Müller, Das Heer und Hitler. Armee und nationalsozialistisches Regime 1933–1940 (Stuttgart, 1969), 42f. Lange reports on the reception of „Mein Kampf" in the Reichswehr, Hitlers unbeachtete Maximen, 47ff.

7. Quoted from Müller, Heer und Hitler, 98f note 62. Compare also Hildebrand, Außenpolitik, 38.

8. Rauschning, Gespräche mit Hitler, 44f, 62, 64, 105, and elsewhere.

9. Hitler's speech in Lemgo on January 14, 1934, is an important source for suggested long-term goals. Compare Schneider, ed., Sieben Reden Adolf Hitlers (Bielefeld-Leipzig, 1934), 62. Hitler spoke of "the eternal quality of our race," of "thinking in terms of long periods of time," "for a "great German future." The Germans had to be brought onto the right path, so that they "would come closer and closer to achieving the goal of their great task. I would like to be the guarantor and the Führer of this people on this path." This was similar to his speech from February 7, 1934, to the Student Union in Berlin: "There is hardly another race with such a broad spectrum of abilities as our German people." W. Siebarth, Hitlers Wollen (Munich, 1935), 19, VB, February 8, 1934.

10. M. Braubach, Der Einmarsch deutscher Truppen in die entmilitarisierte Zone am Rhein im März 1936. Ein Beitrag zur Vorgeschichte des Zweiten Weltkrieges (Cologne-Opladen, 1956).

11. M. Funke, Sanktionen und Kanonen. Hitler, Mussolini und der internationale Abessinienkonflikt 1934–36 (Düsseldorf, 1971), 90ff.

12. Hildebrand, Weltreich, 485ff; Henke, 47ff.

13. Hitler's speech from April 24, 1936 –IfZ Archives Fa 88, Fasz. 52, 12. Cf. this volume, 81 note 10.

14. Speech from January 26, 1936 –Jacobsen/Jochmann.

15. Ibid.

16. BA R 43 II/991a.

17. W. Treue, "Hitlers Denkschrift zum Vierjahresplan 1939," VfZG 3 (1955), 210.

18. Kehrl, 447.

19. Ibid., 445.

20. Ibid. 446.

21. Von Kotze and Krausnick, 112ff –speech from April 29, 1937, here 174.

22. Compare Hitler's efforts at suggestion in his speeches from February 24, 1937, in honor of the seventeenth anniversary of the start of the national uprising, von Kotze and Krausnick, 105; ibid., 221 –speech to construction workers on May 20, 1937. For more information about Hitler's speeches from Jacobsen, see Außenpolitik, 343ff. The opinion of Müller, Heer und Hitler, 244f note 186, cannot be shared. He states that a maturing process of Hitler's foreign policies began in 1937.

23. Hildebrand, Weltreich, 527.

24. IMT XXV, 402ff. To compare the value of sources, see statements by Dülffer, 448 note 54; Hildebrand, Weltreich, 523ff.

25. BA/MA RH 26—10/255 (WK XIII/823); Dülffer, 547. These are hand-written records of an officer and not actually literal quotes of Hitler.

26. Ibid.

27. Speech from November 10, 1938 –Treue, VfZG 6 (1958), 175ff.

28. Ibid., 190f.

29. Ibid.

30. January 18, 1939; January 25, 1939; February 10, 1939; March 11, 1939, May 23,

1939; August 22, 1939; November 23, 1939; January 24, 1940; May 3, 1940; December 18, 1940; April 29, 1941; February 15, 1942; May 30, 1942; September 28, 1942; November 20, 1943; January 27, 1944; June 26 1944; December 28, 1944. –W. Hofer, *Die Entfesselung des Zweiten Weltkrieges* (Frankfurt am Main, 1964), 423. There is a reference to two other speeches from January 30, 1939, and April 20, 1939. Finally Irving, in *Hitler*, 229, gives the contents of a secret three-hour speech given on March 30, 1941, to the supreme commanders of the army in the Chancellery. This outdates the figure given by von Kotze and Krausnick, who name eleven speeches for this period, 288 note 9. To verify the source material of the speeches to officers, compare Hillgruber, *Strategie*, 600.

31. It concerns nine speeches. That is, about half of all known speeches.
32. BA NS 11/28, 86ff. –The authenticity of this speech was already known due to evidence by Groscurth, 166f. Oster passed on to Groscurth a written document which was crowned by a summary: "War goals a) Ruling Europe b) World supremacy for centuries." –Compare also Müller, *Heer und Hitler*, 383, as well as IfZ Archives ED 57 304/52. –The written records of Hitler's military adjutant, Major Engel, 44f, also have a reference to the speech. Engel lists as participants all colonels and captains of the Wehrmacht in order of rank. It is amazing that he hardly mentions the content of Hitler's remarks regarding long-term goals. Maybe those in Hitler's surroundings at this time were already so used to his comments on this subject that the threshold for a reaction was just too high. Engel describes the reactions to the speech as varying: "some were delighted, some were skeptical."
33. BA NS 11/28, 86.
34. Ibid., 87.
35. Compare Weizsäcker's entry about Hitler's comments after the meeting with Chamberlain on September 15, 1938 –Weizsäcker-Papiere, 143.
36. BA NS 11/28, 87ff.
37. Ibid., 96. Hitler connects the idea of Germany's strength with the necessity of a corresponding architecture. Cf,. 80ff with further excerpts from the speech.
38. BA NS 11/28, 92.
39. Ibid., 105.
40. Ibid., 112. –Underlining in the text, obviously Hitler's emphasis.
41. Since Hitler generally used the term "world domination" at this point, then the identity of the two terms must be considered. "World power" therefore does not necessarily mean the second stage in his plan, but probably means "world domination." Cf. note 43.
42. BA NS 11/28, 114.
43. BA Slg. Schumacher, doc. 365, doc 13.
44. BA NS 11/28, 115.
45. Ibid., 119.
46. Term according to G.W.F. Hallgarten, „*Hitler verwirklicht seinen Grundplan. Zur Psychologie und Soziologie der nationalsozialistischen Expansion*, „*Blätter für deutsche und internationale Politik* 10 (1965), 515–522, 690–699.
47. Compare Kuhn, 72ff.
48. N. Schausberger discusses the significance of Austria for Germany's warfare: „*Die Bedeutung Österreichs für die deutsche Rüstung während des Zweiten Weltkrieges.*" MGM 1/72, 57–84.
49. Compare: *Offiziere im Bild von Dokumenten aus drei Jahrhunderten*, ed., H. Meier-Welcker (Stuttgart, 1964), 104.
50. BA NS 11/28, 47ff.

51. Ibid., 52f.
52. Speech from January 25, 1939 –ibid., 63ff, 82. Jacobsen/Jochmann name the partici-pants as those from the speech on January 18, 1939. Obviously they mix two dates up.
53. BA NS 11/28, 120ff.
54. Ibid., 121. Compare the agreement with corresponding remarks in *Mein Kampf*, 234, 439.
55. BA NS 11/28, 122.
56. IMT XXXVII, 546ff, 079-L.
57. IMT XXVI, 338 ff., 798-PS; ibid., 523f, 1014-PS.
58. Ibid., 327ff, 798-PS.
59. Quoted from H.-A. Jacobsen, *1939–1945. Der Zweite Weltkrieg in Chronik und Doku-menten* (Darmstadt, 1961), 97.
60. Ibid., 112.
61. Picker, 186 –February 27, 1942.
62. Groscurth, 414.
63. Ibid., 416.
64. Ibid., 417.
65. This does not contain the Führer's meetings as the KTB Halder does.
66. January 24, 1940; May 3, 1940; December 18, 1940.
67. Domarus, 1499.
68. Ibid.
69. Ibid., 1498; cf. Picker, 320 –May 8, 1942.
70. I thank Dr. von Kotze for letting me use the record of this speech.
71. Stehlin, 191. –The general was K.H. Bodenschatz, chief of the ministry for German air transport.
72. BA Slg. Schumacher, vol. 365, 13f; cf. note 43.
73. IfZ Archives MA 731. Kehrl, 395ff, and Speer, 369. This dates the speech on June 26, 1944, instead of June 22, 1944.
74. Speech from December 28, 1944 –H. Heiber, ed., *Hitlers Lagebesprechungen* (Stutt-gart, 1962), 738ff.
75. Ibid., 741.
76. Ibid., 756.
77. Müller, *Heer und Hitler*; Messerschmidt; finally: H.C. Deutsch, *Das Komplott oder Die Entmachtung der Generale. Blomberg-und Fritsch-Krise. Hitlers Weg zum Krieg* (Zurich, 1974).
78. Hillgruber, *Großmachtpolitik*, 37ff. With regard to this: M. Geyer, *Aufrüstung oder Sicherheit. Die Reichswehr in der Krise der Machtpolitik 1924–1936* (Wiesbaden, 1980).
79. Offiziere im Bild von Dokumenten, 101.
80. E.g., Galland, Rudel, Steinhoff.
81. The following information is based for the most part on the two studies carried out by Müller, *Heer und Hitler*, and Beck. See also: A. Hillgruber, „*Generalfeldmarschall Erich von Manstein in der Sicht des kritischen Historikers.*" Geschichte und Militärgeschichte. Wege der Forschung, ed., U. von Gerdorff (Frankfurt am Main, 1974), 349–362. Also see: Claus Donate, „*Deutscher Widerstand gegen den Nationalsozialismus aus der Sicht der Bundeswehr- ein Beitrag zum Problem der „Vergangenheitsbewältigung.*" (Phil. Diss. Freiburg, 1975).
82. BA/MA N 28/3, 6 –May 29, 1938, „Bemerkungen zu den Ausführungen des Führers am 28.5.38. Cf. Müller, *Heer und Hitler*, 309ff; Müller, *Beck*, 523.

83. Müller, *Beck*, 526, 528. With regard to Seeckt's concept of "intelligent warfare," see Hillgruber, *Großmachtpolitik*, 39f.

84. G. Breit, *Das Staats- und Gesellschaftsbild deutscher Generale beider Weltkriege im Spiegel ihrer Memoiren* (Boppard, 1973), 171.

85. Müller, *Heer und Hitler*, 389.

86. Breit, 200.

87. Hillgruber, *Großmachtpolitik*, 41, with a reference to the memorandum from Stülpnagel dated March 6, 1926. Breit refers to the world power based thought of the generals after WWI, 46, 55, 75, and elsewhere.

88. Compare Hildebrand, *Weltreich*, 594ff; G.L. Weinberg, "German Colonial Plans and Policies 1938–1942," *Geschichte und Gegenwartsbewusstsein. FS für H. Rothfels*, ed., W. Besson and F. Baron von Gaertringen (Göttingen, 1963), 464ff.

89. F. Halder: *Kriegstagebuch (KTB). Tägliche Aufzeichnungen des Chefs des Generalstabes des Heeres 1939–1942*, ed., H.-A. Jacobsen, 3 vols. (Stuttgart, 1962–1964), here: I: 363 –June 19, 1940.

90. Ibid., 2: 11 –July 5, 1940.

91. Ibid., 411 –May 14, 1941. –The test was carried out in the deserts of Libya and was continued in Greece from 1943 on. Compare E. Leeb, „Aus der Rüstung des Dritten Reiches. Das Heereswaffenamt 1938–1945." *Wehrtechnische Monatshefte* 4 (Berlin-Frankfurt am Main, 1958), 14.

92. KTB Halder II, 27 –July 19, 1940; 34 –July 22, 1940; 35 –July 25, 1940; 62 –August 12, 1940; 167 –November 5, 1940.

93. Ibid., 354 –April 7, 1941.

94. Ibid.

95. Ibid., 110 –September 23, 1940: "At the moment it is not clear what one [Hitler] wants." –Already at the end of November 1939, Halder rejected the preparation of drafts for operations in the Nordic countries, the Balkans, and the Near East, since there were no clear political aims –KTB Halder I, 132 –November 25, 1939.

96. B.H. Liddell Hart, *Jetzt dürfen sie reden* (Stuttgart-Hamburg, 1950), 91.

97. This is the way that H. Speidel puts it, *Invasion 1944. Ein Beitrag zu Rommels und des Reiches Schicksal* (Tübingen, 1961), 78. –Compare also: E. Rommel, *Krieg ohne Hass* (Heidenheim, 1950), 390ff.

98. KTB Halder III, 38 –July 3, 1941.

99. Koeppen Reports, 56f –October 8, 1941. –Compare Reinhardt, *Wende vor Moskau*, 49ff.

100. Messerschmidt, 324 –MfT 31, August 1940.

101. Ibid., 325 –MfT 95, April 1941.

102. BA/MA N 118/5 –Engel letter from December 31, 1940.

103. *Deutschlands Rüstung im Zweiten Weltkrieg. Hitlers Konferenzen mit Albert Speer 1942–1945*, ed., and with introduction by W.A. Boelcke (Frankfurt am Main, 1969), 85 –March 21–22, 1942, 18; compare Irving, *Hitler*, 341f.

104. H. Guderian, *Erinnerung eines Soldaten* (Heidelberg, 1951), 251; Leeb, 10; Milward, 22, 92.

105. Boelcke, *Rüstung 2. WK*, 68 –March 5–6, 1942; F.M. von Senger and Etterlin, *Die Kampfpanzer von 1916–1966* (Munich, 1966), 85.

106. Boelcke, *Rüstung 2. WK*, 211 –January 3–5, 1943, 9, 258f –May 13–15, 1943, 22–23. Hitler's viewing of the wooden model built by Porsche took place on May 1, 1943.

107. Boelcke, *Rüstung 2. WK*, 211.

108. Ibid., 259.

109. Ibid. 136 –June 23, 1942, 9; Guderian, 253; F. Halder, *Hitler als Feldherr* (Munich, 1949), 17.
110. Boelcke, *Rüstung 2. WK,* 136.
111. *Gesichter eines Diktators. Adolf Hitler,* ed., J. von Lang (Hamburg, 1968). This picture book contains a photo (no. 62), of Hitler viewing the wooden model of a giant tank.

Chapter 14

THE NAVY'S BATTLESHIP BUILDING PLANS AND VISIONS OF WORLD POWER

In contrast to the corps of army officers, where the old Prussian military nobility, even after 1918, still played a leading role, the majority of the navy had always remained bourgeois.[1] The navy also recruited from all over Germany, so the ranks were more nationally oriented than simply Prussian. However, under the reign of Kaiser Wilhelm II, the navy, as well as other social groups, underwent a process of feudalization which caused the most substantial differences between the naval officers and those in the army to disappear.[2] In spite of this process, the navy still had certain peculiar characteristics. The acquisition of colonies at the same time as the fleet was rapidly expanding led to increased activity throughout the oceans of the world, which in turn broadened the horizon of many a naval officer who in many cases, was promoted to a leading position. In contrast, the army's tasks remained concentrated within the region of central Europe.

Typically, and for that reason, the heavy blows to their self image after the navy revolt of 1918–1919 and the loss of the modern ships in Scapa Flow, as well as the conditions imposed by the treaty of Versailles, didn't last long. Already in the summer of 1920, navy memorandums[3] showed that the Tirpitz tradition in the fleet had continued long after the end of Kaiser Wilhelm's reign. According to the teachings of the great master Tirpitz, the fleet, temporarily out of action, would be an important factor in gaining a position of power and would thus be seen as capable of forming an alliance against Great Britain. Only with Britain's support could an overseas position of global power become feasible. Well before 1933, conclusions were drawn in the leading circles of the navy regarding the opportunities the Kaiser's fleet had missed. Those navy officer circles supported the building up of a war fleet with harbors in the Atlantic that would prevent being cut off in the "wet triangle" of the North Sea.[4] Due to these expectations. the initial position for the leadership of the navy only seemed more favorable toward National Socialism than the one of the army, although there were no competitive party organizations for the navy comparable to the SA for the army, and the small number of coastal locations allowed for a strict control.[5] The broad range of goals therefore set up January 30, 1933, as a "smooth transition" for the navy,[6] a process which additionally found its symbolic embodiment of continuity in the person of Admiral Raeder, who had headed the navy leadership since 1928.

The starting point in global politics shared by he navy officers and the National Socialist politicians, which had been noticed already in 1928–1929 in a contemporary analysis,[7] resulted in close cooperation between Hitler and navy leaders shortly after the seizure of power. Although Hitler's plan for rearmament was one-sided, he did have a plan.[8] By 1934, Hitler had become actively involved in current armament plans,[9] and he increased his interests and his influence in the two years that followed.[10] He began to realize his concepts of ship construction from the 1920s in matters relating to the size of artillery caliber, the speed of construction, and the work of lock gates.[11] In view of the double-track strategy that had been developed in recent years and that was also used in colonial policies, which had both short and medium term goals, the 1935 Naval Agreement with Great Britain most certainly did not sacrifice anything. On the contrary, it had an aggressive, offensive tone. It would be sufficient during the phase of conquering the continent, and it could also be used when necessary to put pressure on Great Britain to accept the new reality, or to be used as a foundation on which to continue expanding a fleet worthy of a world power.[12]

Even more important was Hitler's influence since the beginning of 1937, which clearly corresponded to his decisions relating to architecture. His change in approach, already evident in his speeches, already took into account everything from the continent all the way to global power politics, and finally influenced the planning of the fleet during the May crisis of 1938.[13] Blueprints were drawn up for ships with 53cm guns, a weight of 100,000 tons, a length of 335m, and a width of 50m. Considering the depths of European waters, they could only be given the title of "monuments at sea." Navy leadership probably carried out Hitler's wishes so as not to endanger their position in the competition with the other branches of the armed forces.[14] In fact, Raeder had a sort of a "right of precedence" with Hitler, including the right to speak to him at any time, which wasn't even endangered by the *Blomberg-Fritsch crisis* and which actually put the navy in a special position at that time. A so-called Plan Z[15] which was signed by Hitler on January 27, 1939, called for the construction of an 800-ship fleet by 1948,[16] a date which was later brought forward to 1944 on Hitler's desire. After a temporary halt to construction when war broke out, work was resumed on Plan Z in July 1940, as well as for all the large building projects in Germany then. During the summer of 1942, Hitler kept informed about the progress of the work and discarded the plans from the navy construction authorities.[17] In attempting to conform meticulously with Hitler's ideas, a section of the navy issued an official paper in 1942 about the "building up of the fleet after the war" and left open whether a type of battleship would be built "corresponding to the Führer's ideas" or whether their own concept was to be followed.[18] Plans for the "huge battleships" also continued (H 42 – H 44)[19] until all construction on all warships, cruisers, and aircraft carriers was halted with Hitler's consent at the beginning of February, 1943.[20]

Trondheim had been chosen by the navy to be the biggest German naval harbor of the future.[21] In addition, all German harbors on the North Sea and the Baltic were to be enlarged. At the suggestion of Admirals Dönitz[22] and Raeder,[23] the Trondheim project quickly advanced to become one of Hitler's preferred plans, and it was displayed in the model hall in Berlin.[24] Todt was given the task of surveying the route for a highway from Klagenfurt to Trondheim with bridges over the Great Belt and the straits at Helsingborg.[25] Speer was to rebuild the city completely in a terraced formation according to Hitler's idea that each house should get sunlight.[26] The Trondheim naval base was planned to accommodate 300,000 people and would, according to Hitler's words, make Singapore look like a "toy town."[27] In addition to an enormous port with five harbor basins[28] for the super warships of the Plan Z fleet,[29] everything from the garrison detention center to the naval bakery was planned in detail by the general naval department, after the usual conflicts about authority between the navy, the air force, and groups associated with Terboven, the NSDAP commissioner in Norway.[30] Although Trondheim had been chosen by the naval leadership as a naval base from which to attack Great Britain, the navy was working on still more extensive colonial plans long before war broke out.

Already in 1938, the navy began to organize raid combat units for the future colonies[31] and was chosen by the OKW to be in charge of the preparation for the occupation of the former German colonies in Africa.[32] But already at the time of the Polish campaign, the navy leadership had given up the idea of confining itself to this area. In a letter to Raeder dated September 17, 1939, a high-ranking retired navy officer introduced a program for German naval bases,[33] based on the demand for one hundred percent equality with Great Britain, a program that included handing over the following bases to German control: the Orkneys, the channel islands of Guernsey and Jersey, Whale Bay and its hinterland, Zanzibar and Pemba, St. Helena, and Ascension, as well as the Seychelles. Only a few weeks after his pessimistic forecast at the outbreak of war when he said that one could "only go down fighting bravely,"[34] Raeder obviously approved of this annexation program and encouraged its author to continue working on the details. In October 1939, the aspirations of the navy reached even higher when the former German possessions in the South Pacific were the main focus of a memorandum from the Marinekommandoamt (navy command office).[35]

The navy's image of future German colonies in 1940 also went far beyond what the Foreign Office[36] and interested industrial circles[37] were planning at the same time. It must be reiterated that Great Britain had not yet been defeated when the navy was already dividing up the "spoils."[38]

In a discussion about "expansion and naval base issues"[39] in June 1940, the navy cast its eyes over a colonial empire of central Africa from Senegal to the Congo and to East Africa. The new empire was to be secured by a network of Atlantic bases that would stretch from Norway to Iceland, which would entail the complete suppression of North, Central, and West European countries to Germany. The colonial empire in Africa also included, in addition to chains of bases in the Atlantic and Indian Oceans, a broad territory in front of the main battle-line made up of the groups of islands off the continental coast.[40]

This went beyond simple plans. During an inspection regarding the scarce commodity of aluminum at the end of June 1941, by mere chance a navy program for the construction of barracks in the tropics was found in an airplane factory. The production had already started.[41] A critical observer summarized the condition of the navy at the end of 1940 with the following words: "My impression of the navy officer corps, especially in the upper and middle ranks, doesn't delight me. There is a lack of leadership and good spirit. Now the gallantry of the uneducated *miles gloriosus* is being mixed together with a lack of civic courage and moral values."[42]

If Germany's position against America was already clear in the plans made during the summer of 1940, mainly through the system of bases that had been extended so far into the western hemisphere that they encompassed the islands of Cape Verde and the Azores, then the two world maps, which were probably used for reports on the navy military situations, vividly demonstrate how much the plans of the navy had changed within a short period of a few months.

On the 1939 map[43]—which like the second map, also bore Raeder's signature, revealing his knowledge of it—there were broad areas of the globe that remained white and were therefore located outside of the field of operations. Among these were the Pacific and its adjacent areas of land, the interior of Europe, the entire North and East, including the Soviet Union, and Spain. According to this situation report, the area of activity of the navy was limited. The navy would attack escort ships in the Atlantic and, in the Mediterranean around Malta and Sicily, as well as engage in piracy in the South Atlantic and the Indian Ocean.

In the second scenario,[44] probably set up for the end of Plan Z in the middle of the 1940s, Germany was identified as the leading European power, with Spain, France, Norway, Sweden, and Finland as satellites. Holland, Belgium, and northern France up to the Pas de Calais had been annexed to the Reich. On the African continent, only South Africa and parts of the Portuguese colonies were not among the areas already under German and Italian control. Naval bases from Trondheim to Brest and to Freetown in Sierra Leone, as well as a series of other important harbors on the western and eastern coasts of Africa, were all under German and Italian joint control. In the East, after its victory over the Soviet Union, Germany pushed its sphere of influence forward from the polar sea along the Urals and in the South, in cooperation with Italy, into the Caucasus and the area that had formerly belonged to Turkey. Great Britain was encircled, as Iceland also belonged to the new European block. With the help of the system of naval bases in the Atlantic, the Germans were able to take the war to the coast of North and South America. The only remaining opponents for the navy in the fight for world supremacy were now North America and Japan, both of whom could have potentially relied on North and South America, the Philippines, Australia, India, and South Africa. With that, the fate of the rest of the world was pretty much sealed, even if the map still generously allowed the opposition some possibilities for maneuvering on the Atlantic coast of Europe and Africa.

In a study of "operations for a future trade war in the Atlantic,"[45] which was completed probably at the end of 1942, one of the heads of the navy appointed committee for naval warfare once again considered the important maritime role of Great Britain, although this consideration still happened in the context of megalomaniacal assumptions. For an eventual war between a Germany-controlled Europe against Great Britain and the United States at the end of the 1940s, a fleet of 3.3 million tons, including 300,000 tons of reserves, was planned. The "fleet as it was on paper" included twenty battleships, fifteen carriers for attack, sixteen aircraft carriers, one hundred cruisers, and five hundred submarines. To enlighten the actual war situation, one must point out that the navy ended war operations with overseas units in the Atlantic in February 1942 and therefore gave up the idea of a global war that also would have included America.[46]

Long after the disillusionment caused by the actual war situation had become pervasive in the army, euphoric plans still prevailed among the naval leadership, prompting Halder, after a meeting with Hitler at which the chief of staff of the navy, Admiral Fricke, and Captain Assmann were present, to write in his diary: "The image that the navy has of the situation of the war is far removed from our realistic view of things. Those people are dreaming of continents. Based on previous experience with the army, they are taking for granted that it is absolutely only a matter of our good will as to when or whether we cross the Caucasus by land and arrive at the Persian Gulf or when we go from Cyrenaica across Egypt and break through to the Suez Canal. There is talk of land operations across Italian controlled Africa towards the East coast of Africa and South Africa. The problems that we are experiencing in the Atlantic are being treated with arrogance, and our problems in the Black Sea are been dealt with in a criminally nonchalant manner."[47]

At the end of 1939, it had already become apparent to an outsider within the ranks of the naval officers where things were heading after the Hitler-Stalin pact and the Polish campaign. In a memorandum dated December 1939, Lieutenant Commander Franz Liedig wrote: "Adolf Hitler, the corrupter of Germany and also the destroyer of Europe, sees and follows with the dynamics of a born anarchist the path of apparently least resistance to the goal of world supremacy without any ideas, a purposeless, violent and raiding right of disposal to seize land and raw materials using the most brutal means. A revolutionary dynamic of destruction of all historical connections and all cultural ties that previously defined the honor and good name of Europe are the real and only secret of his political prowess."[48]

Notes

1. To the following, compare H. Rothfels, *Die deutsche Opposition gegen Hitler* (Frankfurt am Main-Hamburg, 1969), 70f.
2. In addition: H. H. Herwig, „*Zur Soziologie des kaiserlichen Seeoffizierkorps vor 1914,*" *Marine und Marinepolitik im kaiserlichen Deutschland 1871–1914*, ed., H. Schottelius and W. Deist (Düsseldorf, 1972), 73–88.

3. Dülffer, 36f; Dülffer, „*Determinanten der deutschen Marine-Entwicklung in der Zwischen-kriegzeit (1920–1939),*" MR 72 (1975), 8–19. –The following explanations are based for the most part on his results.

4. Dülffer, 182ff.

5. Messerschmidt, 9.

6. According to Dülffer, 199.

7. Ibid., 194, 220.

8. Ibid., 204ff, as well as this volume, 35.

9. Dülffer, 283.

10. Ibid., 313ff.

11. E. Raeder, *Mein Leben,* vol. 2 (Tübingen, 1957), 67. –See also Dülffer, 383.

12. Dülffer, 350f.

13. Ibid., 470.

14. Ibid., 385f.

15. Ibid., 498ff. See also M. Salewski, *Die deutsche Seekriegsleitung 1935–1945,* vol. 1 (Frankfurt am Main, 1970), 58ff; Hildebrand, *Weltreich,* 598; C.A. Gemzell, *Raeder, Hitler und Skandinavien. Der Kampf für einen maritimen Operationsplan* (Lund, 1965), 72ff. –An interpretation of Plan Z in the framework of Hitler's final goals will be made in the following chapter.

16. IMT XXXV, 584ff, 855-D.

17. BA/MA Case GE 282 PG 228 –reference from June 2, 1942, Gkdos 13337/42.

18. BA/MA Raeder Collection 13 Skl. Qu. AI Sf Gkdos 6255/42.

19. Ibid.

20. Wagner, *Lagevorträge,* 466 –February 2, 1943.

21. Gemzell, 217ff.

22. IMT XXXIV, 159ff, 005-C.

23. IMT XXXV, 628ff, 879-D.

24. BA R 120/7, 17. –Cf. A. Hillgruber, ed., *Staatsmänner und Diplomaten bei Hitler* (Frankfurt am Main, 1967), 1: 239 –October 4, 1940 (meeting with Duce).

25. Weizsäcker-Papiere, 201 –entry from May 1, 1940; Kehrl, 186; H.-D. Loock, *Quisling, Rosenberg and Terboven* (Stuttgart, 1970), 457.

26. Koeppen Reports, 20 –entry from September 19, 1941. –Speer's *Erinnerungen* makes no mention of this.

27. Seraphim, *Tagebuch Alfred Rosenbergs,* 110 –entry from April 30, 1940.

28. BA R 120/7, 6 –plan for the construction of a harbor basin by OKM headquarters for warship construction, harbor construction section from February 28, 1942.

29. Wagner, Lagevorträge, 108 –entry from July 11, 1940.

30. BA R 120/7, 41; BA/MA Sammlung Raeder 13, letter from the headquarters for warship construction from August 2, 1941 KVT Gkdos 1572/41.

31. Hildebrand, *Weltreich,* 596, 612; Weinberg, "*Colonial plans,*" 468.

32. Hildebrand, *Weltreich,* 601.

33. BA/MA Case GE 536 PG 34 399.

34. Quoted from Hillgruber, *Strategie,* 37 note 46.

35. Hildebrand, *Weltreich,* 634.

36. ADAP D IX, no. 354, 390ff. Written records of Claudius from May 30, 1940; no. 367, 407ff. Written records of Ritter from June 1, 1940. Cf. Hillgruber, *Strategie,* 244; Hildebrand, *Weltreich,* 645f. ADAP D XI, 1, no. 16, 18f. Etzdorf records from September 4, 1940. Cf. Hildebrand, *Weltreich,* 674f. no. 298, 409ff. Bielfeld records from November 6, 1940. Cf. Hildebrand, *Weltreich,* 695f.

37. Compare Hildebrand, *Weltreich*, 646 note 17, with further information: Martin, *Friedensinitiativen*, 266ff; D. Eichholtz, *Geschichte der deutschen Kriegswirtschaft 1939–1945. Volume I: 1939–1941* (Berlin, 1971), 155, 162ff; *Anatomie des Krieges. Neue Dokumente über die Rolle des deutschen Monopolkapitals bei der Vorbereitung und Durchführung des zweiten Weltkrieges*, ed., and introduced by D. Eichholtz and W. Schumann (Berlin, 1969).

38. Seemingly exaggerated in its emphasis, the assumption that Hitler received food for thought from the navy appears in M. Salewski's *Denkschriften und Lagebetrachtungen 1938–1944* (Frankfurt am Main, 1973), 3: 20. As an explanation, Salewski provides a statement allegedly made by Hitler in which he said that the lectures by the ObdM were very important to him, as they would allow him to see if "he was on the right track." This statement without proof is actually on file: BA/MA Case 536 PG 32 624a, 20. It refers, however, only to the "Lagevortrag" on the situation from September 26, 1940.

39. BA/MA Case 562 PG 33 932.

40. Compare Salewski, *Denkschriften*, 105ff; Salewski, *Seekriegsleitung*, 1: 234ff; Hillgruber, *Strategie*, 245f; Hildebrand, *Weltreich*, 646f. Furthermore: Salewski, *Denkschriften*, 121ff, doc 5 –"*Gedanken der Seekriegsleitung zum Aufbau der Flotte nach dem Krieg.*" –According to these documents, the post-war fleet was to comprise 1,200 ships, including 25 large warships, 8 aircraft carriers, 100 cruisers and 400 submarines. –Cf. ibid, 135.

41. Irving, *Luftwaffe*, 192.

42. Hassell, 153 –entry from November 23, 1940.

43. The map can be found on file: BA/MA Case 282 PG 32 228.

44. The map can be found in the attachment to doc. 5A, Salewski, *Denkschriften*, 399ff, from July 4, 1940, with a different interpretation of the map.

45. BA/MA K 10-2/21.

46. With project "Cerberus" and the embarking of the warships "*Gneisenau*," "*Scharnhorst*," and "*Prinz Eugen*" from Brest and their breaking through the canal on February 12–13, 1942.

47. KTB Halder III, 455 –entry from June 12, 1942.

48. BA/MA N 104/2 doc. 56 –also in Groscurth, 509ff. Compare also ibid., 72 and Müller, *Heer und Hitler*, 554f. –Liedig, a friend of Oster and Groscurth, was among the early members of the resistance to Hitler. The conservative politician Ewald von Kleist-Schmenzin already harbored similar fears concerning the extent of Hitler's expansion plans in 1938. –Fest, *Hitler*, 769.

Chapter 15

THE ME 261/264
Hitler's Long Range Bomber

The Americans held an interrogation of the generals and admirals Göring, Dönitz, Keitel, Jodl, Warlimont and Major Büchs, aid to Jodl, at the beginning of July 1945,[1] where those questioned unanimously denied having any knowledge during the war of any plans to attack the United States of North America or the Panama Canal. While Göring and Keitel denied the existence of the long-range airplanes that would have been necessary, Dönitz admitted that there was talk about this within the Lutfwaffe.[2] But he too denied the actual existence of such aircraft types or any specific plans. Jodl admitted that long distance deployments had been discussed and remembered a discussion between Hitler and Göring on this matter, a discussion which Warlimont verified as far as Hitler was concerned. During the war, Hitler had told him about the development of a bomber that could reach the United States.[3] Just like Jodl, he couldn't remember a particular type of airplane. Büchs[4] was the only one to mention the Messerschmitt Me 264, which according to him had the necessary range. The mass production of this plane failed due to a lack of materials.

In contrast to the statements by Büchs, the results of research into the role of the Luftwaffe in the Second World War largely verifies the statements of the military who were questioned in 1945: there was no German bomber with a long enough range to reach the United States.[5] As far as one can even find information about the Me 264 and its predecessor the

Me 261 in any technical "literature"—which is blinded by its fascination for technology and which often has absolutely no sense of the political problems implicit in the armaments industry—then this information is inexact or even completely false in its abbreviated form.[6] But even the big history of WWII of the *Militärgeschichtliches Forschungsamt der Bundeswehr* (MGFA) keeps to the judgment: no bomber intended for use against America. The defeat in the war was too complete. The two planes often become placed in the category of "wonder weapons" that appeared towards the end of the war, even though they had nothing to do with the long-range bomber project that existed shortly before the war ended. It is precisely because of a lack of source materials regarding the Luftwaffe[7] that up to this point no one has taken the opportunity to reconstruct the relationship that existed between the political, military, and industrial levels regarding such a limited object. The theory that Göring ordered the long-range bomber project to be halted in 1938 is still the accepted view today.[8]

Even before the "takeover of power," Hitler and Lufthansa representative Milch, who was later to become secretary of state and chief inspector of the Luftwaffe, agreed to build up a large fleet of bombers, [9] a decision that was completely in keeping with the prevailing theory of air warfare. According to the doctrine of the Italian general Douhet,[10] a fleet of bombers with a high level of deterrence should replace the fighters. This fleet of bombers was meant to be mainly an attack weapon. At the same time, the armed forces on land and at sea would execute defensive operations.[11]

Already in 1933, measures instigated by Milch and Wever, the first chief of the general staff of the Luftwaffe, led to the outline of specifications for long-range bombers. By 1936, the Ju 89 and the Do 19 were ready to fly.[12]

The decision to halt the long-range bomber program that seemed to be so promising for the future came about after Wever's death in 1936, as his successor, General Kesselring, together with Generals Milch and Udet, was successful in fighting another group inside the Luftwaffe. Göring sanctioned the decision with a corresponding order on April 29, 1937.[13] Three years later, the fiasco of the Battle of Britain took place when there were not enough medium-range bombers.

One or two months before war broke out, the German aviation ministry announced a program for the "B" bomber.[14] This led to the prototypes Do 317, Ar 340, Fw 191, and Ju 288, which were built from 1942 onwards, came too late for the decisive phase of the war, as did the prototypes from an announced competition for the construction of long-range surveillance planes in 1940. These were meant to reach an operational height of a minimum of 14,000 meters. Here the Do 217P, Hs 130 and above all the

He 274, which was to be very important for aviation in France after the war,[15] must be mentioned.

If the name Messerschmitt is missing in this list of aircraft types and programs, it was because the previously mentioned order by Göring of April, 1937 did not completely stop the development of long-range bombers. On the contrary, already in 1938 Göring was backing the development of long-range planes, which casts doubt as to whether the decision from April 1937 had been imposed on him.[16] In a speech to members of the aviation industry in Karinhall[17] on July 8, 1938, he demanded of those present that, in addition to a series of strategically meaningful weapons, they should concentrate on the development of a long range bomber "that flies to New York and back with a 5 ton cargo of bombs. I would be very happy with a bomber of this kind," Göring continued, "to finally shut the arrogant faces of those people over there."[18] As if to underline his coarse statements, he then asked those present not to consider his words as just a figure of speech, but really to work toward putting his words into action.[19] Factually, the order of 1937 to stop construction—if it ever existed—was therefore cancelled.

Göring's request was superfluous, for at least one airplane manufacturer: Willy Messerschmitt. In November, 1937, Hitler visited his company, accompanied by Göring, Milch, and Udet, as well as other high-ranking officers of the Luftwaffe.[20] The reason for the visit was the presentation of the Me 109. But Messerschmitt had a surprise up his sleeve. After the presentation of the fighter plane, he took Hitler to the side and said, "My Führer, I have something else that I would like to show you."[21] He took him to a hall where a model of a four-engine bomber had been built.[22] Neither Göring nor Milch nor other representatives of the air ministry had been informed about Messerschmitt's project and were indeed very surprised. The technical department of the air ministry, Udet's department, had not issued a contract for its development. The model was therefore not part of the Luftwaffe LC-plane development program until October 1937.[23] Clearly Messerschmitt had had taken it upon himself to develop this plane without a contract from the air ministry. As one of the people present on that day suspected, he wished to influence the construction plans of the Luftwaffe.[24] This snub of the high-ranking officials of the Luftwaffe was a risk he could take because Hitler admired him as a genius among the German airplane manufacturers and allowed him "poetic license."[25] The parallels to the Hitler-Speer relationship are clear.

The decisive point resulting from the November visit to Augsburg was that Hitler came out of the presentation with the impression that the Luftwaffe was obviously one step ahead in the development of four-engine bombers.[26] His Luftwaffe adjutant of many years believes that Hitler's conviction played an important role in later decisions regarding the armaments of the Luftwaffe. To what extent Hitler had been informed about Messerschmitt's project before his visit remains unclear. The possibility of Messerschmitt's cooperation, or even of Hitler's having given Messerschmitt a direct order, becomes clear from the following points:

The development of the Me 261/264 is closely connected to an old project of Messerschmitt to build an "Antipode plane."[27] As early as 1932, his M 34 project was shown as a model in an air show. The plans became current, though, only after the Summer Olympics in 1936. There was a rumor at the Messerschmitt Company that a courier plane was being planned for the 1940 Olympics in Tokyo. This plane was supposed to ferry the press around as had been done in the 1936 Olympics, only this time not for the relatively short distance between Berlin and Sweden that had been achieved by the Me 108 "Typhoon," but for the distance between Berlin and Tokyo. In 1937, Hitler ordered a plane from Messerschmitt that would enable him to fly nonstop to East Asia. The offer came from Messerschmitt,[28] and it is not clear when the contact with Hitler took place. Neither is it clear whether Udet and Hess, who were always coming and going at Messerschmitt, were involved as middlemen.[29] This issue was certainly a topic of discussion during Hitler's visit to the Bavarian airplane manufacturer (the firm was known as Messerschmitt AG from 1938 on) in Augsburg in 1937.

Not until the beginning of 1938 did the air ministry give Messerschmitt its initial decision that he should develop and build some prototypes. At the same time, the Luftwaffe made the task more precise.[30] The development and production plans required the completion of the first prototype at the beginning of 1939, with the first test flight planned for the same year. They should be finished in enough time for necessary changes and additions to be made to the second prototype. Both airplanes were expected to be ready on time for deployment by the middle of 1940, with the V1 intended as an actual courier plane and the V2 as a "Führer airplane" with which Hitler apparently planned to deliver the Olympic fire to Japan.[31]

It is certainly difficult to suppose that Hitler had a concept or a strategy before 1939 based on these initial signs of influence, or that he had a special interest in matters regarding planes covering long distances. It cannot be disregarded, however, that along with the propaganda effect of a non-stop flight to Tokyo, he would also have considered the military implications, and that he therefore saw the 1940 Olympics as a timely opportunity to put corresponding plans into place. Demands made directly on the technical department of the Luftwaffe would have awoken suspicions, since officially the enemy was still Great Britain. It was possible, however, even at this point in time at the end of 1937, and beginning of 1938, that an arrangement existed that authorized Göring to request, around the middle of 1938, that the airplane industry build a bomber that would be able to reach the US.[32]

Soon after the outbreak of war, proof can be made that a military exploitation of planes was being considered—considerations that clearly reached beyond the European theater of war with its much less demanding requirements for the flight range of planes. A building plan for the long-distance plane Me 261 from August 1940 indicated a range of 11,000 km at an average speed of 400 km/hr, and emphasized that in addition to use in civilian aviation, the plane was also suitable for military use.[33] Due to the outbreak of the war, the first flight was delayed, and took place on December 23, 1940. By the end of 1942, a trial program for the deployment of the two completed planes was carried out, one as a transport plane and the other as a long range surveillance plane.[34]

The Me 264, an Me 261 with four engines,[35] had been developed secretly since the end of 1937. Messerschmitt increased his commitment substantially in 1938 when he created a separate department for its development, but he didn't receive orders to develop the plane until 1940.[36] The contract was for a "four-engine plane for long-range flights with a capacity of 2 tons for disruptive flights to the US."[37] There were to be six versions of this plane, which would reach a maximum speed of 610 km/h:[38]

a) long-range bomber with DB 603 H[39] with fifty tons of weight at take-off, a bomb capacity of 1–8.4 tons, and a range of 15,600 km
b) long-range bomber with Jumo 213 (see above), with a range of 16,300 km
c) Heavy duty bomber with DB 603 H, a bomb capacity of 8–14 tons, and a range of 11,500km
d) Heavy duty bomber Jumo 213 (see above), with a range of 11,900 km
e) long-range surveillance, patrol, and courier plane, with Jumo 213 and a duration of flight up to sixty hours, as well as a range of 20,800 km [40]
f) long-range transport plane

The report of December 1941 states clearly that "the planes, even before the completion of all the tests, are ready to be deployed in special cases."[41] The first flight of the Me 264 took place in December 1942. Two further prototypes were never completed, and the works production that was planned to be done at the "Weserflug" could no longer take place because of the *Reichsverteidigungsprogramm* (German defense program)[42]

The Me 264 had about seventy test flights.[43] Because of the low production costs incurred, this plane was regarded as highly suitable for mass production.[44] On top of that, the plane had "absolutely first class" flying characteristics, as the test pilot stated after the war.[45]

While Hitler was still at the height of his expectations for the outcome of the war, he announced by mid-November 1940 that with this plane he would "attack America" from the Azores "should they join the war, and force them to develop their non-existent air defenses, rather than helping the British with theirs."[46] This idea was clearly on his mind in the months that followed. In April 1941, he informed the Japanese Minister for Foreign Affairs Matsuoka of his intention to wage an "energetic war" against the US with submarines and the Luftwaffe.[47] At the end of May 1941, Hitler again mentioned the importance of occupying the Canary Islands and the Azores in order to "be able to deploy long-range bombers against the US, which would be considered in the autumn."[48] He was speculating on a successful early completion of Operation "Barbarossa" so that he could then use a defensive strategy to keep America from getting involved in the European theater of war.[49]

It became quickly apparent that Hitler had fallen victim to the promises made by Göring and Messerschmitt. After the loss of the 'Battle of Britain', there were no long-range bombers ready to deliver the promised devastating air attack on Moscow on the day the Russian offensive began.[50] Hitler's intention to wage terror attacks on capital cities and city centers in order to deal great, decisive blows that would lead to a quick capitulation and fewer casualties on the German side is one of the peculiarities of his war strategies. Warsaw, Rotterdam, and Belgrade had suffered this fate, which had also been planned for the hugely populated cities of America's East Coast.[51] Hitler also took into account psychological effects. He obviously remembered the effect of the famous radio report from Orson Welles about the Martian invasion, which had spread fear over New York City in August 1938. However, Messerschmitt could not keep his thoughtless promise to Hitler[52] that he could actually have an Me 264 to "carry several tons of bombs to the American Midwest."[53] In love with clever designs, Messerschmitt quickly lost interest in any single development.[54] Despite all his expertise, a high employee turnover, too many plans, the skipping of crucial developmental phases, and the unsatisfactory use of capabilities[55] prevented the realization of the long-range bomber Me 264. Had the plane gone into production in 1940–1941, there can be no doubt that it would have been a very disruptive factor to the American war effort. Only a few planes would have sufficed to wage a terror attack on Washington D.C. and New York, as had been discussed in

Luftwaffe circles[56] in the summer of 1942, and this would have perfectly suited Hitler's notion of psychological warfare.[57]

When Hitler admitted to Japanese ambassador Oshima at the beginning of 1942 that he "did not yet know how to beat the United States,"[58] plans for an air war against the US were already fully underway at the Luftwaffe headquarters.[59] Since the Me 264 was not yet available and the US could not be reached on a non-stop flight with conventional planes,[60] the generals had to resort to other alternatives, such as refueling at sea. Dönitz gave his full support to the Luftwaffe plans.[61] At this time, the plans of the Luftwaffe were very similar to the global plans of the navy. The Luftwaffe, which had already failed to achieve victory in Great Britain, set targets that reached as far as the Great Lakes. The generals dreamed of flights to the Panama Canal, Lagos and Thailand only a few weeks after the British air force started its massive bombing offensive on German cities.

Even in the years that followed, the Me 264 project was still kept going. In March 1943, Göring complained at a meeting with airplane manufacturers that the Me 264 could not be built because of technical problems.[62] In the autumn of 1943, after a desperate plea from Göring for a bomber to attack the US, Messerschmitt offered him the Phantom plane.[63] A few weeks earlier, Hitler had complained that the Luftwaffe had not yet taken the Messerschmitt plane "on board," and that the generals refused to support its manufacture.[64]

Contrary to Göring, Hitler had already given up the idea of bombing the US by the beginning of July 1943, as the few planes that would get through could only result in rallying the population to the cause of resistance. Instead, he saw an important task in the Atlantic for the Me 264 as a surveillance plane in cooperation with submarines.[65] Even in August 1944, Hitler gave great importance to "rapid completion of the Me 264"[66] and demanded that just a few planes be quickly manufactured as a temporary alternative to having nothing. And indeed, Messerschmitt had made a last effort in July 1944 to start production in Augsburg.[67] But at the end of September 1944, the project had to be abandoned once and for all.[68]

Despite the fact that many details of the story of the Me 261/264 are not yet known, the long-range bomber project is an indication that the Luftwaffe, had completely overestimated its capabilities both before and during the war, and not only with regard to the European theater. It is certain that the core plan of Hitler's "program," the war against Russia for *Lebensraum*, had been known to the Luftwaffe leadership since the beginning of 1935.[69] Wever's long-range bomber plans had therefore existed also since 1935, and went under the code word of "Ural-Bomber."

The fact that Hitler appears to have been misled in the matter of the Me 264 is due to his inadequate sources and methods of acquiring information regarding aviation issues. Well into the war, he dealt with all problems that came up by consulting only with Göring, whom he trusted completely.[70] General Jodl and his staff were excluded from the command of the air war and didn't have any background information about the demise of the Luftwaffe.[71] In the case of the Me 264, the relations between Hitler and the military were complicated by Messerschmitt, who had the special right to see Hitler at any time[72] and who was able to play out his own personal interests against his "rival" Göring. Göring, in contrast to Wever, was no Douhetist, and had been skeptical of the long-range bomber project since the early thirties.[73] This conflict of many years between the air ministry and Messerschmitt can explain why Messerschmitt's plane didn't receive priority over the He 177, even though the He 177 was full of defects.[74]

Even the supposed contradiction between the decisions reached by Hitler and Göring is easily cleared up by examining Messerschmitt's role in the confusion. Göring quickly accepted Messerschmitt's suggestions whenever Messerschmitt complained to Hitler or when he took things into his own hands and created practical obstacles, as he did in the case of Me 264, so that he could return to his own concepts when the political situation had changed. Hitler was in no way the instigator in this situation, rather more the uneasy umpire that constantly wavered between his Luftwaffe commander and his much admired aircraft designer, to whom, as a technician, the military aspect remained of secondary importance in his designs. However, Hitler's important contribution to the development of the Me 261/264 cannot be ignored, as it allows conclusions to be drawn about his later intentions. When the Luftwaffe and the long-range bombers suddenly acquired significant importance as part of Hitler's overall war plans in 1940–1941, this weapon, contrary to his expectations and Göring's promises, was not ready for war.[75]

More specialized investigations will discover the reasons behind the Luftwaffe's attempt to swing the war into a global strategy, especially after they had already failed against the British air force, never mind their inability to defend the German territory against hostile attacks. As the youngest branch of the armed forces, the Luftwaffe had undergone a breathtaking development up to the outbreak of war.

Was the Luftwaffe following other motives that resulted from pragmatic constraints in 1942—and probably since 1939[76] when it planned large-scale attacks on America's industrial potential—or were the foundations already present for an outlook toward great power and world supremacy, as had been the case in the navy? Another explanation could be a form of departmental egoism, which led to the air force wanting to demonstrate to Hitler that successful warfare against the United States was possible, in the wake of the navy's announcent that it was unable to seize the Canary Islands and the Azores.

It is possible that the Luftwaffe's concept of controlling or occupying vast areas and strategically important positions with fleets of long-range planes had more of a future than the concept of building up a vulnerable fleet of ships that were already technically out of date the moment they were completed..

In the strategic planning of the Luftwaffe, one can also see the universal stamp of Hitler's ideas, even without Hitler openly appearing as the instigator. The overestimation of its own ability and its unrealistic evaluation of the situation in the war made it impossible for the Luftwaffe either to make its own plans or to distance itself from Hitler's expansionist program.

In the summer of 1938, Göring, in his speech to the young officers corps, certainly the most loyal branch of the armed forces, had not only presented the United States as the enemy, but had also taken the opportunity to hint at the consequences, "if we were to win the fight. Then Germany becomes the biggest world power; then all the global markets belong to Germany; then it comes the hour when Germany is rich. One must, however, take risks, one must show his commitment."[77]

Notes

1. IfZ Archives –US Army Interrogations ZS/A 21, doc. 170–172.
2. Dönitz still denied this during his lifetime. Interview with Dönitz from May 22, 1974; BA/MA N 236/7 and 8 –written correspondence between Dönitz and Professor Morison.
3. Warlimont claimed in a letter to the author that corresponding plans could have only come from the Luftwaffe. Written information from December 29, 1973.
4. Major Herbert Büchs was Jodl's adjutant during the war.
5. Qualifying A. Galland, who named other planes as replacements in a letter to the author from November 27, 1973, just like W. Baumbach, *Zu Spät? Aufstieg und Untergang der deutschen Luftwaffe* (Munich, 1949). Baumbach, commodore and colonel of the fighter pilots, wrote that he himself would have made suggestions to Göring for attacking the Panama Canal and New York. Cf. this volume, 163f –passages are to a great extent also applicable to the creation of the Me 264.
6. G.W. Feuchter, *Der Luftkrieg* (Frankfurt am Main–Bonn, 1964) 237f; R. Lusar, *Die deutschen Waffen und Geheimwaffen des 2. Weltkrieges und ihre Weiterentwicklung* (Munich, 1964), 104, 109; B. Lange, *Das Buch der Deutschen Luftfahrttechnik*, 2 vols. (Mainz, 1970), 366, 340f; F. Hahn, *Deutsche Geheimwaffen 1939–1945. Flugzeugbewaffnungen* (Heidenheim, 1963), 404.

7. In addition: F.C. Stahl, „Die Bestände des Bundesarchivs-Militärarchivs." MGM 2/68, 139–144.

8. Irving, Luftwaffe, 102; T. Osterkamp and F. Bachér, Tragödie der Luftwaffe? Kritische Begegnung mit dem gleichnamigen Werk von Irving/Milch (Neckargemünd, 1971), 68ff; Fraenkel and Manvell, Göring, 213; K. -H. Völker, Die deutsche Luftwaffe 1933–1939 (Stuttgart, 1967), 30, 75, 133ff, 209; C. Bekker, Angriffshöhe 4000 (Oldenburg-Hamburg, 1964), 289f.

9. Cf. this volume, 35.

10. G. Douhet, Il dominio dell'aria (1921); German version: Die Luftherrschaft (1935).

11. Typically, Raeder was against building a fleet of bombers, since he feared an early reaction from Great Britain. –Osterkamp and Bachér, 31.

12. Bekker, 164f.

13. Ibid., 289f; Baumbach, 26.

14. Information from: K. Kens and H.J. Nowarra, Die deutschen Flugzeuge 1933–1945 (Munich, 1961), 217ff.

15. In addition to this, albeit with some reservation: A. Marchand, "Le Heinkel 274. Il devait bombarder New York." L'Album du Fanatique de l'Aviation 49 (1973), 20–24.

16. Compare Osterkamp and Bachér, 68ff, which acknowledges Milch's shady behavior in this situation.

17. The text of the speech in: IMT XXXVIII, 375ff, 140 R.

18. Ibid., 397.

19. Ibid.

20. The following report comes from a statement by Hitler's Luftwaffe adjutant, Group Captain Nicolaus von Below –IfZ Archives ZS 7. The visit to Messerschmitt took place on November 23, 1937. Compare Domarus, 760, and VB, November 23, 1937.

21. Quote taken from Below's report, cf. Irving, Hitler, 192.

22. It's not quite clear which airplane is meant. Von Below presumes it was the Me 264.

23. Written information from H.J. Ebert, Messerschmitt-Bölkow-Blohm Company, dated February 25, 1974.

24. IfZ archives ZS 7.

25. R. Suchenwirth, Ernst Udet, 57f –Archiv Führungsakademie der Bundeswehr; Milch-Documents, 158.

26. IfZ archives ZS 7.

27. For the following information I thank Mr. Ebert, who helped me to reconstruct the history of the development of the Me 261 ("Adolfine"). It was written by an employee of Messerschmitt and verified through questioning of other employees.

28. Information from Mr. Ebert.

29. Suchenwirth, Udet, 57f.

30. Messerschmitt-Chronik Me 261 (H. Kaiser).

31. This can be concluded from the material on hand –Messerschmitt-Chronik. Information from Dipl. Ing. D. H. Schwencke, from January 1, 1975; Information from Mr. Nicolaus von Below from December 2, 1974, who denies this intention.

32. L. Gruchmann, „Völkerrecht und Moral. Ein Beitrag zur Problematik der amerikanischen Neutralitätspolitik 1939–1941." VfZG 8 (1960), 397. Gruchmann refers to Göring's speech somewhat hastily as "impulsive comments."

33. I thank Mr. Ebert for the document from the archives of Messerschmitt-Bölkow-Blohm MBB GmbH in Munich.

34. H.J. Ebert, ed., Messerschmitt-Bölkow-Blohm. 111 MBB-Flugzeuge 1913–1973 (Stuttgart, 1973), 156.

35. Information from Mr. Ebert; Ebert, MBB, 180.

36. Irving, *Luftwaffe*, 219; Baumbach, 157.

37. Information from Mr. Ebert. Quoted from *"Gesamt-Ablauf des Baumusters Me 264,"* from the central planning office of Messerschmitt.

38. The following information comes from the files for the Me 264 in the PRO London AIR 40/203 IIG/132/7/127. The binder Me 264 from December 1941, 33 pages, ed., Messerschmitt AG in Augsburg, Geheime Kommandosache.

39. The abbreviations DB 603 H and Jumo 213 represent airplane motors from Daimler-Benz and Junkers.

40. PRO London Air 40/203 IIG/7/127. –The distance from Brest to New York is only about 5,500 km!

41. Ibid.

42. Ebert, 180; Kens and Nowarra, 462f.

43. Information from the test pilot Baur –PRO London AIR 40/203.

44. Information from Messerschmitt, PRO London AIR 40/203.

45. Information from test pilot Baur: "An absolutely first class aircraft,"—ibid. The British secret service was well-informed about the development of the Me 264 and recognized the aim of the task (operation against the United States) very early on. –PRO London AIR 40.

46. Wagner, *Lagevorträge*, 154 –entry from November 14, 1940. Compare also the *Kriegstagebuch des Oberkommandos der Wehrmacht (Wehrmachtführungsstab)*—ed., P.E. Schramm in co-operation with A. Hillgruber, W. Hubatsch, and H.-A. Jacobsen, 4 vols. (Frankfurt am Main 1961–1965), 1: 177 –entry from November 15, 1940 –Hillgruber, *Strategie*, 324; IMT XXV, 391ff, 376 –PS.

47. IMT XXIX, 70ff, 1881 –PS –meeting from April 4, 1941.

48. Wagner, *Lagevorträge*, 229 –entry from May 22, 1941.

49. With regard to the war against the United States, cf. this volume, 160ff.

50. Hitler complained about this in a situation report meeting at the beginning of 1943, when the long-range bombardment of the Soviet Union was once again being discussed. –*Lagebesprechungen*, 141 –Mittagslage from February 1, 1943. With regard to the first air attacks on Moscow from July 22, 1941, see Bekker, 283.

51. Compare Speer, *Spandauer Tagebücher*, 126f.

52. Suchenwirth's characterization, *Udet*, 57f, IfZ archives ZS 7.

53. Irving, *Luftwaffe*, 318.

54. Suchenwirth, 57f.

55. The criticism from Milch. –Milch Documents, 158. –The catastrophic mismanagement in German air industry describes: Milward, 123f; Baumbach, 65ff.

56. Irving, *Luftwaffe*, 235.

57. The documents of the PRO in London also have indications that the Me 264 was going to be used in "a leaflet campaign against the United States."

58. Staatsmänner, 2: 41 –January 3, 1942.

59. Baumbach, 157; BA/MA III L 313. In addition: O. Groehler, „*Globalstrategie der Luftwaffe. A Document from the Files of the German Air Force Ministry from 1942,*" *Militärgeschichte* 11 (1972), 445–459; B. Martin, *Deutschland und Japan im Zweiten Weltkrieg* (Göttingen, 1969), 118 note 61.

60. Details in Irving, *Luftwaffe*, 225f, 235.

61. Ibid.

62. Milward, 124.

63. Irving, *Luftwaffe*, 318.

64. Boelcke, *Rüstung 2. WK*, 295 –September 11–12, 1943. –According to the statements of a prisoner-of-war, three prototypes of the Me 264 were being built in Sep-

tember 1943. This was to be the next plane to go into mass production. –PRO London AIR 49/203.

65. Wagner, *Lagevorträge*, 518 –entry from July 8, 1943.
66. Boelcke, *Rüstung 2. WK*, 399 –August 5, 1944, 1.
67. PRO London AIR 40/203; Baumbach, 159.
68. Boelcke, *Rüstung 2. WK*, 410 –September 21–23, 1944, 1a.
69. This reference is found in the memoirs of H.J. Rieckhoff, *Trumpf oder Bluff? 12 Jahre deutsche Luftwaffe* (Geneva, 1945), 142f. The date of publication makes the memoirs of the Luftwaffe general an important historical source.
70. R. Suchenwirth, *Göring als Oberbefehlshaber der deutschen Luftwaffe*, 43 –Archiv Führungsakademie der Bunderwehr. In general, with regard to this: P. Diehl-Thiele, *Partei und Staat im Dritten Reich* (Munich, 1969).
71. W. Warlimont, *Im Hauptquartier der deutschen Wehrmacht 1939–1945* (Frankfurt am Main, 1962), 433.
72. Suchenwirth, *Udet*, 57f.
73. G. Bidlingmaier: „*Die Grundfragen für die Zusammenarbeit Luftwaffe/Kriegsmarine und ihre Erprobung in den ersten Kriegsmonaten,*“ *Vorträge der 7. Historisch-Taktischen Tagung der Flotte* (Darmstadt, 1964), 74.
74. Kens and Nowarra, 292ff, BA Slg. Schumacher vol. 315, page 17ff –Göring's meeting with representatives of the air industry on September 13, 1942 in RLM.
75. Compare Hillgruber, *Strategie*, 270ff, 380f.
76. Baumbach, 157.
77. IMT XXXVIII, 383.

Chapter 16

SUMMARY

Since 1937–1938, Hitler had revealed his global expansion program as a framework for future wars to the supreme commanders of the three German armed forces. The indication that the population of the United States was smaller compared to that of Germany and that the Third Reich's military potential was greater indicates how, starting at that time, North America became part of his consideration as a future enemy that would required the development of battleship construction and long-range planes. Even if the limited perceptions of the generals toward Hitler's "message" must be accepted, notes made by general Oster, by younger officers such as Groscurth and Liedig, and by other critical listeners present at Hitler's speeches show that it was possible to infer what his long-term plans were. The officer corps of the army felt a particularly strong influence, because within this framework, they were the first line of Hitler's multi-stage plan, before the Luftwaffe and navy became available for further plans.

If the armament program and the colonial plans of the three armed forces are compared with Hitler's overall "program," it can be seen that even before the outbreak of war in 1939, the army, navy, and air force had been ruled out as factors of control for Hitler, as the generals and admirals had only reached Hitler's world supremacy stage in their thinking, meaning a continental empire with colonial African annexes. Their concepts, however, had nothing to do with wars of extermination based on racist ideologies, nor with the idea of a ruling racial elite. The naval plans that were the first to come to light, at least chronologically speaking, were at the same time those carried out most thoroughly. After 1940, these plans can be described as absolutely extreme in the intensity of their demands and incomprehensible in their political blindness. Typically, it was the navy that adhered to this world of dreams the longest. The army, originally assuming a much longer struggle to reach a position of world power that had not yet even been put into concrete terms, was in 1940 far behind the navy in formulating its operations. The army came to terms with the reality of the situation much earlier and was the only sector of the armed forces, apart from some exceptions, that was involved in measures to kill Hitler. As far as the Luftwaffe is concerned, the scarcity of source material—the archives were destroyed to a great extent—still allows for the statement that it, at least from 1942 on, the same course as the navy, and shared the latter's extravagant plans. It is difficult to discern to what extent any political objectives existed. The Supreme Commander's early turning against the United States leads to the suspicion that as a specialized and technical unit *par excellence*, the air force did not understand the political aspects of its job and as Hitler wished, was ready for deployment to any theatre of war.

Hitler's interventions in the armament plans, as shown in several examples, were usually intended to set records, of size and distance. As with architecture, he saw weapons as having a symbolic psychological effect on the masses. For that reason, right up to the end of the war he could still believe in the success of individual "miracle weapons." The Me 264 in a certain way belonged to that faith. To the luck of the US, the world, and ultimately Germany, it didn't attack New York City during the days of Pearl Harbor, as Hitler had hoped it would. Otherwise, the first atomic bomb might have fallen upon a German city.

Part IV

HITLER IN 1940–1941
When Visions Become Reality

Chapter 17

AXIOMATIC GEOPOLITICS:
1950 As the Objective

Besides searching for new types of sources for investigating Hitler's ultimate goals, it is necessary once again to systematically examine the traditional sources. In describing these, H.R. Trevor-Roper has used the image
of a few windows that allow us to view Hitler's true goals.[1] Thanks to the
intensive analysis of Hitler's "program" during the last decades, one can
reflect on the period from 1920 to 1939 and compare it with a panoramic
view, conveyed by an unbroken chain of evidence, indicating Hitler's ultimate political goals.

In addition, it seems meaningful to examine the concrete realization of
Hitler's plans against the backdrop of the mere eighteen months between
the armistice with France on June 22, 1940, and the failure of the "Blitzkrieg" in the Soviet Union at the end of November and the beginning of
December, 1941, coinciding with the entry of the United States into the
war. At no other time was Hitler closer to achieving his goals and expectations than during this period. Therefore, a scrutiny of those months, in
addition to the examination of the previous results of this study, would
serve not only as a reinforcement, but would add to the density of the
available evidence, and thus allow for a more solid interpretation.

It is first necessary to summarize several of the most important results
of this study on the months preceding what Hitler saw as an imminent
victory that should be included in our reflections.

Hitler's statements about world domination by the Aryans, led by the dominant German core race—this exponential *"ceterum censeo"* of the years 1920–1945—offers an initial impression of his ideas about Lebensraum. They could be referred to as a vulgar form of geopolitical theories with an additional doctrinal feature. The parallels to Karl Haushofer[2] and above all to Halford Mackinder's "Heartland" theory cannot be ignored. It was Mackinder who stood for the view that modern means of transportation and information exchange had transformed the continents into islands. The "world islands" of Europe, Asia, and Africa alone covered two twelfths of the Earth's surface, while what was left of the land masses accounted for only one twelfth; the rest was ocean. Mackinder thus concluded that control of the "world islands" by a continental power could certainly mean the opportunity for a world supremacy from which the naval powers were excluded. "Whoever rules Eastern Europe commands the Heartland. Who rules the Heartland commands the World-Island. Who rules the World-Island commands the world."[3]

A confirmation that Hitler was thinking in this direction is offered by the evidence presented in the previous chapters. Even in 1943, Goebbels reproduced Hitler's fundamental assumption in an essentially classical manner when he made the following entry in his diary: "The Führer expresses his unerring certainty that the Reich will one day rule over all of Europe. We will still have to fight many battles, but they will doubtlessly lead to the most fantastic successes. From that point on the path to world supremacy is practically drawn. Whoever rules Europe will grab the leadership of the rest of the world."[4]

From the few comments that Hitler made about ruling the world,[5] it can be concluded that he imagined the future world as being made up of a series of Aryan core race, with Europe as their center of power and inspiration. Inevitably, just by the "law of numbers"—Germany would present the strongest group numerically—the role of leader would have to go to Europe. Therefore, Hitler planned to build an adequately strong seat of government and power in Berlin, later to be named Germania.[6] He imagined Aryan global rule in the form of a colonial regime that would spread throughout the second half of the twentieth century, similar to British rule in India.[7] The mix of archaic elements he used in his plan must be kept in mind. "The distorted reality of the socially estranged intellectual"[8] which Hitler's ideas here reveal can hardly be exemplified more clearly. Only the subjugated inferior races were still to be productive in Hitler's "New World," while the new ruling race would take care of the distribution of products.[9]

An ephemeral building and armaments boom, which would begin to decrease by 1950, would once again summon all the energy of the Western capitalist system combined with all the slave labor from the East, before one could—thanks to the resources acquired in the East—begin to overcome the system and revert to an agrarian utopia and the biological myth. Economy, for Hitler, was reduced to the question of feeding the people.[10] With a cynicism that could have hardly been outdone, Heinrich Himmler, in a speech to the officers corps of the dictator's body-guards, the SS-Leibstandarte "Adolf Hitler," summarized an aspect of that future development in September 1940 as follows: in times of peace, the "Untermensch" (slave) would be needed once again to break and burn stones for the Führer's buildings. The resulting earnings and profit for the noble race would increase the quality of life and the breeding of good blood, for "if it doesn't multiply, we will not be able to rule the world."[11] In a letter to Mussolini in 1941 Hitler wrote that the last 1500 years had been nothing but an interruption. History was about to "return back on track."[12]

With this obvious evidence of Hitler's vision of an Aryan global supremacy with its predominance in the European center, the opportunity can be taken to examine the thesis of "living space in the East" in order further to speculate about Hitler's ultimate goals. Concentrating on 1940–1941, one can already formulate the theory that Hitler's ultimate political goals were a mixture of his "program" and of "pseudo-regularity law." Up until the European stage, namely the conquest of the Western areas of the Soviet Union, Hitler had planned a deliberate series of closely limited operations of conquest. After reaching the continental phase, there was no fixed order which these conquests would occur, as they would, for the most part run automatically to the new European seat of power. Hitler's comments made solely about Europe when speaking of his ultimate goals do not, then, present a contradiction, rather—according to the theory outlined in this study—they only refer to the first part of his doctrine, which was in short: whoever controls Europe, will conquer the world. The expansion into the East was clearly the absolute priority, but it also provided the basis for all the further steps that could not be realized without that foundation. In the moment following the conquest of Soviet Russia, there would be an automatic reorientation of the world toward Europe.

For this study, several of Hitler's "far-off dates" are materially important, since they placed Hitler's visions at least partly in the near future. Among these there were:

1. Hitler's statement at the Hossbach meeting that by 1943–1945 at the latest the continental conquest phase should be completed
2. the build-up of a huge fleet of ships by 1944 (Plan Z)

3. the creation of a bomber fleet with a core of long-range bombers that could attack the United States by 1941–1942
4. the construction of victory monuments to begin in 1946 and to be completed at the same time as the representative buildings in 1950
5. Hitler's planned move from the New Chancellery, which had just been completed in 1939, into a gigantic governmental palace in 1950
6. victory parades and a world exhibition in Berlin, also planned for 1950[13]
7. after 1940, the successor games of the Olympics to be held in Nuremberg for all time: the "*Racial Spartakiade*" of the new mankind.

Additonal observations that must also be recorded:

1. The leadership of the navy prepared themselves for a war with the United States and Japan, which would take place in the 1940s.
2. The leadership of the air force also prepared itself for the possible event of a transatlantic war with the United States.

This allows us to draw the following conclusions, even before the discussion of Hitler's ultimate plans in 1940–1941:

1. Hitler planned as far ahead as 1950 in more concrete terms than was previously known.
2. The plans for the production of arms were geared particularly for a date in 1944–1945, a point that coincided with the projected conclusion of the expansion to the East and the resulting establishment of the new balance of power in Europe.

From these statements, the question arises: did Hitler still view Great Britain as strong opponent, after he had been pointing out to his officers since 1937–1938 the supposed numerical inferiority of the opponent United States and that the Luftwaffe was to be the first of the armed forces after 1941–1942 to be equipped for global battles? This issue should be dealt with in connection with the short list of the enemies that would remain after a victory over the Soviet Union. Hitler's path to his goal of world supremacy will be analyzed through three case studies. After that, several aspects of the techniques of control and domination that Hitler intended to use for the large territory he was seeking will be discussed. Observations on the assessment of Hitler's ultimate goals regarding his most important opponent in the first two years of the war, Great Britain, will close these considerations.

Notes

1. Trevor-Roper, *Hitlers Kriegsziele*, 121f.
2. In addition: U. Laack-Michel, *Albrecht Haushofer und der Nationalsozialismus* (Stuttgart, 1974); E.K. Bird, *Hess. Der "Stellvertreter des Führers"* (Munich-Vienna-Basel, 1974), 41ff, 251. –Hess made a statement at the Nuremberg trials to the effect that Hitler just took the theories of Haushofer on board without really understanding them, and that he had simply changed them to fit his own purposes. Compare further: G. Bakker, *Duitse Geopolitiek 1919–1945* (Assen, 1967), K. Lange, „*Der Terminus "Lebensraum" in Hitlers Mein Kampf*," *VfZG* 13 (1965), 426–437.
3. H.J. Mackinder, *Democratic Ideals and Reality* (New York, 1942), 65, 150, –quoted from L. Gruchmann, *Nationalsozialistische Großraumordung. Die Konstruktion einer „deutschen Monroe-Doktrin"* (Stuttgart, 1962), 51; furthermore: P.M. Kennedy, *"Mahan versus Mackinder. Two Interpretations of British Sea Power,"* MGM 16 (1974), 39–66.
4. *Goebbels Tagebücher. From 1942–1943. With other documents* ed., L.P. Lochner (Zurich, 1948), 327, –entry from May 8, 1943.
5. Compare with the quoted documents in the preceding 16 chapters.
6. Picker, 398, –June 8, 1942.
7. Koeppen Reports, 15f, September 18, 1941. –In addition: J. H. Voigt, „*Hitler und Indien*," *VfZG* 19 (1971), 49.
8. Fest, 527.
9. Compare Hitler's corresponding comments to Strasser, *Mein Kampf*, 64.
10. Weinberg, *Foreign Policy of Germany*, 349; Bracher, Sauer and Schulz, 746.
11. IMT XXIX 1918 –PS, 108.
12. Quoted from Fest, 148.
13. Speer, *Spandauer Tagebücher*, 233f.

Chapter 18

THE REMAINING POWERS AFTER VICTORY OVER THE SOVIET UNION

An assessment of Hitler's ultimate goals during the years 1940–1941[1] can hardly be considered speculation. All of Hitler's comments and all his decisions were based on the axiom that a war with the Soviet Union would be child's play and that with a "Blitzkrieg" it could be won quickly.[2] In France, the German infantry divisions had covered distances up to ninety kilometers within twenty-four hours. With a victory over the Soviet Union, the central idea of his "program" would be achieved. All other plans for military operations were based on the fulfillment of this goal by early autumn 1941.

The important observation that Hitler had withdrawn from politics since the outbreak of war in 1939 and never actually returned to it,[3] makes it appear difficult to rationalize and justify Hitler's decisions, especially in 1941. Rather, an extremely doctrinal position and a static-fatalistic view on the part of the Führer can be supposed, which might explain the sudden changes of direction which appear more as reflexes than as resulting, from political calculation. Not just from 1939 onwards, but already from the beginning of his leadership in 1933, Hitler's political stance was more strongly limited by eschatological premises than the first six years of his involvement in foreign affairs seem to reveal. This is not to deny the fact that during the war, Hitler continued to be active in politics, both in internal and external affairs. Especially in warfare, right down to the tactical level or even the politics of armament, he showed rational behavior for a long time until, in this area too, with the progressive worsening of the situation and the approaching fronts of the enemies, he became in-flexible. Only in long-term plans is he seen as willing to take a step back, although these, with lessening intensity until 1945, continued to appear from time to time in form of eruptions, revealing how Hitler intellectu-ally held on to them once they had been formed. For this reason, the most important question in this area relates to Hitler's stereotypical views and judgments regarding his long-term analysis of the war, and less the chang-ing decisions he made based on the changing situation.

Before Hitler's ideas can be inspected in detail, it is necessary to ex-amine the powers that, according to Hitler's calculations, would have re-mained after a victory over the Soviet Union, namely Great Britain, the United States, and Japan.

It isn't necessary to follow Hitler's relationship with Great Britain dur-ing 1940–1941 in a long series of stages.[4] Despite his temporary tactical changes and comments about the ideal partner for an alliance, it seems clear that Hitler never deviated from his positive view of Great Britain with respect to its "racial quality."[5] However, he did occasionally fear that the United Kingdom would swing around to form a coalition with the United States, and therefore enlarge the military conflict. But on the other hand he hoped—with the timely conclusion of Operation "Bar-barossa" in the fall of 1941—to quickly win Great Britain over as an ally and junior partner.

When the attempt to make contact with Great Britain "for the pur-pose of dividing the world" failed at the end of May 1940,[6] it led to Hit-ler's decision to eliminate the Soviet Union without securing the front in the West. He described some of the many consequences that would result from this toward the end of July 1940: "If (the British) expectations on Russia are no longer relevant, then we can also forget about America, because a Russian defeat automatically means an immensely strength-ened position for Japan in East Asia. If Russia is destroyed, then Britain's last hope is wiped out. With that, the dominant power in Europe and the Balkans will be Germany."[7] Since the months that followed brought no change in Britain's position, Hitler placed his expectation that the United Kingdom would join the continental block temporarily on the back burner and demanded a consolidation of Europe during the year of the Russian campaign in order to "look forward to a war against Great Britain (and America.)"[8]

As the date for the attack on Russia came closer, Hitler was becom-ing more optimistic about the resolution of Anglo-German relations. At the end of May 1941, he told his old confidant Hewel that victory over the Soviet Union would create a situation that would "even force Britain to make peace."[9] Two days before the beginning of the invasion of the USSR, he told Hewel, that he believed Britain had to give up. "This year, he hopes."[10] At the beginning of July 1941, in the weeks of the stormy advance, Hitler's trademark wishful thinking surfaced once more: his hope of a miracle, "salvation" by an action that he had forecast, whereby Churchill would be ousted by an opposing faction. "Then an incredibly strong wave of anti-Americanism would arise and Britain would be the first country in the European struggle to stand up against America."[11]

Indeed, Hitler didn't dismiss the idea of a short war against the island kingdom in principle. But he remained convinced that the pro-German sentiment of the British people would quickly realign Great Britain in favor of Germany. "I believe that the end of the war will mark the beginning of a lasting friendship with Britain," he forecast during those weeks. "At first we have to knock Britain out. Only in this way can we live together in peace. The English only respect the opponent that makes them powerless to fight."[12] These utterances clearly show Hitler's attitude towards Great Britain: not fierce enmity, but "fair play" among equals that must end with a "handshake" after the stronger of the two has won. Hitler's cliché image of education and the value of "public schools" as well as the indestructible gentleman stereotype, were driving his ideas. Hitler often made a comment at this time that should also be understood this way, that Germany and Great Britain would learn to appreciate each other in the "present duel" so much "that later they would be able to proceed together against the United States."[13] In September 1941 he once again expressed his warm feelings towards his opponent: "A German-British alliance would be an alliance of one nation to another. The British would only need to keep their hands off the continent. They could keep their empire and the world!"[14] He often brooded at this time that he wouldn't be around to see it, Germany and Great Britain one day step up against America as a united front.[15] The almost unbelievably rapid swings alternating from optimism to pessimism with regard to the timing of the common elimination of the United States appeared in a comment at the end of October 1941, when he said: "If the British are clever, they will seize the psychological moment, switch sides, and march with us."[16] According to Hitler, if Great Britain gave up, America would be out of the game for thirty years.[17]

By this statement he indicated that he might indeed still carry out the decisive conflict with the United States during his lifetime.[18] He also took the opportunity to outline which tasks Great Britain would fulfill over the short term, besides providing its racial value. During the consolidation phase in Europe, Great Britain would have to take on the role of a future Aryan leadership overseas. With the defeat of the United Kingdom, the enemy would gain positions that would sooner or later force Hitler into unnecessary wars. The Soviet Union would annex India, Japan would swallow up East Asia, and the United States would get a foothold in Canada and Africa.[19] He already had made similar comments in June and July of 1940 when he spoke out against the destruction of the British Empire.[20] Hitler's underlying principle not to harm his future ally, and therefore not to harm himself overseas, explains his hesitation at instigating subversive measures in the Near and Middle East, even though preparations for this had already begun in the summer of 1939.[21] Hitler was highly irritated at the development of the war once the United States had taken part: "Strange that we, with the help of Japan, are destroying the positions of the white race in East Asia and that Britain with the Bolshevik pigs is fighting against Europe."[22] He reacted to the news a few weeks later that Singapore had fallen to the Japanese with more depression than his comments to Antonescu implied.[23]

Basically, Hitler's plans were roughly to reset the balance of power in Europe in a solo run,[24] and at the same time to be accepted as a joint owner of the British Empire. After several "years of learning" from the "right ally,"—he admired his "unparalleled cheek ... we still have a lot to learn"[25]—and a silent partnership, the time would then come to take over British capital, shipping, colonial administration, and international contacts.[26] Thanks to Germany's bigger and stronger core race and the rearmament which at that stage would have been completed, Great Britain could be rendered obedient without too much effort. The division of the world was in Hitler's eyes a temporary measure in order to avoid the appearance of a danger zone. Should the British Empire be destroyed, he stated at a reception for a highly decorated fighter plane pilot at the end of September, 1940, "a vacuum would be created that could not be filled."[27]

Hitler was convinced, according to the manner with which he drew his most important conclusions, that the forty million British citizens, as the second largest core of the Aryan race in Europe, represented the absolute prerequisite for dominating the Earth in an alliance with the other Aryans of Europe. As already partially explained in earlier chapters, Hitler derived statistics from historical models and projected these onto a future world order. Therefore, he was impressed with the idea that 6,000 Greek Spartans had ruled over 345,000 Helots,[28] and that Great Britain, kept 300 million Indians under control with 60,000 men.[29] With its total population, which corresponded to one half of the German population, Great Britain could control a quarter of the world with about 500 million people.[30] Many comments made by Hitler indicate that he, by adding the German and British populations, had extrapolated these calculations, and that they matched his important vision of a future world supremacy or world domination.[31]

Since Hitler, apart from labeling things, no longer thought in national, but rather in racial terms,[32] a few comments must be made on his position about acquiring colonies. By the end of 1940, he had already expressed his concern regarding the goals of colonial policy,[33] which partially clashed with his ideas about ruling conquered territory: His view of the world was limited to control and exploitation. In simplified terms, control meant colonial policy. There is, however, an interesting contradiction in these terms. Without pinning himself down to a finite number of demands for colonies in Africa,[34] Hitler was an advocate for colonialism from the first moment, but one who viewed overseas possessions more as a status symbol than an economic one. In the autumn of 1941, he commented that colonies "only had a limited value for him," and because of that "he would come to an agreement with Great Britain on this matter very quickly." Germany just needed some colonial land for the cultivation of coffee and tea, everything else would be produced on the European continent. The Belgian Congo would suffice for Germany's colonial needs. "Our Mississipi must be the Volga, not the Niger."[35]

The stereotypical views in Hitler's assessment of America also deserve a short outline and introduction. Even though Hitler wasn't consistent in his judgment of the racial quality of North America, he did have, starting in 1928, a rather one-sided respect for the United States. As far as he was concerned, America was an extension of Europe whose racial core was made up of sixty million people of predominantly German origin. The great migration towards the west, which had taken place since the days of the pilgrims, was for Hitler, just part of early German imperial history, because the whole Anglo-Saxon world was for him "a branching off of our German race." First came the conquest of England, and then German involvement in the development of the Americas.[36] Hitler did not view the rest of the American population as being worthy of his respect, and generally he omitted it when he was tabulating population numbers in his war statistics.

In the thirties, the "records" set by the New World in the areas of technology and engineering impressed Hitler, for example the building of skyscrapers and bridges, as well as the high numbers reached in the production of automobiles.[37] On the other hand, he concluded from the racing successes of German sport cars—if this statement has any credibility—that German industry had to be superior to that of the United States.[38] Hitler's bias in evaluating data in this area was drastically evident, especially during the first years of the war. For example, he was not prepared to acknowledge the potential of the US arms industry, as in his view, it wouldn't become an important factor until 1942 and would not develop fully until 1946. Furthermore, other impediments and logistical problems would, in his view, prevent the United States from entering the European theater of war.[39] Warnings from the German embassy in Washington were tossed to the four winds, and only positive reports were considered.[40] Upon receiving a memo from a leading figure in the German arms industry dated October 1940, which was delivered to Hitler by Todt, Hitler supposedly commented with the words: "What's written here is all very nice—it might even be true that these gentlemen are right, but I already [have] the victory in my pockets."[41]

He stubbornly stuck to his own version of reality, and in September 1941 he relished in the pictures from an American weekly news show that came to him from South America. It contained photographic material of "one of the two fully motorized divisions of the US army which were simply laughable."[42] Hitler's conclusions about the quality of US weaponry were along the same lines. According to him, the production of large guns, tanks, and ships from 1940 to 1942 was in some areas lower than the corresponding monthly German production.[43] Even in 1943, when the American capacity for arms production had long been common knowledge, he clung to his preferred picture of America, and while passing around photos of poor American farmers stated that this was proof of the internal condition of the United States.[44]

This impression, however, didn't keep Hitler from keeping a nervous eye on his opponent across the Atlantic.[45] Already in the late summer of 1940, after the failure of the "Battle of Britain," he concerned himself with the occupation of islands in the Atlantic and of strategic points along the north and west coasts of Africa. At the beginning of September 1940, he demanded that the Luftwaffe occupy the Canary Islands.[46] He later extended this to Cape Verde, the Azores, Dakar, and Casablanca.[47] Hitler apparently had a double objective in securing a foothold on the Atlantic coasts in the winter of 1940–1941, one that would allow for a defensive strategy against the United States in the summer of 1941, during the decisive weeks of the Russian campaign, a strategy that could be carried out with long-range bombers flying sorties against the cities and industrial centers that were producing arms on America's East Coast. On the other hand, this would prevent the Americans from getting a foothold on the periphery of Hitler's future great empire and would give Hitler an offensive position from which he could launch a possibly necessary conflict with the United States after the consolidation of Europe. But the ideological component cannot be ignored either: in Hitler's view, the American financial world was pressing for war against Germany. For that reason alone, he hoped for a timely supply of long-range bombers to use in terror attacks against the huge American cities in order to teach the Jews living there a "lesson."[48] Incidentally, he regarded the United

States as a power whose interests would also include inheriting the British Empire.[49] He therefore saw a natural antagonism between the two naval powers, one that one day would have to end in the destruction of one of the adversaries.[50]

Fixated on the person of Roosevelt—someone "whose soul you could not see into,"[51] as he complained in the weeks before the beginning of Operation "Barbarossa"—Hitler was constantly calculating America's chances against him. He was perfectly clear about the risk his actions entailed: "Should we fail, it's all over anyway."[52] With the "all or nothing" motto on his mind, he resisted the prompting of the navy to engage in an early war with the United States. Even with the US-occupation of Iceland, he didn't allow himself to be provoked. He did, however, announce that he would punish the Americans with appropriate measures as soon as possible, even if this meant years of war.[53]

The question of Hitler's relationship to Japan[54] certainly culminated in a conversation with General Oshima on July 14, 1941.[55] On that occasion, Hitler offered the Japanese ambassador a comprehensive alliance for the purpose of jointly destroying the Soviet Union, the United States, and Great Britain.[56] However, the United Kingdom, which was regarded here as a component of the other naval power, on other occasions in the same month of July had received a completely different assessment by Hitler.[57] Therefore, the isolated instance of Oshima may be viewed as somewhat problematic for the moment in terms of its value as proof of Hitler's ultimate goals.[58]

There are arguments indicating that Hitler's offer to the Japanese was simply bait, similar to the offer he made to Soviet foreign minister Molotov in 1940, to jointly enrich themselves from the "massive world bankruptcy" of the British Empire.[59] Hitler aimed at persuading the Japanese into rash activity in East Asia to demonstrate to Great Britain how necessary and inevitable it would be for her to change sides "in its own interest." At the same time, he was also aiming to keep the Americans out of Europe. An overly nervous "Führer," who already had powerlessly stood by and watched as Iceland was occupied, gave up any reservations he had with the Japanese. He was lacking the military means to hit the Americans in their own hemisphere. To disguise the situation, he took refuge in a completely exaggerated account of what was happening in the East: in six weeks at the latest, he maintained, it would be all over.[60] Hitler's offer of an alliance to Japan was therefore more a gambler's last stake than a calculated decision.

More difficult than the attempt to follow Hitler's probably policies toward the United States after a victory over Russia, is the fundamental question of his assessment of Japan. Since Japan would probably be the last opponent he would face before ultimate world dominance, Hitler's comments on this subject are rarely to be found. In any case, his animosity towards the "yellow race" is revealed in a decision of his after the fall of Singapore. He is reported to have rejected an announcement by Foreign Minister von Ribbentrop for the press and radio about the Japanese victory with the words: "I don't know, Ribbentrop, whether this is good. One must think in terms of centuries. Sooner or later the conflict between the white and the yellow race will break out."[61]

Hitler's comments already mentioned elsewhere regarding the undesirable alliance with Japan underline the theory that Hitler's offer to the Japanese to work together to eliminate Great Britain was certainly not intended seriously. On another occasion, he also referred to the fact that it would be necessary to fight against the Japanese should there be an uncontrolled collapse of the British Empire.[62]

Even the wartime alliance with Japan held back on solving current problems in favor of racial considerations.[63] The German-Japanese war alliance never reached a level of real cooperation.

Notes

1. The chapter relies for the most part on the results of Hillgruber's studies; *Hitlers Strategie*; *„Faktor America"*; *England in Hitlers außenpolitischer Konzeption*; Hildebrand, *Weltreich*; *Deutsche Außenpolitik*; Martin, *Friedensinitiativen*.
2. Hitler, when speaking to the Bulgarian ambassador, Draganoff, on December 3, 1940, referred to the Russian army as a "joke." –Hillgruber, *Staatsmänner*, 1: 385; similar statement to Keitel on June 28, 1940, Speer, 188: a campaign against Russia would be "child's play."
3. This is one of the most important theories of Fest, 526 ff, 836 ff.
4. While Henke's analysis still is to be agreed upon for the pre-war period, it should be employed for Hillgruber, *England in Hitlers außenpolitischer Konzeption*, especially with regard to 1941. Compare also A. V. N. van Woerden, "Hitler Faces England: Theories, Images and Policies," *Acta Historiae Neerlandica* (1968), 141–159.
5. In addition: Irving, *Hitler*, 127, 135, 145, 154 (!), 246.
6. KTB Halder I, 308, –May 21, 1940; Hillgruber, *Strategie*, 144ff; Martin, *Friedensinitiativen*, 243f.
7. KTB Halder II, 49, –July 31, 1940.
8. Ibid. 244, –January 16, 1941.
9. Hewel Diary, –May 29, 1941.
10. Ibid., June 20, 1941.
11. Ibid., July 10 or 11, 1941; Hillgruber, *Strategie*, 147 note 11.
12. *Libres propos*, 13, –July 22–23, 1941.
13. Weizsäcker-Papiere, 263, –August 13, 1941, 269, –September 15, 1941.
14. Hewel Diary, –September 8, 1941.

15. Picker, 145, –September 8–9, 1941.
16. *Libres propos*, 92, –October 26–27, 1941.
17. Ibid.
18. Compare Hillgruber, *England*, 80, with a different interpretation. Especially the stages he designated as 6–8 present other possibilities for interpretation based on the sources.
19. *Libres propos*, 92.
20. KTB Halder II, 21, –July 13, 1940; compare also Martin, *Friedensinitiativen*, 252.
21. A satisfactory monograph has yet to be made. The Lahousen Diary is an important source. –BA/MA RW 5/497 and 498.
22. Hewel Diary, –December 16, 1941.
23. Hillgruber, *Staatsmänner*, 2: 48, –February 11, 1942; Hillgruber, *England*, 81.
24. Compare the comment of Hitler to Sven Hedin, –Hillgruber, *Staatsmänner* 1: 395, –December 5, 1940.
25. Picker, 145.
26. Compare: A. Sohn-Rethel, *Ökonomie und Klassenstruktur des deutschen Faschismus* (Frankfurt am Main, 1973), 161.
27. A. Galland, *Die Ersten und die Letzten. Die Jagdflieger im Zweiten Weltkrieg* (Darmstadt, 1953), 104.
28. *Libres propos*, 115, –November 5, 1941.
29. Picker, 239, –April 1, 1942.
30. One of many examples 1939–1941: Hitler's speech from January 30, 1941, in Berlin.– P. Bouhler, ed., *Der großdeutsche Freiheitskampf. Reden Adolf Hitler* 3 vols. (Munich, 1940–1942), 381.
31. Compare Martin, *Friedensinitiativen*, 335f.
32. Compare Hitler's speech from May 3, 1940, –Domarus, 1499.
33. Engel-Tagebuch, 91, –December 11, 1940.
34. Cf. this volume, compare 181.
35. Koeppen Reports, 46, –October 4, 1941.
36. Two representative examples: Hitler's speech from December 18, 1940, –Domarus, 638f; Reichstag speech from December 11, 1941, –ibid., 1797.
37. Hitler made revealing statements at the Tempelhof airport on October 29, 1934, which indicate an observation of conditions in the United States. –BA R 43 II/1181, 62, back side of the page. See also this volume, 87f.
38. Dietrich, 181f.
39. KTB Halder II, 165, –November 4, 1940, 335, –March 30, 1941; Hillgruber, *Staatsmänner*, 1: 506, –March 27, 1941 (Matsuoka).
40. Hillgruber, *Strategie*, 195ff, 374ff, 399f.
41. Information gathering and its analysis for the Luftwaffe administration. A study done by retired Lieutenant-General D.A.L. Nielson in Karlsruhe, –Archiv der Führungsakademie der Bundeswehr, 17: 117.
42. Koeppen Reports, 21, –September 19, 1941.
43. Ibid.
44. Heiber, *Lagevorträge*, 171, –March 5, 1943.
45. Hillgruber, *Strategie*, 195.
46. Wagner, *Lagevorträge*, 137, –September 6, 1940; KTB OKW I, 80, –September 17, 1940.
47. Wagner, 143f, –September 26, 1940, 147, –October 14, 1940, 149f, –November 4, 1940; KTB OKW I, 132, –October 28, 1940, 137, –October 29, 1940; Hillgruber,

Staatsmänner 1: 214, –September 17, 1940 (Serrano Suñer), 235, –October 4, 1940 (Duce); compare also Hillgruber, *Strategie*, 188ff.

48. Engel-Tagebuch, 99, –March 24, 1941.
49. Hillgruber, *Staatsmänner*, 1: 214, –September 17, 1940 (Serrano Suñer), 300f, November 12, 1940 (Molotow), 358, –November 22, 1940 (Antonescu); Picker, 145, September 8–10, 1941.
50. *Libres propos*, 15, –July 25, 1941.
51. Hewel Diary, –May 22, 1941.
52. Ibid., –May 29, 1941, June 8, 1941.
53. Wagner, *Lagevorträge*, 263f, June 21, 1941, July 9, 1941; Hillgruber, *Staatsmänner*, 2: 547, 550 –July 14, 1941 (Oshima).
54. Fundamental: T. Sommer, *Deutschland und Japan zwischen den Mächten 1935–1940* (Tübingen, 1962); B. Martin, *Deutschland und Japan im Zweiten Weltkrieg* (Göttingen, 1969).
55. Hillgruber, *Staatsmänner*, 2: 543ff.
56. Ibid., 549.
57. Compare this volume, 162.
58. Against Hillgruber, „*Faktor Amerika*," 17, and Hildebrand, *Außenpolitik*, 113f.
59. Hillgruber, *Staatsmänner*, 1: 313f, –November 13, 1940.
60. Ibid., 2: 543, 546.
61. Zoller, 157.
62. *Libres propos*, 92, –October 26–27, 1941. See also Martin, *Friedensinitiativen*, 453. During a meeting with Lord Kemsley on July 27, 1939, Hitler mentioned his fears that a war between Germany and Great Britain could so weaken the two opponents that it would mean an excellent starting position for Japan to further the realization of its own ambitions. –W. Lenz and L. Kettenacker, "*Lord Kemsleys Gespräch mit Hitler Ende Juli 1939*" *VfZG* 19 (1971), 319.
63. B. Martin, „*Zur Vorgeschichte des deutsch-japanischen Kriegsbündnisses*," *GWU* 21 (1970), 609f; Martin, *Deutschland und Japan im Zweiten Weltkrieg*, 50ff.

Chapter 19

HITLER'S PATH TO WORLD SUPREMACY

The difficulties that have already been briefly mentioned in trying to precisely understand Hitler's thoughts in 1941, as well as the controversial evaluation of a key source, prevent the forming of a single interpretation of the path to world supremacy, upon which Hitler had already embarked. It is certainly more fitting to his calculating character if one insinuates that he possessed a number of possible solutions to reach his goal, the most suitable of which would be launched at the right moment. The time period 1940–1941, despite the structures worked out by research that is still considered valid, shows at least three variations in Hitler's ideas regarding his ultimate goals. Even though the third model of thought is favored when considering the complete overview, the first two should not be excluded from discussion. All three scenarios are very close in terms of their political consequences, but for the sake of precision and differentiation, a special listing and examination of each seems necessary.

Hitler's ultimate goals in 1940–1941 could be achieved through these three possible scenarios:

1: The military solution, or war with America
2: The trade war—half way between a cold and a hot war
3: The "annexation" of the world, or the psychological war with a surprise solution

The Military Solution

One of the logical consequences of an untrammeled development of National Socialism without the extensive war that happened after 1939 is that a conflict with the western democracies, principally the United States, was unavoidable. National Socialism under Hitler was incapable of pitting itself ideologically against the political, economic and social norms of the states in the rest of the world without threatening or using violence. It could reach its "fulfillment" only through the world's embracing and commiting, to the principles of anti-Semitism, social Darwinism, and racism.

A series of Hitler's relevant public pronouncements during 1939–1941 show that he had intensively dealt with the issue at that time, even after having already called the conflict "unavoidable" in 1937. But at the same time, Hitler had expressed hope to determine the timing of the war with the democracies himself.[2]

Even his New Year's appeal to the party and the German people in 1939–1940 contained Hitler's informative prognosis that "Jewish capitalist society ... would not survive the twentieth century."[3] In a speech given at the end of February 1940 in Munich, he announced that a global development would take place resembling what had already taken place in Germany, but without the participation of democracies. "The creation of a new world will take place without them!"[4] Therefore, Germany's aims had to go far beyond those of the present war, as he emphasized in his speech at the opening of the 'Winterhilfswerk' (winter aid project) on September 4, 1940 in Berlin: a new state must be created to counteract the resistance of the "plutocrats" and "Judaism." "And I am convinced that the world, the future belongs to this global event. I am convinced that countries that do not join this change will sooner or later fall apart. ... And now they know our objectives and they know that we will persistently and rigorously advocate and also reach this goal."[5] The fundamental nature of the conflict that made it necessary for the world to align itself on the "German model" was emphasized by Hitler in a speech at the end of 1940 as he characterized the war with the western powers as the "fight between two worlds."[6]

The appeal for the New Year 1940–1941 contained the direction for the force that would be applied against the "Systemfeind" (enemy of the system): "The democratic war interests that have created world unrest for many decades and have been casting the population into one crisis after the other must be destroyed. It is our irrevocable decision to let this judgment fall so that Europe may once again find peace from within."[7] Along with his defensive justification for his aggressive actions, it is worth mentioning how Hitler thought he could convince the public objectively, of his impartiality as a judge or arbiter in a "fateful" conflict.

All these remarks still convey no concrete statements about the final conflict with the Western democracies, with the United States at their head. Only the previously mentioned meeting with Oshima in the middle of July, 1941 contains an indication of direct military aggressions against the United States in the very near future. A few days later, however, Hitler spoke in a less forceful manner of "serious action even against the United States"[8] after the end of the Eastern campaign. This was a choice of words that was similar to other comments made during those weeks and months when Hitler said that after completion of the operations in the East, the Americans "will get their war if that's what they want."[9] In other words, Hitler was prepared to go to war with America. But the initiative would now come from the other side.[10]

Separate decisions for military measures directed against the United States point more toward sanctions that could have been put in place in the autumn of 1941. Hitler's comments to Oshima, on the other hand, seem to be referring to a special constellation and do not convey any information about his actual plans for the United States. At any rate, the following three possibilities for an interpretation of his offer to Japan are:

1. Exuberant expectations of victory, even in the case of a conflict with the United States, in view of the rapid advance in the East, which would generally prove the theory about the fighting strength of the Red Army in particular, and the superiority of the strongest "Aryan" core in the world in general. (offensive)
2. The presentation of common enemies: Great Britain, the Soviet Union, and the United States, as bait for Japan so that in the end, he alone would benefit from this short-lived alliance, modeled on the Hitler-Stalin accord (covertly offensive)
3. Hitler didn't want to admit his inability to win a war against the United States, and at the same time was requesting help from Japan. (defensive)[11]

Hitler's volatile behavior during these weeks eludes a precise interpretation. But with regard to his aggressiveness against the United States, it leads to the conclusion that from 1940 onward he thought that in 1941, with the help of long-range bombers, he could keep America away from involvement in Europe, and that he could make up for the lack of military potential for transatlantic operations within the army and navy by taking economic measures against North America.

The Trade War

The frequently quoted passage from Hitler's *Second Book*, where he writes "we must show our horns to America," cannot be used as evidence that Hitler had already forecasted a military conflict, as can be proven by a speech also given in 1928. Rather, it is more a way of describing his idea of a fight for world markets, in which the defensive stance would be paramount.[12]

Hitler's considerations concerned not only self-sufficiency in Europe, above all, he was thinking about South America. This sort of mixture between "war" and "annexation" was an idea Hitler developed consistently with the world view that started to emerge in the mid-1930s. A fierce trade war with the United States broke out at this time over the "New Plan," launched by Nazi Germany. It foresaw in the trade with South America the possibility of operating without foreign exchange payments on the basis on settlements of debts, at a time when the US share of the South American market was continuing to fall.[13]

Hitler's assessment of South America's future role, obviously based on this plan, appeared in a number of comments made since 1940 that boil down to the basic idea of antagonistic commercial policies between North and South America. Hitler's exploratory comments were made in June of 1940, when he encouraged the Spanish government to build up South America as a counterbalance to the influence of North America.[14] A year later, he was much clearer in his views with the Turkish ambassador when he expressed his hopes that a far-reaching change would soon take place in America. "South America would not be able to survive without Europe, because it has to get rid of its outrageous amounts of goods such as grain, livestock, and wood. America cannot buy these, however, because they have such a surplus of the same products themselves. The United States would live by the crazy idea of exporting as much as possible and walking off with the money. On a long-term basis this could only lead to a catastrophe."[15] Hitler's comments of October and November 1941 were of a similar nature. He predicted a new orientation of commercial policies in Central and South America after the war. In light of the trade competition that would now emerge, South America would be incapable of buying American products without hard currency.[16] Only with Europe could an exchange of goods make sense for the southern part of the continent.[17] Should the British join the new European hegemony, America would in time suffer mass unemployment and incur huge debts.[18]

"After getting rid of the Asians, Europe would never be dependent on a foreign power again. Even America could "go hang."[19] Europe would supply all of its own raw materials and have a market for its sales in the Russian territories. In this way we would no longer need the rest of world trade," Hitler said. "The new Russia right up to the Urals will be 'our India,' but closer to home than the British one. The new great German Empire will have a population of 135 million and rule over 150 million more."[20]

The "Annexation" of the World

It is not only the frequency of relevant evidence but also Hitler's idea of war, which was outlined at different times, that supports the theory that he believed in an automatic development towards world domination. His racial ideology, his anti-Semitism, and his key geopolitical ideas caused him, already at the outbreak of war, to trust fate. Hitler therefore started to withdraw from politics and to devote himself to his interests. Since the significant victory over France, he had hoped that his theories would "take hold." His comment to the French Admiral Darlan—that he would have been happy if the war would have ended in June or July 1940 because he had no ambitions to be a military leader, but rather "as the leader of his people, only interested in securing the cultural and social rise of the German nation,"[21] appears believable. In November 1941, he also complained to the Finnish foreign minister that he had been pulled away from his formative and cultural work and could no longer dedicate himself to his architectural plans.[22]

With very few interruptions, this idea of achieving his ultimate political goals without a major war dominated his thinking until the end of 1941 and allowed him to hope for a favorable end to that war year. In his eyes, by mid-1940 Germany and its allies would represent a power "that no combination in the world could attack, much less conquer."[23]

A "European Monroe Doctrine," such as Hitler suggested[24] in an interview a few days before the French capitulation, was apparently the key formula for the new balance of power in Europe that would also impress America. The graphic statistics, 500 million Europeans against 230 million Americans,[25] were very clear for Hitler. It was the wording of his invitation to hesitating European politicians, and it was the opium that went into his public speeches. "The path from now to the future," he promised his audience in February 1941, would be easier "than the path from February 24, 1920 to today." With "fanatical confidence" he now would look "towards that future."[26] Even if it came to a grandiose struggle among nations, the last battalion left on the battlefield would be German.[27]

Especially in the months leading up to the attack on Russia and during the weeks that followed, Hitler developed his ideas in detail with regard to his extreme expectations. In a letter to the German consul general in New Orleans, Hewel, one of the confidants who best knew Hitler's plans for the future, wrote: "At any rate we don't fear America in any way whatsoever. Even the Führer hardly concerns himself with this problem since there are others that seem much more acute and decisive in nature. I am sure that the low morale in America sooner or later will settle among this politically stupid people, will have extraordinarily far reaching consequences."[28] The biggest decisions would have been made by the time they would meet again, Hewel told the German diplomat. A few weeks later, Hewel made a note after a conversation with Hitler that without the United States, the "war would be over this year."[29] From the fight with Russia, Germany "will emerge as the most powerful state in the world."[30] After Churchill's sudden fall, Great Britain, riding on an enormous wave of anti-Americanism, would be the first country to enter the coalition of the victor.[31] In Hitler's estimation, the effect of a victorious Eastern campaign on the United States would be "immense."[32] Most of all, the mutual admiration of Germany and Great Britain after their duel would have to result in a united front against America.[33] The United States would have to obey the new Europe. Thus Hitler concluded, "the war will quite surprisingly just be over."[34]

In the previously quoted meeting with the Turkish ambassador, Hitler's geopolitical argumentation was expressed in two basic assumptions, as he explained: "1. That Europe, Asia Minor and Africa all represented one economic region that belonged together due to its thousand-year history. 2. That this region, if we used it cleverly, would still be the best region in the world today."[35] Regardless of Germany's claim to a colonial empire in central Africa, its future tasks would be "emphatically continental."[36]

After the victory over the Soviet Union, this would lead to a complete reorientation of Europe and the Near East.

The area around the Mediterranean was at no time a real strategic alternative for Hitler.[37] The triumph over the Soviet Union as the pivot for all other developments would correct "mishaps" such as the failed occupation of Gibraltar or the spring events in the Near East. This is why Hitler took the events in Iraq in April 1941 relatively calmly, as the forthcoming Russian campaign hindered him from effective involvement. This "cosmetic flaw" would automatically be corrected in the autumn of 1941, as he indicated during a conversation with Hewel. "As soon as it [Russia] is taken care of, then Iraq and Syria will be solved automatically. Then I will be free enough to advance down through Turkey. If the French lose Syria, and I am sure that Syria is lost, there is only the danger that they also lose Algeria. Then I will advance immediately through Spain and cut the British off from the Mediterranean."[38] In a directive issued a few days later, a change in emphasis toward the navy and the air force was ordered with regard to tasks after the autumn of 1941.[39]

Hitler's idea about the importance of Europe to his ultimate goals was expressed most clearly in the weeks of September and October, 1941. "The struggle for global hegemony will be decided in Europe's favor by the possession of the Russian space," he predicted. "In this way, Europe will become an impenetrable fortress, secure against every threat of a blockade. All of this will open up economic perspectives that, one can assume, will orient the most liberal Western democracies towards the new order of things."[40]

By reversing the status quo, Hitler intended to make the old world into the new world. "Europe will gain importance in itself. Then Europe and not America will be the land of unlimited opportunities. If the Americans are clever, they will understand that it is in their own interest to participate in this work."[41] A large-scale return of emigrants from the former "New World" would, in Hitler's opinion, correct the flawed European development that had taken place since the Thirty Years War. This would hasten the shift of power by, on the one hand, weakening America's economic potential and on the other, strengthening Europe. There would be a huge area for activity and pioneer tasks in the new and greater Europe. If Germany were to offer American engineers big projects, for example, Hitler assumed that they would come, since two thirds of them were of German stock anyway.[42]

According to Hitler, America would have no chance in the face of the new hegemonic power that would held "the dominant position in the world."[43] 130 million Americans would face 130 million in Germany, and 90 million in the Ukraine, as well as the countries of the new Europe: together a population of 400 million.[44]

With the development of this new world order, the fate of world Jewry would also be sealed. This was revealed at previously unknown meetings with Goebbels at the Führer headquarters in the middle of August, 1941. Hitler announced to Goebbels the rapid stand-by of transport capabilities for the deportation of the Berlin Jews to the East. Apparently Goebbels had requested this. There they would be "worked over by the harsher climate."[45] Hitler promised his henchman that he would not rest "until we take the final appropriate steps with the Jews."[46] The prophesy contained in the Reichstag speech of January, 1939,[47] that the end of Jewry would come with the outbreak of another world war, would now be confirmed. "This prophesy is coming true in these weeks and months with a certainty that appears almost eerie," as Goebbels wrote, summarizing his meetings with Hitler. "In the East the Jews will have to pay. In Germany they have partially done so already and they will pay even more in the future."[48] There would be, however, still the refuge of America, but even "there, sooner or later, they will also have to pay. ... At any rate, in the coming world, the Jews won't have a lot to laugh about."[49]

The above statements make it clear that Hitler was hardly dependent on subversive measures, such as a "fifth column."[50] Other countries' fear that such preparations existed was enough to create a situation in foreign affairs that Hitler found very useful.[51] Therefore, the fear of attack by fleets of German long-range bombers existed everywhere in Great Britain,[52] France,[53] and the United States,[54] a fear that was nonetheless not completely without foundation, as the introduction of the long-range bomber project and Hitler's intentions have shown.

The increase in the number of members the 'Auslandsorganisation" (AO), the foreign organization of the Nazi Party, which was now ten times the size it had been five years earlier,[55] and its potential growth, had been more successes in foreign politics, must be seen as an instrument that Hitler would have used if needed. In a speech at the party convention in Nuremberg in 1935, Hitler addressed Germans living abroad and touched upon this intention, emphasizing that Germans living overseas were still members of the national community and as such had a duty to consider themselves to be compatriots. The logical consequence would be that they too must do everything that National Socialism demanded of the individual.[56]

Hitler's intention to intimidate his opponents with non-existent military potential and completely exaggerated figures was expressed in April 1940, as he instructed Goebbels not to hesitate in the future about allowing the term "fifth column" appear in the press and even to talk about it so that the fear in enemy countries would increase."[57] Nothing should even be done to repudiate articles written about it in the United States.[58] It was only in April, 1941 that the propaganda was changed again in order to reduce the hysteria within American public opinion that Germany was planning an attack on America after the victory over Great Britain.[59]

The actual existence and importance of the fifth column to Hitler's plans is for the most part limited to the question of propaganda, just incalculating the assumption that an open conquest and occupation of the United States was being planned.[60] Rather, Hitler had hoped for a much more effective apparatus that did indeed contain a series of possibilities for military pressure, including the arsenal of psychological and doctrinal warfare, the magnetic effect of a German final victory that would involve the use of violence to force people to accept the new reality, and other diabolic instruments like treason, all in order to break the will of individuals and nations.

Notes

1. This is valid mostly for the study by Hillgruber, *Hitlers Strategie*, which points to the direction regarding Hitler's strategy.
2. von Kotze and Krausnick, 174, –cf. this volume 112f.
3. Bouhler, 135.
4. Ibid., 168. –Speech from February 24, 1940, on the twentieth anniversary of the announcement of the party program, cf. Domarus, 1407.
5. Bouhler, 276f, Domarus, 1583.
6. Bouhler, 333f, –Hitler's speech from December 10, 1940, to workers in a Berlin arms manufacturing factory; Domarus, 1627.
7. Bouhler, 374.
8. Wagner, *Lagevorträge*, 271, –July 25, 1941.
9. Etzdorf records from July 13, 1941.
10. Compare Hitler's statements from the end of March 1941 as recorded by Engel Diary, 99, –March 24, 1941.
11. Compare A. Hillgruber, „*Grundzüge der nationalsozialistischen Außenpolitik 1933-1945*," *Saeculum* 24 (1973), 328ff.
12. Compare this volume, 47f.
13. In addition: H.-J. Schröder, *Deutschland und die Vereinigten Staaten 1933-1939* (Wiesbaden, 1970), 127ff, 254ff and elsewhere; Martin, *Friedensinitiativen*, 133.
14. Hillgruber, *Staatsmänner*, 1: 136, –June 16, 1940 (Vigón).
15. Ibid., 2: 539, –June 19, 1941 (Gerede).
16. Ibid., 1: 634, –October 25, 1941 (Ciano).
17. Ibid., 1: 654, –November 27, 1941 (Scavenius).
18. *Libres propos*, 92, October 26-27, 1941.
19. Compare with the amazingly similar phrasing of the quartermaster general of the army, General Wagner, in a letter to his wife from September 20, 1941: "A region that will not be ruled by people, the idea of a German India, I believe is what one has in mind: autarchic Europe, so that we won't have to give a hoot about America." –E. Wagner, ed., *Der Generalquartiermeister. Briefe und Tagebuchaufzeichnungen des Generalquartiermeisters des Heeres, General der Artillerie Eduard Wagner* (Munich-Vienna, 1963), 202.
20. Hitler's comments to Abetz on September 16, 1941. –Etzdorf records; Koeppen Reports from October 18, 1941 confirm the content of the meeting of Hitler with Abetz, ibid., p. 70.
21. Hillgruber, *Staatsmänner*, 1: 539, –May 11, 1941.
22. Ibid., 1: 643, –November 27, 1941 (Witting).
23. Hillgruber, *Staatsmänner*, 1: 275, –October 24, 1940 (Pétain); compare also the speech from November 8, 1940, –Domarus, 1605, as well as the speech from November 14, 1940, –Bouhler, 327.
24. Interview with K. von Wiegand on June 13, 1940, –Domarus, 1524 (with wrong date); Hillgruber, *Strategie*, 198; Martin, *Friedensinitiativen*, 259ff.
25. He mentioned this relation to Ciano on October 25, 1941, –Hillgruber, *Staatsmänner*, 1: 634.
26. Bouhler, 426, –speech from February 24, 1941.
27. Domarus, 1178, –November 8, 1941.
28. Political archives of the German Foreign Office, Hewel file, Deutschland S-St –April 5, 1941.
29. Hewel Diary, –May 22, 1941.
30. Ibid., July 11, 1941 –(maybe also July 10, 1941).

31. Ibid.
32. Etzdorf records from July 16, 1941.
33. Weizsäcker-Papiere, 263, 269.
34. Ibid., 270, –September 16, 1941.
35. Hillgruber, *Staatsmänner*, 2: 539; compare also KTB Halder II, 243, –January 16, 1941.
36. KTB Halder III, 29, –June 30, 1941.
37. Compare Hillgruber, *Strategie*, 190ff. With regard to this, Gerhard Schreiber, *Revisionismus und Weltmachtstreben. Marineführung und deutsch-italienische Beziehungen 1919-1944* (Stuttgart, 1978).
38. Hewel Diary, –May 31, 1941; HA Hewel, Deutschland T-Z, –June 14, 1941. Compare Engel-Tagebuch, 101f, –April 24, 1941.
39. W. Hubatsch, ed., *Hitlers Weisungen für die Kriegsführung 1939-1945* (Frankfurt am Main, 1962), 129ff, –Instruction 32 from June 11, 1941.
40. *Libres Propos*, 33f, –September 17–18. 1941; Picker, 146, September 8–10, 1941.
41. *Libres propos*, 54, –October 13, 1941.
42. Ibid., 44, –September 25, 1941, 68, –October 17, 1941; Koeppen Reports, 65, –October 17, 1941; Picker, 174, –February 4, 1942.
43. *Libres propos*, 92, October 26–27, 1941; Bouhler, 106, –Hitler's speech from November 8, 1941.
44. *Libres propos*, 92; compare this volume, 178 note 25; Domarus, 1778, –November 8, 1941.
45. *Goebbels Diary Fragments*, 1: 225f, –August 18–19, 1941.
46. Ibid., 1: 240.
47. Domarus, 1058, –January 30, 1939.
48. *Goebbels Diary Fragments*, 1: 237f.
49. Ibid. This would be also proof against Adam, *Judenpolitik im Dritten Reich*, 360 and elsewhere. Even though Hitler never mentioned the annihilation of the Jews nor made any anti-Semitic comments as specific as this over the years this point was always an integral part of his idea of world domination.
50. Fundamental: L. de Jong, *Die deutsche Fünfte Kolonne im Zweiten Weltkrieg* (Stuttgart, 1959).
51. P. Kluke, „*Politische Form und Außenpolitik des Nationalsozialismus,*" FS for H. Rothfels (Göttingen, 1963), 437; L. Gruchmann, „*Völkerrecht und Moral. Ein Beitrag zur Problematik der amerikanischen Neutralitätspolitik,*" *VfZG* 8 (1960), 402f.
52. D. Aigner, *Das Ringen um England* (Munich-Eßlingen, 1969), 246.
53. Martin, *Friedensinitiativen*, 64.
54. Ibid., 331.
55. Jacobsen, *Außenpolitik*, 137.
56. *Reden Reichsparteitag 1935*, 46f, –September 13, 1935; cf. Jacobsen, *Außenpolitik*, 144.
57. W. A. Boelcke, ed., *Kriegspropaganda 1939-1941* (Stuttgart, 1966), 330, –April 25, 1940, 2.
58. Ibid., 470, 4.
59. Ibid., 703f, –April 25, 1941, 4.
60. In addition: G.L. Weinberg, "Hitler's Image of the United States," *AHR* 69 (1964), 1013; as a contemporary source: W.L. Shirer, *Berlin Diary. The Journal of a Foreign Correspondent 1934-1941* (New York, 1941), 591ff, –entry for December 1, 1940. –Extensive material regarding the mood in the United States can be found in BA/MA: RW 4/v. 335, 336. Case GE 334, 335 PG 32 323-326, also Case GE 348ff. PG 32 383ff. Polit. Übersicht 1. SKL Part D.

Chapter 20

RULING THE NEW WORLD

Detailed statements about how the planned rule of territories would be carried out turn out to be much more difficult to find than statements about the global extent of Hitler's ultimate goals. However, the popular accusation that these stages of Hitler's "program" were purely visionary must be countered with the fact that already in the Russian campaign in 1941, no broad idea of the situation after victory existed. Despite occasional bragging about the treatment of territories in the East, as is well-known from records of the '*Tischgespräche*', a typical characteristic of Hitler does emerge in the inability, or perhaps only unwillingness, to really carry a thought through to the end. After conceiving the first steps, he left reality and decided things in a visionary rather than a rational way.[1]

Another explanation is the fact that the National Socialist system was still in its expansion phase at the time. Hitler followed a basic direction without settling any specific details: the arrangements were to be left open for a reaction to the situation that would develop later on.[2] Despite all the activities of Hitler's satraps in the conquered territories, the political plans after the war remained temporary[3] and were, at least in Hitler's view, to be considered with great circumspection.

The activities of leading groups within the Third Reich, which were described at the end of May 1940 by a critical observer as "unreservedly triumphant followed by grandiose plans to divide the world,"[4] don't seem to have corresponded completely to Hitler's ideas. They are much more the evidence of the internal authoritarian anarchy that existed within the

Third Reich itself. In any case, Hewel, who was always well-informed, felt obliged in August 1940 to answer the questions of an old friend from his days in East Asia with regard to the colonial future as such: "At the moment throughout the entire German Reich, many colonial plans are being made. Official departments are being formed, and posts are being handed out. In reality this is maybe very useful work, but it is, at the moment, of no practical use, because as you write yourself, everything is still so unsure. The Führer isn't saying anything about it, because all decisions in this area depend on how the conflict with England develops. Indeed it depends completely on that issue. When everything is ready, the Führer, as I know him, will make his own decisions and then in a sovereign manner dismiss many well thought out plans. Nasty people are looking forward to that moment."[5]

A look at Hitler's European allies, the neutral countries and those occupied by the Germany in 1940–941, reveals some of the political contours of Europe's future. As long as the Soviet Union remained yet undefeated, Hitler showed a certain interest in allies. After a victory, these partners would have nothing more in common with Germany. Hitler's intentions are revealed in his comment that the diverging interests of the European powers in Africa were only to be solved by a "grand fraud."[6] The most important prerequisite right now was to gain more time.

Already in May 1941 he explained that after a victory over Russia "he would no longer have to show consideration for Italy!"[7] The fate of the Latin race would be sealed, it must be put back in its rightful position.[8] Already at the end of 1940 he had also announced a hard line against France: after taking Gibraltar one could "speak clearly with the Vichy government; there's no more getting away from it then."[9] In a conversation with Ambassador Abetz on September 16, 1941, he went one step further: "In the tactical handling of the French he [the Führer] didn't want to change anything as long as the campaign in the East wasn't "finished," because it wasn't his style to do two things at once. He also had the patience to observe the French a little longer." "Of course they should participate in the 'new Europe', however, they must adapt themselves "without reserve" into the 'new order of things.'"[10]

Franco's Spain was, after his hesitation about Hitler's offer and the failed plans to take Gibraltar away from the British at the end of 1940,[11] also finished as far as Hitler was concerned. In February of 1941, Hitler announced that he was going to drop Spain, and he had already predicted its downfall.[12] Still, in the first weeks of the Russian campaign, he regretted deeply that Gibraltar hadn't already been taken care of. "What would our position be now if last winter we had taken Gibraltar with his [Franco's] agreement?"[13]

There was a bitter fate in store for Turkey as well, even if they were to "come in" once an imminent victory over Russia was in sight. Then their wishes would no longer be acceptable, Hitler said. One of the first measures to be taken would be to drive the Turks out of the Crimea.[14]

Unclear ideas about Hitler's ultimate goals can also be found among Hitler's closest political confidants.[15] None of them seems to have had a real global concept comparable to Hitler's.

Himmler was certainly the only one who gave some coherent elaboration to Hitler's plans,[16] which according to traditional views were "empty," inhuman, and only aimed at a pure state of conquest with the might of the stronger. Himmler also partially outlined the framework for those plans.[17] Himmler's ideas, however, were predominantly concerned with the East. Therefore, one can only regard him as a "partial interpreter." He wanted, for example, to bring all people of Germanic origin back to Europe, "because every drop of Germanic blood that is not on our side can one day be our own destruction."[18]

Göring, one of the closest confidants of Hitler, was not exactly a politician with a precise concept, and though much more within the conventions of a liberal imperialist. Only his anti-American attitude can be seen already as of 1938 in his willingness to take part in a military conflict with the big power.[19]

By contrast, it can be said of Hess, Hitler's deputy, that he had known of Hitler's plans for global supremacy since the twenties, as the written correspondence with Hewel during the years 1927–1928 shows.[20] Hess' comments in Great Britain after his flight prove, however, that he saw himself simply as his master's voice. This becomes obvious even in his choice of words.[21] The decision to fly to England would have come during a visit in Hitler's headquarters in June, 1940, he reported to his interrogators:[22] "I have to admit that I found myself faced with a very difficult decision, the most difficult in my life of course."[23] Hess further explained that he was hoping to have found, albeit without official permission, the peace-loving British opposition to Churchill. Had he succeeded, Germany's victory would be now clear. That's why the Empire must be kept intact. Hitler would be lord over Europe,[24] and the Americans would come in too late. By the time they could help, Great Britain would be starving because of a blockade.[25]

In comparison, Goebbels' speeches and comments indicate that he not only knew Hitler's "program," but also that he understood it. As early as 1933, in a speech in Hamburg, he developed the idea of Germany as having a "global mission to fulfill." "The development that has spread here in Germany will also gain ground in a changed form in other countries. Revolution flows across borders like spring tides."[26] When at the party convention of 1937 Goebbels again used the term "new world mission" in order to describe the struggle against "global enemy number one," Bolshevism, Hitler showed consideration for Italy and had a number of passages deleted from the official version for interdepartmental publishing.[27] The speech made to the German press on April 5, 1940, in the propaganda ministry shows that Goebbels knew Hitler's goals very well.[28] The fragments of his diary entries in summer 1941, however, clearly indicate that during the first successful phase of the Russian campaign, he was already not sure what was going on. Goebbels' writings reveal skepticism and concern about how the war would end. Not until he returned from a visit to Hitler's headquarters and had been formally pepped up by Hitler did the optimism return to his writing. It seems as though Hitler had directed his pen.

An analysis of the school and educational system within the National Socialist regime can hardly reveal better insight into the form of rule envisaged by Hitler.

Hitler apparently never deviated from the principles on education given in Mein Kampf, giving the priority in education to the development of completely fit bodies,[29] over the development of mental skills. Also remarkable in this area, however, is that it was only after 1936 that Hitler showed a certain interest in education.[30] It is in a way a further parallel to the changes seen at that time in foreign policy, architecture, and armament—an overall activity which Hitler touched everything of importance for the future. However, we cannot conclude from this that Hitler showed much attention to educational issues.[31] All the same, one of the "Ordensburg speeches"[32] given in 1936–1937 should be singled out in order to elucidate Hitler's basic principles concerning education. Human achievement, explained Hitler, is generally a collective achievement, whereby a concentration of the will to work must appear first. He said it was necessary to have "a certain similarity in the way of thinking and thus of planning, which creates a common intention and unanimous decision."[33]

The political leadership had to be consistenty "made up of brave, also personally courageous men," Hitler said. "During the struggle, one could have taken "his parachute jump … into the political] assembly." "Unfortunately I can't do that now. This fellow now must show some other way that he is a person, that he is tough, that he is committed, that he has courage that is what is necessary. Only with this type of planned selection, an absolute appeal to manhood, will it be possible for us, also in the future, to have political leaders that are really tough, and who, of this you can be sure, will be respected by the nation."[34]

Although Hitler was reserved concerning the elitist educational system of the Third Reich,[35] these comments show at least the intentions and the general ideas of the National Socialists on elitist education. In addition to Himmler, who, with the SS, wanted to start a biological breeding of the elite, the results of which would eventually be carried over into the general population,[36] the three sections of the party's own school system should be briefly described at this point.[37] However, the chaos in terms of competence that existed between Rust, Ley, Schirach, Rosenberg, Bormann, and Himmler, as well as the short span of the National Socialist rule, prevented any kind of setting of a clear direction.

The schools that came closest to the SS model with its ideas about elites were the Adolf Hitler Schools (AHS) founded in 1937.[38] Their creation as the official party schools competed with the national political education institutions (NPEA),[39] already founded in 1933, the lesson plans of which resembled those of a normal secondary school and which were the responsibility of Rust, the German minister for education. Graduates from the AHS could only follow a career in the party. During the war, they were posted as apprentices to party offices in the occupied Eastern and Western territories to receive their first practical training.[40] The curriculum, which in 1941 involved a total of thirty-seven hours a week, fifteen hours of which were allocated to sports,[41] reveals how the regime intended to produce an administrative corps of fanatical, narrow-minded, and presumptuous functionaries. During the war, the politics of education appealed first and foremost to the lower-middle class, who found for their children in the party schools reputation, boarding houses, equal opportunity, mobility, and security within the hierarchy.[42] The AHS was a kind of a pre-school for the Ordensburg[43] system that was also established in 1933. Already the architecture of an Ordensburg school, just like that of the uncompleted party university, the "Hohe Schule der NSDAP," on Chiemsee,[44] gave an impression of the future tasks it was to fulfill. Within the atmosphere of colonialism, the schools' shape of a medieval castle and their barracks pointed in the general direction of myths, styled after the Middle Ages, absolutism, and the ancient world.

After the victory over Russia, Hitler assumed that German would become the vernacular of Europe.[45] The Roman consul Marius and King Frederic II ("Der alte Fritz") were the inspiration behind his idea of using non-commissioned officers of the army who had served for twelve years to work as teachers. For their comrades in the motorized divisions, Hitler planned jobs such as gasoline pump attendant. If they came from rural areas, they should marry farm girls. The resettling of city boys into the countryside was pointless as far as Hitler was concerned.[46]

Although these were not the only path to the goal, Hitler's dreams of world domination were generally filled with thundering cannons, military campaigns, and defeating rebellions, even though at one point in *Mein*

Kampf he didn't quite dismiss the idea of a pacifist world, in which the Aryans were sole rulers of the globe.[47] Almost frightened by this view, he quickly had put it into perspective. "For the good of the German people," he would wish for a war every fifteen to twenty years,[48] he said at the end of August, 1941, and he indicated the general direction of these wars later in monologues at his lonely headquarters: They would take place off beyond the Urals, where there would still be a never-ending possibility for action.[49] But also internal struggle within a world political system based on socio-Darwinian principles is conceivable. The party that Hitler once referred to as the "greediest animal in the history of the world"[50] would especially have made demands after the war. Following the extermination of the Jews, the elimination of other minorities, which in principle could have included the native populations, would have been a consequence of this rule. In the end, it was the *"raison d'être"* of the regime to create a permanent outlet for aggression both internally and externally. If the result of an examination about the form of Hitler's efforts at world domination remains unsatisfactory in the end, made up of fragments and beginnings, and explanation of Hitler's intentions does indeed show that his ideology was not simply a matter of a one-dimensional conglomeration of ideas. His multi-faceted ideas, his amateurism, and his fanaticism make it clear that a certain summation of his ideas on foreign policy can be reached here, even if the retractions, the false analogies, and the general abstruse thinking make it impossible to discuss the points of his program one-by-one.

As already proven by his speeches to the officers up to 1944, Hitler never gave up the idea of conquering the world with Europe's help. Even in his political testament, there are traces of ideas of world domination: the evil of Christianizing the Germanic tribes, the religious wars, and the German inferiority complex that he had wanted to fight against all his life.[51] His concept of war, to destroy an enemy with '*Blitzkrieg*' tactics that involved a low loss of life on his own side, is to be found once again here.[52] His notion of America as a land of German immigrants with the highest concentration of Nordic blood also offered a contribution to the well-known picture.[53] The ways in which he had wanted to persuade his officers, found its use: the rightful place of Germany could not be achieved by him alone nor in the course of one generation,[54] but Germany would have its future ahead of it.[55]

The war that was actually raging presented a different picture, but Hitler's thoughts were dominated by myths right up to his death, after he had demanded blind obedience at the front and at home. After having failed to gain a victory, one was expected to await the end in a fortified castle, one that recalled the Germanic *"Wagenburgen"* of the Teutons.

Notes

1. Fest, 878.
2. Compare Jacobsen, *Außenpolitik*, 451. From here there is a general criticism of works such as the two volume study by N. Rich, *Hitler's War Aims*.
3. With regard to Germany's occupation policies, compare the extensive bibliographical references in Hildebrand, *"Hitlers Ort,"* 584f note 3.
4. Hassell, 137, –entry from May 29, 1940.
5. PA AA HA Hewel Privat H-Q, –August 31, 1940.
6. KTB Halder II, 124, –October 3, 1940.
7. Hewel Diary, –May 29, 1941.
8. Weizsäcker-Papiere, 252, –May 1, 1941 (note Hewel).
9. KTB Halder II, 212, –December 5, 1940.
10. Etzdorf Records.
11. In addition: D.S. Detwiler, *Hitler, Franco und Gibraltar* (Wiesbaden, 1962).
12. Hewel Diary, –February 14, 1941.
13. *Goebbels Diary Fragments*, 233, –August 18–19, 1941.
14. Koeppen Reports, 45, –October 4, 1941.
15. With regard to his circle of confidants, compare Jacobsen, *Außenpolitik*, 352ff.
16. Compare Bollmus, *Amt Rosenberg*, 250.
17. Fest in his introduction to: Himmler, *Geheimreden 1933 bis 1945*, 13. –Compare also J. Ackermann, *Heinrich Himmler als Ideologe* (Göttingen, 1970), 177f.
18. *Geheimreden*, 38, –November 8, 1938. Compare also ibid., 157, –speech to the Supreme Zone Commanders and heads of the central offices on June 9, 1942.
19. Compare Hildebrand, *Außenpolitik*, 21; Martin, *Friedensinitiativen*, 92f. A satisfactory scientific biography of Göring has yet to be written at the time of this study.
20. Compare this volume, 45f, 51.
21. It would be worth doing a study on the voluntary and involuntary adoption of Hitler's vocabulary and use of aphorisms amongst civil servants in the Third Reich.
22. PRO London PREM 3 219/ 1–7; cf. Martin, *Friedensinitiativen*, 426ff.
23. PREM 3 219/5, 9.
24. PREM 3 219/4, 6.
25. PREM 3 219/4, 7.
26. Forschungsstelle NS Hamburg –*Hamburger Fremdenblatt*, June 17, 1933. –Compare also this volume, 49; as well as Goebbels, *Vom Kaiserhof zur Reichskanzlei*, 292, –entry from April 2, 1933.
27. Jacobsen, *Außenpolitik*, 460.
28. Forschungsstelle NS Hamburg; compare Hillgruber, *Strategie*, 14 note 5.
29. *Mein Kampf*, 452ff and more often. –Compare K. C. Lingelbach, *Erziehung und Erziehungstheorien im nationalsozialistischen Deutschland* (Weinheim-Basel, 1970), 27ff.
30. D. Orlow, *The History of the Nazi Party: 1933–1945* (Pittsburgh, 1973), 191.
31. H. Scholz, *NS–Ausleseschulen. Internatsschulen als Herrschaftsmittel des Führerstaates* (Göttingen, 1973), 18.
32. What is meant are the speeches in the Ordensburgen Crössinsee on April 24, 1936 (IfZ archives), Sonthofen on November 23, 1937 (Picker), and Vogelsang on April 29, 1937 (von Kotze and Krausnick). Another fundamental speech was that of December 10, 1940 (Domarus/Bouhler).
33. von Kotze and Krausnick, 112.
34. Ibid., 145.

35. Scholtz, *Ausleseschulen*, 240.
36. In addition: L.V. Thompson. *"Lebensborn and the Eugenics Policy of the Reichsführer-SS,"* *Central European History* 4 (1971), 59.
37. In general: D. Schoenbaum, *Die braune Revolution. Eine Sozialgeschichte des Dritten Reiches* (Cologne-Berlin, 1968), 342ff; K.D. Bracher, *Die deutsche Diktatur. Entstehung, Struktur, Folgen des Nationalsozialismus* (Cologne-Berlin, 1969), 287ff; H.J. Gamm, *Führung und Verführung. Pädagogik des Nationalsozialismus* (Munich, 1964), 80ff.
38. D. Orlow, *„Die Adolf-Hitler-Schulen,"* VfZG 13 (1965), 272–284; Scholz, *Ausleseschulen*.
39. In addition: H. Ueberhorst, ed., *Elite für die Diktatur. Die Nationalpolitischen Erziehungsanstalten 1933–1945. Ein Dokumentarbericht* (Düsseldorf, 1969). –All in all, one hundred NPEA's were planned.
40. Orlow, *„Adolf-Hitler-Schulen,"* 283f.
41. Ibid., 282.
42. Scholtz mentions this, *Ausleseschulen*, 267f.
43. Scholtz, *„Die „NS-Ordensburgen","* VfZG 15 (1967), 269–298. –Photos in: *Bauten der Bewegung*, 1:130f.
44. BA NS 10/65, 94; compare Bollmus, *Amt Rosenberg*, 242. –Other elite schools were the SS-Junkerschulen and the Heimschulen.
45. *Libres propos*, 109, –November 2–3, 1941, Koeppen Reports, 50, –October 5, 1941.
46. Koeppen Reports, 47, –October 4, 1941.
47. *Mein Kampf*, 315f.
48. *Libres propos*, 29, August 19–20, 1941.
49. He said to Goebbels in August 1941that Russian centers of power beyond the Urals, for example Omsk, had to be destroyed. –Ibid., 212, –August, 17–18, 1941; Koeppen Reports, 36, –September 23, 1941.
50. *Libres propos*, 92, –October 26–27, 1941.
51. *Le testament politique de Hitler. Notes recueillies par M. Bormann* (Paris, 1959), 82, –February 13, 1945.
52. Ibid., 106f, –February 17, 1945.
53. Ibid., 123, –February 24, 1945.
54. Ibid., 131, –February 25, 1945.
55. Ibid., 132.

Chapter 21

THE BRITISH ASSESSMENT OF HITLER'S ULTIMATE GOALS

A close examination of the British assessment of Hitler's ultimate goals in the years between 1939 and 1941 should indicate how the nation that was to feel the immediate effect of Hitler's plans for world domination recognized the program behind Hitler's behavior with amazing clarity. This part of the investigation can only deal with limited and selective material that can only partially do justice to the traditional use of many sources and the critical assessment of these sources relative to other documents. It is, however, justifiable to examine the available material in order to seek answers within the framework of bilateral relations. Independent of the daily fluctuations of politics, the basic underlying views expressed by different official departments regarding Hitler's foreign policies needs to be examined. The British judgment of Hitler's ultimate program can serve as indirect evidence that even from a relatively removed view coming from a foreign power, the single pieces from the mosaic of Hitler's ideological pronouncements could be pieced together to form a picture corresponding more or less to the model of the goals that has been discussed in the previous chapters of this investigation.

Hitler's *Mein Kampf* had been known in Great Britain since 1933, and it had formed an uninterrupted underlying thread in German-British relations.[2] Especially after 1936, the year that marked the flare up of Nazi activity in foreign policy, it can be clearly determined that the British understood and agreed to pay close attention to the shift in Hitler's program. Passages from *Mein Kampf* were being circulated within the Foreign Office (FO) in London.[3]

In its assessment of the Third Reich, three main currents can be observed in the British Foreign Office:

1. one that remained oriented toward the political thoughts and patterns of action of traditional foreign affairs
2. one that made occasional warnings against Hitler's foreign policy actions
3. one that consistently warned against Hitler's foreign policy

It was especially during the first three months of 1939 that one can observe lively activity within the Foreign Office with regard to Hitler's ultimate goals. The information coming from British military intelligence and from the high-ranking officers in the armed forces was astonishingly incomplete in its analysis of Hitler's intentions. In a report from the intelligence service dated in mid-January, 1939 regarding Germany's present situation and its future goals, Hitler's personal significance in matters of foreign policy was greatly emphasized. "Germany's future policy is in the keeping of one man." Until that point the "Führer," a visionary and megalomaniac individual, had made no mistakes, although his actions showed a series of rushed and hasty decisions. *Mein Kampf* contained the clear announcement of the goal of "Lebensraum in the East" and the consequences of such policies were to be a global hegemony, as Hitler would also see.[4] Furthermore, Hitler's building projects in Berlin and other cities were clearly understood as being significant measures in preparation for a comprehensive expansion.[5] The report summary stated that the political system of the Third Reich was based on the principles of economic and territorial expansion.[6] A memorandum from the British War Office dated January 24, 1939, that dealt with an analysis of *Mein Kampf* reached the same conclusion, namely that Hitler intended to create a global hegemony.[7] A week later, a memorandum from the British military attaché in Paris also included a warning that Hitler's goal was world domination. The basis of this statement was a comment of the head of the Secret Service of the French Air Force, Colonel de Vitrolles. The conflict with the western powers was seen as secondary, while the clash with the East was the priority for Nazi Germany. The colonies were actually only a pawn to be used for trading: a "bargaining counter" for German policy.[8] A report written on June 19, 1939, based on meetings by the British military attaché in Berlin contained remarkable information about the thinking of the German generals at that time. The Army's supreme commander, General von Brauchitsch, explained, according to this source, that a European war would be a catastrophe, but that on the other hand he emphasized the "military rebirth" of Germany and his certainty that the army would carry out its duty and both willingly and effectively do whatever was necessary. General Halder would have made similar statements and referred to many letters from officers whose common message was that Germany had found its path and must continue marching.[9]

A memorandum by Foreign Minister, Lord Halifax, about possible German intentions, dated January 19, 1939, underlined Hitler's leading role in the shaping of German foreign policy. Germany's attempt at reaching European hegemony would be a step for Hitler toward ruling the world.[10] In February, 1939, the main ideas of Rauschning's book, *The Revolution of Nihilism*, a further indication of Hitler's goal of world domination,[11] were of great interest to the British Foreign Office.[12] Shortly afterward, a letter to the Foreign Minister from Henderson, the British ambassador to Berlin, showed the real difficulty for the British in understanding Hitler's goals. A policy that sought to achieve world domination or even only hegemony in Central and Eastern Europe, wrote the diplomat, meant conflict with the entire world, or at the very least with all neighboring European countries. No matter how strong a country was, it would not be able to stand up to a united defensive front. For that reason alone, Hitler could hardly afford to devote himself to such insane dreams. Up until the early nineteenth century, a European hegemonic power could have attempted to seek the goal of world domination, but such a view was an anachronism in the twentieth century.[13] At the end of March, 1939, the British ambassador to Paris, Phipps, reported to the FO from a meeting with his American colleague, Bullitt, who informed him of a war council held by Hitler on March 9, 1939. The German dictator was planning to attack the United States in 1941 with the support of the British, French, and Italian fleets. Bullitt would be convinced of the authenticity of his source.[14]

A detailed report regarding Hitler's address to the generals on August 22, 1939, on the Obersalzberg received a great deal of attention at the British Foreign Office. Hitler had apparently spoken of world domination, even if certain details were met with skepticism by the FO.[15]

With the outbreak of the war with Germany, such observations became rare. In a memorandum issued at the end of November 1939, the permanent undersecretary, Vansittart, referred once again to the passages in *Mein Kampf* about conquering the world, in a criticism aimed at the naïve attitude of Berlin ambassador Henderson toward Hitler's policies, probably an internal rearguard action.[16] Already on November 16, 1939, the British government, in agreement with its ally France, had determined that it was pointless to speculate about Hitler's intentions. One must be prepared for anything.[17]

Just as when war broke out, it also became apparent in 1940 that the energy of British political leaders was temporarily being absorbed by immediate problems. Once at war with Germany, one thought only of the next immediate step, and an analysis of the situation as a whole was put on the back burner. After defending themselves against the German air offensive in the late summer of 1940, everyone in London expected a German attack on the British Isles by the end of the year,[18] without really having a concrete reason to believe such an attack would take place.[19] A possible advance by the enemy into Spain and North Africa was also expected with concern.[20]

The fear of an unstoppable German expansion continued to become even stronger when Germany attacked the Soviet Union in 1941. Information coming from the Swiss embassy in London in March, 1941 about German preparations for an attack, prompted a diplomat in the British Foreign Office to comment with a side note that Hitler was returning to his "program" and that the principles of Mein Kampf were becoming the basis of his policies.[21] At the beginning of August 1941, British leaders expected Hitler's real plans to get underway after the completion of the Russian campaign. There was actually no sign of a Russian defeat, but afterward pressure on Turkey and Persia would be expected. In the West, Vichy France was expected to face greater problems, and an advance into Spain as a first step towards North Africa was thought to be possible at any moment.[22] Not until December 10, 1941, one day before Germany declared war on the United States, was there a sigh of relief in the British cabinet. At the same time, it was widely believed that the severe defeat of Germany on the Eastern front could have important consequences.[23]

Notes

1. For the period until 1939, the fundamental study by Henke about Great Britain in Hitler's political calculations must be pointed out, especially 100ff, 132f.
2. Aigner, 84.
3. A. Eden, *Angesichts der Diktatoren* (Cologne-Berlin, 1964), 379f, 436f.
4. Public Record Office (PRO) London WO 190/745, –January 17, 1939; also Churchill claims to have recognized Hitler's goals of world domination using his analysis of *Mein Kampf*. –W.S. Churchill, *Der Zweite Weltkrieg* (Bern, 1950), 1: 78f.
5. PRO WO 190/745; PRO FO 371 24 380/C 3867/5/18, –Report of the British ambassador Kelly, in Bern on March 12, 1940, with detailed information about Hitler's building plans for Berlin. Hitler was reported to be incessantly occupied with this.
6. PRO WO 190/745; PRO WO 190/746, –January 23, 1939, Germany—General Situation.

7. PRO FO 371 22 962/C 1194/15/18, Brigadier Beaumont-Nesbitt to Under-secretary Strang.

8. PRO FO 371 22 964/C 1432/15/18, –Memorandum from February 1, 1939, to Minister for Foreign Affairs Halifax.

9. PRO WO 190/824.

10. PRO FO 371 22 961/C 939/15/18 –Anlage 1. –A summary of information available by the middle of December, 1938.

11. Rauschning, *Revolution des Nihilismus*. The usual judgments regarding this book need to be somewhat corrected as a result of this study. Though Rauschning emphasizes the lack of principles in the foreign policy, 39, this refers solely to the goal of world domination, 384ff, 477. The significance of Eastern Europe is indeed well understood, 332, 384.

12. PRO FO 371 22 965/C 2070/15/18.

13. PRO FO 371 22 966/C 3184/15/18, Henderson on March 9, 1939, to Halifax.

14. PRO FO 371 22 968/C 4604/15/18, Letter of Phipps from March 28, 1939, to Halifax. –Similar rumours; PRO FO 371 22 968/C 4604/15/18, –March 30, 1939.

15. PRO FO 371 22 979/C 12 341/15/18, Ogilvie-Forbes to Kirkpatrick on August 25, 1939; PRO FO 371 22 981/C 12 825/15/18, Ogilvie-Forbes to Kirkpatrick on August 27, 1939, –Compare with Hitler's speech, this volume, 120.

16. PRO FO 371 22 986/C 19 495/15/18, –November 28, 1939.

17. PRO CAB 65, 2 W.M. 85 (39), 108.

18. PRO FO 371 24 385/C 10 703/5/18, FO Minutes from October 7, 1940.

19. PRO FO 371 24 385/C 13 703/5/18, December 13, 1940. Report from the War Cabinet, –Joint Intelligence Sub-Committee.

20. PRO CAB 65, 16 W.M. (40) 306. Conclusions, Minute 3, Confidential Annex, –December 16, 1940.

21. PRO FO 371 26 518/C 2222/19/18. Report from Kelly on March 5, 1941, –marginal note by Cavendish Bentinck.

22. PRO FO 371 26 523/C 9529/19/18, August 8, 1941. Report from the War Cabinet. –Joint Intelligence Sub-Committee. "*German Intentions up to the End of 1941.*"

23. PRO CAB 65, 20 W.M. 126 (41).

Chapter 22

SUMMARY

The examination of the years 1940–1941 has produced absolute confirmation of the findings from the preceding time period. It has become clear therefore that for Hitler, the terms *"Weltherrschaft"* (world domination) and *"Weltvorherrschaft"* (relative world supremacy) were assumed to be identical. This meant that for him, up until 1945 there was to be Aryan rule over the world with the help of the two most numerous Nordic peoples, to which the enormous reservoir of immigrants to the United States from central and Northern Europe from the last centuries would be added. In Hitler's opinion, Europe would then develop into a new "New World" and become the centre of the globe thanks to a combination of "programming" and "natural law." This aim of Hitler's was very clearly recognized and understood by his desired partner, Great Britain.

Though his behavior indicates variations with respect to achieving his ultimate goal, the predominant impression is that in 1940–1941, Hitler believed that he could achieve his theories in the short-term, the most important elements of which originated from the areas of geopolitics, anti-Semitism, and social-Darwinism. The thesis must be advanced hat Hitler expected to reach his goals, if all went well, by 1950. His instructions for the completion of his huge architectural projects were all too clearly and precisely aimed politically toward that specific date. The second most important year would be 1945, in a completely different sense than what happened in reality—which suggests that after 1941, Hitler did not expect to have to fight extensive wars with the remaining powers.

Although the principle of permanent war was the basis for his conception of the world, it must rather be assumed that he imagined future conflicts more as sanctions, reprisals, and anti-insurrectionist warfare that would have the characteristics of a "*Blitzkrieg*," where the psychological impact was a priority. That is why long range bombers, the Plan Z fleet, and the armaments program in general should be viewed more as a symbol of the strength and power of the supreme world power rather than as specific instruments of warfare against the United States, and hardly against Great Britain. Like the French fleet which was destroyed by the British in July, by 1940 Hitler hoped to put his hand on the Royal Navy as well. The material and troops he got from Austria and later from Czechoslovakia had brought the Wehrmacht deep into Russia. This was the thinking of a gambler.

The arrangements in occupied Europe, the colonial plans, and the educational and training system all reveal certain tendencies toward establishing a "*Herrenrasse*," master race meant to rule the world. But these plans all had a temporary character and are therefore, to a large extent ruled out as direct evidence of Hitler's ultimate goals. The principle that must be assumed is that the National Socialist system was in a phase of development and expansion and that any consolidation or commitment that was to take place would happen after a framework had been set, as long as the social-Darwinist principles would allow for it. Any exact commitment is problematic, since Hitler left almost everything open and offered competing groups only outlines of his doctrine, and only as he saw fit.

Therefore, the lack of a war plan against the United States or Japan is not surprising, as even the war of 1939 had the character of something that was improvised. Even the "plans" for the Soviet Union, which was to be conquered, and for the already occupied regions were, according to traditional ideas, "empty" with respect to their content. On the other hand, Hitler's overall objectives were taken seriously. They were extremely airtight and in fact had a brutally banal consistency to them that went beyond all known historical precedent. The acquisition of more "*Lebensraum im Osten*" was, according to Hitler, the answer to all Germany's problems. This solution was the passkey and the decisive point of the "program" at the same time, the prerequisite for the ultimate goal of world domination for the Aryan race. With this development, humanity would have been brought to a historical stop, and the status quo would be in the future guaranteed by the breeding of a biologically elite race. Hitler's dream of doing away with the "challenge cup" principle of the world would have been achieved.

Chapter 23

FINAL OBSERVATIONS ON HITLER'S GLOBAL STRATEGY

This investigation has shown that Hitler's "ultimate goals," as they were conceived and developed in their global framework, can be dated as far back as 1919 and 1920. They were thus formed much earlier than the determination of his "short-term goals" when he was writing *Mein Kampf* in the years from 1924 to 1926.

The starting point of Hitler's ultimate global ambitions were two supposedly fundamental observations of the role of "Judaism" and the current, unjust division of the world:

1. "International Judaism" was basically be "pure" in terms of race and sought, although small in number, to achieve world domination.
2. Great Britain, despite having a smaller population than Germany, ruled large areas of the world. Other world powers, compared to the German Reich, possessed many times the amount of land Germany did.

Despite these points, there were "positive consequences" for Hitler, which became his doctrine: Even small nations had the opportunity, if they were "racially pure" or if they worked toward that kind of purity, to conquer and rule large territories, and even the whole world. The Aryans, who gave the term "Judaism" a corresponding negative position, allowed

Hitler at the same time to place Germany as Europe's "Aryan raiding unit" also for the whole world, one with which "Jewish Bolshevism" could be fought and defeated. As the representative of all mankind, Hitler intended to be its "savior," through world domination by the "Aryan race," and at the same time to secure a biological final state of the world which would end the "free interplay of forces," and the role the Earth played as a "challenge cup" that was forever being offered to the strongest nation. History, too, gave Hitler a supposed justification for his axiom. Ever since the Teutons invaded the Roman Empire, in his view the only empire that had ever existed, there had been an imperial German history that had developed incorrectly in the years since the Thirty Years War. In its first attempt, Germany was robbed of its world domination, and Great Britain had instead benefited from the last three hundred years of history.

The second and irrevocably the last chance to achieve world domination was found in the situation that currently existed in the world. Hitler's worries about the closing of this small path that would lead Germany to its final goal were caused by the events in the already "Jewified" Soviet Union and by similar tendencies in the United States.

Basing his assumptions on historical examples of the rule of pure race minorities (Sparta, Rome, Great Britain in India and in the world), Hitler hoped in good time to finish the Soviet Union with help from the racially similar British ally, and at the same time to gain "Lebensraum in the East" for the largest population of Aryans in the world, which was currently crowded together in a very small area of central Europe. Geo-political axioms completed to the anti-Semitic and social-Darwinist foundation from which Hitler never deviated. These axioms led Hitler to be of the opinion that a European hegemony would result in Asia and Africa and then the whole world re-orienting itself towards Europe, and that domination by the "Aryan race" would automatically take place. *Mein Kampf* therefore logically contains not only references to the short-term, and intermediate stages within the framework of the "program," but also has very clear indications of the ultimate goal being "Aryan" world domination. For Hitler, the terms "world domination" and "(relative) world supremacy" always had a conceptual identity. Other words, such as "world power," were simply synonyms.

The field of architecture shows how concretely Hitler took his political visions of world domination. Parallel to the writing of *Mein Kampf*, Hitler also made decisions about representative buildings, the realization of which he began with great commitment from the moment he took power. Hitler's long-term thinking and "planning," apart from his verbal announcements, can be shown as continuous after January 30, 1933, for the first time in this study, particularly in the field of architecture. During the years 1933–1936, Hitler showed a subdued behavior for tactical reasons. All in all, this is the decisive indication that there was no difference between the theorist and the practical man. From the very first day of his rise to power, Hitler was torn between calculation and dogma. At no time between 1920 and 1945, as is clearly shown by his personal comments, did he lose sight of his goal of world domination. At the same time, Hitler's decisions in the field of architecture go beyond him as a person and display the unbridled social utopian driving power within the Nazi power system as a whole, which allows a glance into the possible further development of the Third Reich, had history taken a different course, a ride into a pre-modern Utopia by means of a highly industrialized society.[1]

Hitler's architectural plans from 1933 to 1936 were in fact politics through a different medium. The buildings had a functional importance and were a preview of the aggressive, expansionist foreign policy that began in 1936. Working on drafts was never a substitute or a diversion of Hitler's energy in view of the actual political situation. It was much more a way of bringing to fruition his ultimate visionary goals in one tangible area and making them happen according to a specific time table. Hitler's policies covered the entire timing of his short and long-term goals since 1933. His big building projects, striking proof of rational actions and prudent planning, began in 1936, the same year that the National Socialists started to implement their foreign policy. Along with his understanding of history and art, which were closely connected to examples from the ancient world, the decisions Hitler made in architecture indicated his intention to outline the framework of a German role as world leader and to commit both his successors and the population to his global concept. Berlin's gigantic buildings were to symbolize the new world capital. Nuremberg was to have the future domestic social function of conveying to the gathered masses a feeling of fanaticism, unity, and willingness to fight. These buildings that were designed for eternity underlined Hitler's eschatological expectations of racially based world domination.

Hitler's speeches to the high-ranking officers of the army, navy, and air force, which he began to make in 1937–38, had a comparable function to the party conventions in Nuremberg. A number of speeches through 1944 show Hitler's attempt to instill the goal of world domination in his officers. The attempt to portray the United States as a numerically inferior opponent especially reveals Hitler's calculating nature, which hurried far beyond any current issues and which was expressed in the armaments sector by his demands for a huge oceangoing fleet and the development of long-range bombers to attack the United States. The officer corps of the army must be seen as the group to whom Hitler revealed his ultimate goals most thoroughly and most frequently.

The armament programs and colonial planning that the three branches of the armed forces themselves carried out all show the kinds of expectations they had on the political front. Before 1939, the army, the navy, and the air force were ruled out as control factors in the face of a globally oriented expansion program. After 1939, the opposite was the case. Hitler was never obliged to place massive emphasis on his ideas with this audience. Up to the intention to establish a continental position of world power, Hitler and the military had extensive convergence of interests. The navy was even planning for a German position of world supremacy by 1941.

Especially in 1940–1941, when Hitler figured that he was just shy of reaching an important stage within the framework of his "program," namely a victory over the Soviet Union, his entire projection became very clear. Despite the war with Great Britain, which theoretically hadn't been planned for, it seemed that in the autumn of 1941, a situation that a few years before Hitler had only thought possible by 1945 would become reality. Germany would be the unrivalled hegemonic power in Europe. The big change, which he had expected in the summer of 1940 after the defeat of France, would then come about. Great Britain, because of the changed global situation, would sooner or later join the "new Europe," just in time to keep the United States form getting involved in Europe and to prevent Japan from getting rich on the spoils of the Russian and British "massive bankruptcy" in Asia. Then the entire world would "rightfully" orient itself toward Europe, whereby the transition period could alternatively be entered through a short and hefty trade war with the United States or through sanction-like military attacks using the military potential that would be available as of 1944. In 1941, Hitler wasn't expecting a big war any longer. In his wildest dreams, he even must have hoped to have completely reached his goal by 1950. The instructions that the most important buildings be finished by this date were clearly politically motivated.

Neither the administration of the occupied areas of Europe nor the colonial plans nor the education and training system of the Third Reich can be used as direct evidence of Hitler's ultimate goals. All the way up to its defeat, the Nazi system was in a developmental and expansionist phase. Final restrictions could only be worked out after the framework (i.e., world domination) had been achieved, insofar as social-Darwinist principles even allowed for such considerations. For this reason, Hitler left organizing any general guidelines for the world after his goals had been achieved to competing groups, and to a large extent he avoided getting personally involved, as long as it wasn't a subject that directly interested him, such as architecture, armaments issues, or most of all the extermination of the Jews in Europe. World domination and the extermination of his opponents had always formed an inseparable unit for him.

The lack of war plans aimed at the United States and Japan lay in the consistency of Hitler's foreign politics, against his will, he had to improvise in this area from 1939 onwards. Plans, in the traditional sense, didn't even exist for the invasion of Soviet Union in accordance with the "program," nor were there plans for the occupied countries in Europe. The conquest of the Soviet Union was to be the answer to all pending problems: as the closing of the "program phase" and as a "grab bag" for all unresolved social, economic, and diplomatic problems. All the prerequisites for world domination would have been achieved, and the "*Lebensraum*" for the greater part of the Aryan world population would have been opened up. At the same time, a biologically fixed status quo would bring mankind to its desired end: Hitler's dream of stopping the "challenge cup" principle of the Earth.

Hitler's axiomatic ideas on anti-Semitism, gaining area for living space, and anti-Bolshevism were the driving powers behind a foreign policy which saw its only task in the goal of establishing world domination for the "Aryan race." Hitler's decisions in this area, which represented a combination of "program" and "natural law," were autonomous, calculated, and intended for the long term. The accompanying tendencies that were bound to the ultimate goal, which were only slightly discernible in the building policies and in the corresponding growth of SS power since 1937–1938, spared Hitler to a large extent from the need for domestic approval. It became not as much about the conservation of a social or ruling order, as the old German leading political and social groups had hoped, but rather about carrying out a foreign policy and a racial policy goal, both of which would be unthinkable without the "Führer." Despite a variety of connecting lines of people, concepts, and programs between Germany under the rule from the Kaiser to Hitler, Hitler's goals both in quality and quantity went far beyond all previous forms of rule. Because he was much too convinced of his role as "savior" and under pressure to hastily complete points in his "program" at any cost, Hitler never succeeded in having a policy of secrecy regarding his ultimate goals. It was the dilemma of his contemporaries to hear his exaggerated vocabulary and to use it to some extent, but, contrary to Hitler, not to take it "literally." The motto "world power or defeat" therefore didn't mean the fulfillment of the goals of Germany under Kaiser Wilhelm, but as Hitler had clearly stated in public long before his seizure of power, meant either world domination or the demise of the German people, as the answer to the "challenge." The conflict with the Anglo-Saxon democracies and the fierce resistance on the part of the population of the Soviet Union to the war of extermination waged against them were the logical consequences of a long planned policy that did not run according to the "program." Only by bringing the National Socialist system to its knees could the danger of an atavistic collapse and decline of the world be avoided.

Notes

1. Hildebrand, *Weltmacht oder Untergang*, 15.

SELECT BIBLIOGRAPHY

Berghahn, Volker, „NSDAP und ‚geistige Führung' der Wehrmacht 1939-1943." VfZG 17 (1969), 17–72.

Bracher, K.D., M. Funke, M. and H.-A. Jacobsen, eds., Nationalsozialistische Diktatur 1933-1945. Eine Bilanz (Düsseldorf, 1983).

Broszat, Martin, Der Staat Hitlers. Grundlegung und Entwicklung seiner inneren Verfassung (Munich, 1969).

Bullock, Alan, Hitler. Eine Studie über Tyrannei (Düsseldorf, 1967).

Das Deutsche Reich und der Zweite Weltkrieg. Edited by Militärgeschichtliches Forschungsamt. 10 vols. (Stuttgart, 1979–2008).

Dülffer, Jost, Weimar, Hitler und die Marine. Reichspolitik und Flottenbau 1920-1939 (Düsseldorf, 1973).

Dülffer. J., J. Thies and J. Henke, eds., Hitlers Städte. Baupolitik im Dritten Reich. Eine Dokumentation (Cologne, 1978).

Durth, Werner, Deutsche Architekten. Biographische Verflechtungen 1900-1970 (Stuttgart, 2000).

Fest, Joachim C., Hitler. Eine Biographie (Frankfurt am Main-Berlin-Vienna, 1973).

Georg, Enno, Die wirtschaftlichen Unternehmungen der SS (Stuttgart, 1963).

Funke, M., ed., Hitler, Deutschland und die Mächte. Materialien zur Außenpolitik des Dritten Reiches (Düsseldorf, 1976).

Giesler, Hermann, Ein anderer Hitler: Erlebnisse, Gespräche, Reflexionen (Leoni, 1977).

Haffner, Sebastian, Anmerkungen zu Hitler (Munich, 1978).

Henke, Josef, England in Hitlers politischem Kalkül 1935-1939 (Boppard, 1973).

Hildebrand, Klaus, Vom Reich zum Weltreich. Hitler, NSDAP und koloniale Frage 1919-1945 (Munich, 1969).

———, The Foreign Policy of the Third Reich (London, 1973).

———, „Hitlers Ort in der Geschichte des preußisch-deutschen Nationalstaats," HZ 217 (1973), 584-632.

———, Das Dritte Reich (Munich-Vienna, 1979).

———, Das vergangene Reich. Deutsche Außenpolitik von Bismarck bis Hitler 1871-1945 (Stuttgart, 1995).

Hillgruber, Andreas, Hitlers Strategie. Politik und Kriegführung 1940-1941 (Frankfurt am Main, 1965).

————, *Deutschlands Rolle in der Vorgeschichte der beiden Weltkriege* (Göttingen, 1967).

————, *„Der Faktor Amerika in Hitlers Strategie 1938-1941" Aus Politik und Zeitgeschichte. Appendix to „Parlament" B 19/66* (May 11, 1966).

————, *Kontinuität und Diskontinuität in der deutschen Außenpolitik von Bismarck bis Hitler* (Düsseldorf, 1969).

————, *Endlich genug über Nationalsozialismus und Zweiten Weltkrieg? Forschungsstand und Literatur* (Düsseldorf, 1982).

Hillgruber, A., ed., *Staatsmänner und Diplomaten bei Hitler. Vertrauliche Aufzeichnungen über Unterredungen mit Vertretern des Auslandes 1939-1944*. 2 vols. (Frankfurt am Main, 1967–1970).

Hirschfeld. G. and L. Kettenacker, eds., *Der „Führerstaat": Mythos und Realität. Studien zur Struktur und Politik des Dritten Reiches* (Stuttgart, 1981).

Irving, David, *Hitler's War* (New York-London, 1977).

Jacobsen, Hans-Adolf, *Nationalsozialistische Außenpolitik 1933-1938* (Frankfurt am Main-Berlin, 1968).

Jäckel, Eberhard, *Hitlers Herrschaft. Entwurf einer Herrschaft* (Tübingen, 1969).

————, *Hitlers Herrschaft: Vollzug einer Weltanschauung* (Stuttgart, 1986).

Jäckel, E. and A. Kuhn, eds., *Hitler. Sämtliche Aufzeichnungen 1905-1924* (Stuttgart, 1980).

Joachimsthaler, Anton, *Die Breitspurbahn Hitlers* (Freiburg, 1981).

Kershaw, Ian, *Hitler, 1889-1945*. 2 vols. (London, 1998–2000).

————, *Fateful Choices. Ten Decisions that changed the World, 1940-1941* (New York, 2007).

Kuhn, Axel, *Hitlers außenpolitisches Programm. Entstehung und Entwicklung 1919-1939* (Stuttgart, 1970).

Martin, Bernd, *Friedensinitiativen und Machtpolitik im Zweiten Weltkrieg*. 2 vols. (Düsseldorf, 1974–1976).

Messerschmidt, Manfred, *Die Wehrmacht im NS-Staat. Zeit der Indoktrination* (Hamburg, 1969).

Michalka, Wolfgang, ed., *Nationalsozialistische Außenpolitik* (Darmstadt, 1978).

Moltmann, Günter, *„Weltherrschaftsideen Hitlers" Festschrift für Egmont Zechlin* (Hamburg, 1961), 197–240.

Müller, Klaus-Jürgen, *Das Heer und Hitler. Armee und nationalsozialistisches Regime 1933-1940* (Stuttgart, 1969).

Ogan, B. and W.W. Weiss, eds., *Faszination und Gewalt. Zur politischen Ästhetik des Nationalsozialismus* (Nuremberg, 1992).

Picker, Henry, *Hitlers Tischgespräche im Führerhauptquartier*. Edited by P. E. Schramm together with A. Hillgruber and M. Vogt (Stuttgart, 1963).

Rich, Norman, *Hitler's War Aims*. 2 vols. (London, 1973–1974).

Schreiber, Gerhard, *Hitler. Interpretationen 1923-1983* (Darmstadt, 1984).

Speer, Albert, *Erinnerungen* (Frankfurt am Main-Berlin, 1969/ 1993 with an introductory essay by Jochen Thies).

Speer, Albert, *Spandauer Tagebücher* (Frankfurt am Main-Berlin-Vienna, 1975).

Weinberg, Gerhard L., *The Foreign Policy of Hitler's Germany. Vol. I: Diplomatic Revolution in Europe 1933-36. Vol. II: Starting World War II 1937-1939* (Chicago and London, 1970 and 1980).

————, *A World at Arms. A Global History of WWII* (New York, 1994).

Zitelmann, Rainer, *Hitler. Selbstverständnis eines Revolutionärs* (Hamburg-Leamington Spa-New York, 1987).

INDEX